WATERLOO ROAD
ST. PETER'S STREET
ST. PETER'S GREEN
St. Peter
LURKE LANE
ST. CUTHBERT STREET
THE GROVE
DUKE STREET
GADSBY STREET
HOWARD STREET
NEWNHAM STREET
MILL STREET
SILVER STREET
HIGH STREET
Howard Chapel
Baptist Chapel
Old Meeting
St. Cuthbert
Castle Rooms
CASTLE LANE
Castle Hill
THAMES STREET
ST. PAUL'S SQUARE
St. Paul
ST. PAUL'S SQUARE
County Hall
WATERLOO
4
6
11
14

Map of the Town of Bedford from Actual Survey in the Year 1841

KEY TO M. REYNOLDS' MAP OF BEDFORD 1841

1. Developing residential area.
2. Earlier or "best" almshouses.
3. Later almshouses.
4. Former residence of Clerk.
5. Harpur Street, developed by the Trust.
6. Field hired for games.
7. Commercial and junior commercial schools.
8. Children's home (hospital).
9. Clerk's house, office, and boardroom.
10. "National" (elementary) school for boys.
11. Grammar school.
12. Boarders' premises.
13. House of headmaster of grammar school.
14. Brewery and brewer's house.

THE HARPUR TRUST

1552–1973

JOYCE GODBER

THE HARPUR TRUST, BEDFORD

First Published 1973

ISBN 0 9502917 0 6

Printed by White Crescent Press Ltd, Crescent Road, Luton, England

CONTENTS

PLATES AND MAPS

GOVERNORS OF THE HARPUR TRUST

1973

The composition of the Governing Body is as follows and the dates in brackets are those when the respective categories were introduced.

Ex-officio Governors, 5: the Mayor (1566), the Lord Lieutenant (1793) and 3 members of Parliament (1793).

Nominated Governors, serving for 5 years, 13: New College, Oxford (2) (1552), Cambridge University, (1873), London University (1873),

Parents of day pupils (1873) 4, Permanent staff of the Schools (1873) 4.

Representative Governors 12: 6 from Bedford Corporation (1566) and 6 from Bedfordshire County Council (1919).

FOREWORD

by Sir John Howard, D.SC., F.I.C.E., Chairman of the Harpur Trust

In 1930 the Reverend Charles F. Farrar, a relative of mine and himself then a Governor of the Harpur Trust, wrote the history of Harpur's benefaction of 1566. Since then, additional information has come to light, and the last 100 years have seen a period of remarkable growth in the Trust's educational work.

The occasion for this history is the centenary of the revision of the Trust which took place in 1873. Under Government direction the course was changed, with the result that the four main schools gained a national reputation and have increasingly served this country and the Commonwealth.

The Harpur Trust has a primary responsibility to make full use of its resources, and it has now embarked upon one of the most challenging ventures in the life of the Harpur Charity, the rebuilding of the Modern School on a new site at Manton Heights and the redevelopment of the old site in the centre of Bedford, preserving the existing Blore façade. This is a demanding task, but the Governors are convinced that the greatly increased revenue, which will flow from this operation, will benefit in the future the children of Bedfordshire.

On the non-educational side of the Charity, the Trust have in the past decade modernised 25 of the almshouses in Dame Alice Street, and built in Cardington Road, Harpur House, a modern block of 24 almshouses, and look forward to expansion of this work.

In bringing the record of the Harpur Trust up to date, the Governors approached Joyce Godber to undertake this important task. She was educated at Bedford High School and at St. Hilda's College, Oxford and is a Fellow of the Society of Antiquaries and the Royal Historical Society, and was for twenty years County Archivist of Bedfordshire. She comes from a Bedfordshire family, her father, Mr. Isaac Godber, a farmer of Willington, had no less than 19 of his children and grandchildren at the Harpur Trust Schools, and his children have reached eminence in agriculture, medicine, law and politics. She has spent over a year on this task, which she has undertaken as a labour of love, and has unearthed much new information, particularly evidence of the Chancery Proceedings of 1654 when the Trust's estate was consolidated into one piece. On behalf of the Governors I tender our grateful thanks to Miss Joyce Godber for her devoted skill and enthusiasm in the completion of this work.

John Howard

Crossland Fosse,
Box End,
Bedford.

ACKNOWLEDGEMENTS

My chief gratitude is to Sir William Harpur, without whose help I should not have been equipped to write this book. I am deeply grateful to the Governors of the Trust for entrusting the task to me. More especially I pay tribute to the unfailing courtesy, helpfulness, knowledge and wise advice of their Clerk, Mr. R. N. Hutchins. I thankfully acknowledge the patience and forbearance of the Heads of the four schools, Mr. W. M. Brown, Mr. B. H. Kemball-Cook, Miss E. K. Wallen, Miss S. M. Morse, when each school really needs a volume to itself. For Bedford School I am also indebted to Michael Barlen; for the Modern School to Andrew Underwood; for the High School to Dorothy Kitchener; for the Dame Alice Harpur School for Girls to Hilda Long (*née* Howe); and for elementary schools to David Bushby. To some colleagues and old friends, with whom for years I have shared the pursuit of Bedfordshire history, I should like to say once more what a pleasure this association has been to me: to Patricia Bell, Alan Cirket, Ralph Conisbee, Denis Gilmore, Bill Kuhlicke and Gordon Tibbutt. It is good to have young friends coming forward to carry on the work; in particular I refer to studies undertaken by the Modern School Local History Group, both previously and for this volume, and for their help, and that of Bedford School's History VI with Appendix 5. For the Holborn estate I am under special obligation to Frank Kelsall of the Historic Buildings Division of the Greater London Council: he it was, through intimate knowledge of Chancery records, who solved the baffling problem of the 1654 exchange. For making available the important MSS. at New College I am grateful to the Rev. Canon G. V. Bennett, Librarian, and to Francis Steer, Archivist. I also acknowledge the courtesy shown me at Merchant Taylors' Hall, at the Guildhall Library, and at the Corporation of London Record Office. I thank my former colleagues at the County and Town Halls, Mr. P Shallard and Mr. T. S. Lucking, present and former Directors of Education, and Dr. E. C. Walker, former Borough Education Officer, for their readiness to be of service. A former Governor and my lifelong friend, Kathleen Major, has once again, as with previous publications, read part of my text.

With regard to illustrations and maps, nearly all the London maps are reproduced by courtesy of the Guildhall Library, but Pl. 2b from a volume in possession of Mr. H. Newman. Most Bedford photographs are by Mr. F. Jewell Harrison; but Pl. 17a is by Mr. K. Whitbread for the Bedford Masonic Lodge; Pls. 6b, 7 and 26a are from the County Record Office collection and by him as County Council photographer; while the following kindly lent old photographs: Mr. S. W. Noble (Pl. 17b), Mrs. Ward (Pl. 17c), Mr. R. A. Butt (Pl. 17d). The Town Council gave permission to reproduce Pl. 1a (redrawn by Alan Cirket), 8a-c, 9a-b and 12a.

J.G.

GUIDE TO EDUCATION SECTION

Origins

before 1180 An existing school transferred to the control of Newnham Priory.
1535 Newnham Priory dissolved.
1552 Bedford corporation obtained powers to receive endowment.
1566 Harpur's deed of gift to Bedford corporation.
1764 Harpur Trust established; revised 1793, 1826, 1853, 1873.

Harpur Schools

The old free school or grammar school, which in 1891 moved to its present site, became Bedford School in 1917.
The writing school, established 1764, later English or commercial, became Bedford Modern School in 1877, and moves to Manton Heights in 1974.
Bedford High School was established 1882.
Girls' Modern School was established 1882; moved to St. Paul's Square, 1892; and to Cardington Road, 1938; it became the Dame Alice Harpur School for Girls in 1946.
The general preparatory or "National" school was established 1815;
The girls' school was opened 1836;
These in 1902 became voluntary;
in 1921 became Harpur Central School;
in 1946 became Harpur Secondary School;
in 1965 were transferred by the LEA to Chester Road under the name of Westfield School.
The infants' school, 1839–68; re-opened 1874.
Ampthill Road School opened 1876; transferred to the LEA 1900.
Clapham Road School opened 1894; transferred to the LEA 1902.

Department of Education and Science

Was formerly the Ministry of Education, previously Board of Education, and originated as a committee of the Privy Council.

Commissions

Clarendon; reported 1861 on 9 public schools (Charterhouse, Eton, Harrow, Merchant Taylors', Rugby, St. Paul's, Shrewsbury, Westminster, Winchester).
Taunton: reported 1868 on endowed grammar schools. (Copy in Trust office.)
Samuelson; reported 1884 on technical education.
Bryce; reported 1894 on secondary education. (Copy in Trust office.)
Newsom; reported 1968 on independent boarding schools.
Donnison; reported 1970 on independent day and direct grant grammar schools.

Acts

1869 Provided for old endowed schools to submit new schemes.
1870 Schools where necessary to be established with rate support.
1902 (In Bedfordshire) The County Council became responsible for "higher" (secondary) education, and Bedford corporation became responsible for "elementary" education within the borough.
1918 Age raised and fees abolished.
1944 Each child to receive education according to ability.

GUIDE TO WELFARE SECTION

Almshouses: 1793 (20 – more if surplus), 1826 (66), 1853 (65), 1873 (1/11 of income).
Apprenticeship: (1566 "informing poor children"), 1764 (£600), 1793 (£700), 1826 (£1,500), 1853 (£1,200); 1873 discontinued.
Benefactions on completing apprenticeship: 1764, 1793, 1826; 1853 discontinued.
Donations to those going out to service: 1793 (girls £60), 1826 (10 boys and 30 girls); 1853 discontinued.
Hall money or alms in mid-winter: 1566 (residue), 1764 (residue), 1793 (£500), 1826 (£500); 1853 discontinued.
Hospital or children's home: (1566 "nourishing poor children"), 1764 (£200), 1793 (£300: 25 children), 1826 (26–50 children), 1853 (26–50 children); 1873 discontinued.
Marriage portions: (1566 unspecified), 1764 (£800), 1793 (£800), 1826 (£800), 1853 (£560); 1873 discontinued.

1 *Prologue 1552–1764*

EARLIEST YEARS

Before 1166 there was a school in Bedford. It was connected with the canons of St. Paul's church, and the Archdeacon made it his especial care. About 1166 the canons moved outside Bedford to Newnham, where Simon de Beauchamp of Bedford castle built them a priory. By 1180 the Archdeacon decided to resign to the priory oversight of the school.[1] Probably the school remained in Bedford; whereabouts is not known at this date; however the town was then very small, huddled round castle and bridge. In 1224 the boys must have seen exciting days, when a rebel secured the castle and the king came to besiege it, and finally ordered it to be pulled down, so that the Beauchamps had to construct a house on the site. The last Beauchamp, a likely young man, was killed at Evesham in 1265, when the property went to his sisters.

THE HARPER FAMILY[2]

About the time of the first known mention of Bedford school there was living at Southill some miles to the southeast a modest family of the name of Harper, one of them a William. Two were benefactors of Warden Abbey nearby. Gradually the family moved northwestward to Ickwell, Cople and Renhold; and about 1500 a William is found at Bedford and other Harpers at Biddenham. They were still of modest status: the Biddenham ones were husbandmen. William of Bedford however was of sufficient standing to be churchwarden of St. Paul's church in 1510. He also acted as bailiff for Warden Abbey's property in Bedford. The Bedford property was not extensive: a few houses and four acres. In 1509 as bailiff he had to bring a case at Bedford court of pleas for arrears of rent. Though at this date the spelling of names varied, Harper seems the normal form; but as the form Harpur has become entrenched since 1764 it will be used henceforward.

SIR WILLIAM HARPUR[3]

It seems likely that, about the time Henry VIII came to the throne, young William Harpur attended the school in what is now Mill Street, then School Lane. Later he went to London. It may be that he was apprenticed to a tailor, but there is no certainty about this; nor is there evidence of his connection with any other trade. If he was so apprenticed, in those days of gorgeous dress, the qualities required would be manual dexterity, and (for high-class trade) artistic skill in the manipulation of colours and materials – silk, velvet, jewels and gold thread. To be able to judge men and to interpret their wishes would be an advantage, when everything was individually made and dress expressed the wearer's personality; and this in the capital in an age of vitality and national confidence. But whatever Harpur's original trade, he must have shown business sense and the capacity to organise; and it is almost certain that he developed wide business interests, probably like those of his friend and contemporary Sir Thomas White, who traded in cloth, and made loans to Coventry and Bristol. The Taylors' Company's new charter in 1502 made them Merchant Taylors[4] and allowed them to admit other persons. Harpur was admitted in 1533.

The livery companies had grown up to supersede the older craft gilds. They consisted originally of the richer members, i.e., those who could afford to wear the livery; while the smaller members of the trade set up yeomanry or bachelor gilds. They had an annual feast and chose master and wardens; these rights were confirmed to the Taylors in 1299. By 1371 they were making ordinances to regulate the trade. As a fraternity dedicated to St. John the Baptist they had a religious side, and had a special mass at his festival. The medieval crypt under their former chapel still exists, though their hall has been twice burnt in 1666 and 1940. At least from 1502 their connection with tailoring lessened. Harpur, after his admission in 1533, held the various grades of office, and in 1553 became master. The Merchant Taylors came seventh in order of precedence among the twelve great livery companies. Meanwhile on 18 November 1547 he had married (somewhat late, being then over 50), a widow, Alice Chauntrell.[5] The later association of Alice with Harpur in his deed of gift to Bedford has a legal explanation in that her right of dower would be involved, but she may also have shared his interests. Possibly she brought him an accession of income, but by this time his fortune would appear to have been made.

Harpur would come in contact with the leading London citizens of his day. In 1553 he became alderman for the ward of Bridge Without, chosen by the other aldermen. This was a new ward without electors, created in 1550, to which apparently less prestige attached; so when in 1556 there was a vacancy in the older ward of Dowgate, Harpur was elected alderman for this ward in preference to three other candidates, one of whom was Thomas Gresham. He served a year as treasurer of St. Bartholomew's Hospital (after the dissolution of the monasteries aldermen were appointed as governors to the royal hospitals). He was sheriff 1556–7.

Harpur must above all have been a man who learnt from life, from other men and from events. When he went to Merchant Taylors' Hall (appropriately enough in Threadneedle Street) he would see on the opposite side of the road St. Anthony's school, once attended by Sir Thomas More. Perhaps he knew that some years ago a schoolmaster had rented the Taylors' Hall for a school. Other members of his company were interested in education, such as Sir Stephen Jenyns who in 1508 had endowed a school at Wolverhampton, and Sir Thomas White who in 1555 founded St. John's College, Oxford; and more particularly Richard Hilles whose radical religious views made it expedient for him to go abroad for a few years.

These were unsettled times in religious matters. In 1535, when he was approaching the age of 40, Harpur would have heard that, like monasteries elsewhere, Newnham Priory had been closed, the canons pensioned off, and the property confiscated. When he visited Bedford again he would find the priory site desolate, with much of the stone carried away and what was left was before long converted to a house; while at Warden Abbey, which he may have visited in earlier years with his father, the site was leased and a fine brick house in process of building. At Bedford it would seem that he found the school still existing, probably under an aged master; but it was clearly at risk, like similar schools elsewhere; for the building was up for sale with a number of other ex-monastic properties.

And now Harpur seems to have got in touch with John Williams alias Scott, perhaps once his schoolfellow in School Lane. Williams in 1545 obtained a large grant of former monastic property, and with it the schoolhouse in School Lane; and probably Harpur and Williams talked the matter over. Williams gave the schoolhouse a new door (one that he had come by cheaply when the church of St. Peter Dunstable was pulled down), but did not want the responsibility of the school. Perhaps it was now that the old schoolmaster died. At all events, in 1548 Edmund Green came from New College, Oxford, to teach at Bedford. Probably Harpur arranged this and paid his stipend. But at this stage he did not commit himself further. The boy king Edward VI was delicate, and it might well be that the old ways would return if his elder sister, Mary, with quite other views, succeeded.

If indeed it was Harpur who arranged the coming of Edmund Green – and in view of later events no other explanation seems tenable – he must already have given a good deal of thought to the school and to its possible future, should he endow it. When he went back to Bedford on a visit, he must have been aware that he had far out-distanced the lads with whom he used to play, though probably he courteously concealed this awareness. He could not have felt happy about leaving the school entirely to the corporation's care.

He would know of recent foundations like that of St. Paul's by Dean Colet in 1509. As a knowledgeable man of affairs, who probably numbered among his associates nobility and men of education, he would be aware of the high reputation of Winchester, which indeed on its foundation by Bishop Wykeham in 1382 marked a new era in education and was the model for the later royal foundation at Eton. Perhaps he knew that one of the earliest printed school textbooks, *Vulgaria*, 1519, was compiled by John Stanbridge of Winchester and New College, and headmaster of Winchester. William Warham (d.1532), who was Archbishop of Canterbury when Harpur first came to London, had been educated at Winchester and New College. Scholars of Winchester normally proceeded to William of Wykeham's other princely foundation, that of New College, Oxford, where indeed after two years' probation they became Fellows. It was likely that, if New College appointed the master at Bedford, it would often happen that this master had been educated at Winchester. Thus Bedford would be in touch with one of the best, if not the best of the models. Further, Bedford corporation already had a link with Oxford, in that its customs were based on those of Oxford; and in fact in 1556 the corporation addressed to Oxford some queries on doubtful points.

Edmund Green came from Hounslow in Middlesex and was a Fellow of New College 1542–8. There was in the village of Biddenham near Bedford a family of Green who were apparently Harpur's relatives; it is conceivable that they were connected with the Greens of Hounslow; but Green is a common name, and this is conjecture.

The coming of Edmund Green to Bedford was in the reign of Edward VI, and it was in this period that religious gilds and fraternities were suppressed. Land in St. Paul's Square which had belonged to the Trinity gild seems to have been secured by Williams, and to have been bought by Harpur from him for a school site. Here Harpur erected a sizeable building, with a large room below, and another above where the usher might lodge; for to do the thing handsomely there must be an usher or assistant to help the master. The first usher was Robert Elbone. Beside the school Harpur also built a house for the master, Green. Though these buildings preceded the endowment, it was not unusual then or later for a benefactor to administer a project himself during his life, and only in old age to make provision for what should happen subsequently. Besides, though Harpur was now in late middle age, it was conceivable that he and his wife Alice might yet have a son.

Williams was mayor in 1551, and prepared the way for endowment, almost certainly in full consultation with Harpur. In 1552 the corporation obtained from Edward VI letters patent authorising them to accept an endowment for a free and perpetual grammar school for the education, institution and instruction of boys and youths in grammar, literature and good manners. Instruction in grammar meant in Latin and Greek grammar. Latin was still the almost universal language of learning and of business. Though the Bible had recently been translated into English, and the first and second prayerbooks appeared respectively in 1549 and 1552, works of learning or literature in English were so few that education in English would have been impracticable. The great change, speeded up by printing, that was to come in the use of English for all purposes was largely ahead. Greek had at this time almost the excitement of a new discovery. The fact that the school was called "free" did not mean that there was necessarily no payment for scholars; they did in fact, at least later, pay a few pence; but as building and teaching staff were provided, the sums were minimal. The letters patent authorised the Warden and Fellows of New College to appoint master and usher.

Should there be a balance left over from the school, it was to be used for marrying poor maidens, nourishing and educating poor boys, and for alms. The whole coincides with Harpur's later deed of gift.

Then came the reign of Queen Mary, 1553–8, and reversion to older practice in religion. Where Harpur stood is not entirely clear. While some men on either side at an early date took up hard and fast positions, there were many who hesitated and who thought that these were temporary troubles which would subside. From the fact that Harpur's two decisive steps were taken respectively in the reigns of Edward VI and Elizabeth I, one might hazard a guess that, though he was not doctrinaire, he inclined towards that body of opinion which was to form the Anglican church. However, in Mary's reign, when the Merchant Taylors again had their corporate mass on the festival of St. John the Baptist, he attended with the others. He may well have had a kindly feeling for the Newnham canons and the Warden monks whom he would remember from his boyhood. Perhaps in 1556, when his predecessor as sheriff of London had to preside at the burning of 13 Protestants, he was relieved that his term of office did not begin till Michaelmas.

Queen Mary's brief reign passed. It was the turn of the young Queen Elizabeth I, generally beloved; could it be that things were now settling down? Now came the zenith of Harpur's career. In 1561 he was Lord Mayor of London. The Lord Mayor's show represented harpers in history and legend.[6] "The new mayor took his barge towards Westminster, my new lord mayor, Master Harper, with the aldermen in their scarlet, and all the crafts of London in their livery and their barges . . . and landed at Paul's wharf and so to Paul's churchyard, and there met them a pageant gorgeously made with children with divers instruments playing and singing, in the midst David with his story about him, on the right side Orpheus with his story." In February 1562 he was knighted by the queen.

One or two light-hearted glimpses of his mayoralty are given by a contemporary.[7] One is of the revival of that medieval method of merrymaking by appointing a lord of misrule after Christmas. On 26 December there "came riding through London a lord of misrule, in clean complete harness (armour), gilt, with a hundred great horse and gentlemen riding gorgeously with chains of gold, and their horses goodly trapped, unto the Temple, for there was great cheer all Christmas . . . and great revels"; and again on 12 January, when Harpur and the aldermen "went to Paul's, and all the crafts in London in their livery . . . and after came into Cheapside a lord of misrule from Whitechapel with a great company".

Another such glimpse is in September 1562 when, after an inspection of the conduit heads of London's water supply, "after dinner they hunted the fox, and there was a goodly cry for a mile, and after the hounds killed the fox at the end of S. Giles', and there was a great cry at the death, and so rode through London my Lord Mayor Harper with all his company home to his place in Lombard Street".

This house in Lombard Street, said to be the largest and stateliest in the city, had been left to the Merchant Taylors' Company by a former Lord Mayor, for leasing to members. It was conveniently near the Guildhall and the Merchant Taylors' Hall.

However, there were also serious times during his mayoralty. On 12 May a disturbance caused the constables to send for the lord mayor and the sheriffs, "and they had ado to pacify the people, and divers were hurt, and certain carried to Newgate". Harpur ordered some constables to stand armed on duty all night "to see who would be so bold to come . . . and my lord mayor and the sheriffs did walk about Smithfield to see whether any would make any assault". This showed resolution for a man of 65. And the city in July was ordered by the Queen to provide soldiers for service in Normandy. This was done through the companies, and on 25 July Harpur had ready for service the Merchant Taylors' complement of 35 armed men, including 17 pikemen with corselet, pike, sword, dagger and cloak.

It was while Harpur was Lord Mayor that the Merchant Taylors' School was founded on the urgency of his contemporary, Richard Hilles, master of the company in that year. A site was available for £565; Hilles contributed £500 towards this; and the masters' salaries were to be a charge on the common box or funds. This foundation was a notable instance of cooperation; for Hilles and White were of differing views in church matters, yet White arranged a connection from the school to his college at Oxford (St. John's). Statutes, modelled on those of Colet for St. Paul's School, were adopted 24 September 1561 by thirteen members of the court of assistants (i.e. committee or council) of the company, and second among the recorded names of those present is that of Harpur.[8] As Lord Mayor he, with Edmund Grindal, Bishop of London, held the first visitation of the school on 21 August 1562. Incidentally, once at least on 19 March 1563 the members paid a surprise visit to the school "this present afternoon to see if the scholars are there or no".

Now Harpur arranged Bedford's endowment. He bought on 30 September 1564 for £180 13 acres and 3 roods of meadow outside the city at Holborn. It was ex-monastic land and had formerly belonged to Charterhouse, but had passed through several hands before he acquired it. Country land was cheaper to buy; yet if not too far from London there was a chance that it would grow in value; this was the kind of thing one or two London contemporaries were doing in the same neighbourhood; Sir Andrew Judd of the Skinners' Company had already done it for Tonbridge; and Laurence Sheriff of the Grocers' Company was about to do so for Rugby. On 22 April 1566 he and Dame Alice conveyed the purchase to Bedford corporation on terms similar to those in the letters patent.

Harpur's purchase was not in one compact block but in four separate parcels, only two of which adjoined for a short distance. The two larger blocks (7 a. 1 r.

20 p. and 3 a. 3 r.) were in Lyon Field, slightly to the north of the road running through Holborn village, along which road stood a few houses with their gardens or crofts. These houses had also belonged to Charterhouse, but since had come to various owners. The two smaller blocks of land (1 a. 2 r. and 1 a. 0 r. 20 p.) were further to the north in Little Conduit shot. There was also a right of way from Holborn. Interspersed among Harpur's four plots were four plots belonging to a certain Micklow.

Harpur continued his active life till he was over 70. In 1565 he was a contributor to the purchase of a site for Gresham's Exchange. The Merchant Taylors' minutes usually record his attendance among the first three names, other two being Sir Thomas White and Sir Thomas Offley (Offley had been one of the first pupils at St. Paul's School). White and Harpur seem to have been old friends, for when White died in 1566 he left to both Harpur and Dame Alice black hats and gowns.[9] There appears to be in the minutes at this date nothing relating to tailoring; but there is administration of property, purchase of armour, admissions to the school, and often financial transactions in connection with the corporation of London, especially in connection with corn in times of scarcity, or royal loans, for such matters were often levied by the city through the companies as the easiest way to reach the most substantial citizens. Harpur's last recorded attendance was 11 July 1569. His wife Alice died on 10 October of that year.

He had now only a few years to live, but he married Margaret Lethers in September 1570. He died 27 February 1574 at the age of 77. He expressed a wish to be buried in St. Paul's church, Bedford; and directed that several of his friends, if they would be at the trouble of going to Bedford for his funeral, should be provided with black gowns. Presumably the funeral was a stately affair. The chamberlains of Bedford provided 3 gallons of Gascon wine and one of sack. By an oversight which seems almost incredible his burial was not recorded in the register. Yet it seems certain that he was buried in St. Paul's church; for Margaret, now widowed, and incidentally reluctant to leave the Lombard Street house though the lease had fallen in, put up a brass to him with the inscription: "Hereunder lieth buried the body of Sir William Harper, knight, alderman and late Lord Mayor of the city of London, with Dame Margaret, his last wife"; and also one of herself in readiness for her own time. Though she remarried twice, she was in fact buried at Bedford 3 November 1596.

A lad from a country town who was shrewd and became a successful man of business; of repute in matters relating to the city of London; with a wide interest in education; in religious matters not doctrinaire, but tending towards that body of opinion which came to be Anglican; a co-operative man who could work with others of differing views; one not averse to pageantry and sport; resolute when need required; a hale man, active until after the age of 70; such are the shadowy indications that have come down to us of Harpur.

BEDFORD CORPORATION[10]

For the first two centuries after its establishment in the new building provided by Harpur, the free school was run by a partnership between the corporation and New College, the former administering the endowment and the latter appointing the staff. There was nothing to distinguish the school from similar ones in other county towns, for instance in Huntingdon, Hertford and Northampton; that is to say, it remained small and it was subject to periodic lawsuits. But the relation between corporation and college in this period has a bearing on that of Trust and college from 1764, since some of the same attitudes were to continue and some factors were to influence the future.

It was in this period that a pattern of town government was worked out which was to continue till the municipal corporations act of 1835, that is to say, its form crystallised as an oligarchy. The setting for this oligarchy was a small town of probably less than 2,000 population. In Elizabethan Bedford many townsmen combined farming with other occupations; common right depended on the amount of land held; and there was a municipal herdsman and a swineherd. Many townsmen were occupied in the clothing trades or in food supply or in various crafts; there was the occasional attorney, but it was usual to have a country gentleman legally qualified for the occasional small duties which were all that was required of the town clerk. It was even becoming the practice to have a country gentleman to represent the borough in parliament, and often he held the office of recorder as well.

This small community did not need much administration. Its officers were the mayor, who had most power, and went to church in state; the two bailiffs; the chamberlains who kept the modest accounts; the bridge-wardens who saw to repair of the bridge. These offices were held by burgesses (burgessdom came by inheritance or election), all of whom could attend the common council. There were also inferior offices held by freemen, such as wood-searchers and bucket-searchers (i.e., supervising fire precautions). Each of the five parishes had its parochial officers, its churchwardens and overseers who collected rates for church repair and for the poor; St. Paul's was much the largest; next came the parish of St. Mary; and the other three were trifling.

The London land system was to let on long leases. The Holborn estate was let on 6 December 1565 for 40 years to Richard Bacon at £12 p.a., oddly enough before Harpur's deed of gift to Bedford had been signed.[11] It must have been arranged by him. The lease (a copy survives) set out in intricate detail the boundaries of four separate plots in Lyon Field and Conduit shot:

a.	r.	p.
7	1	20
3	3	0
1	2	0
1	0	20
13	3	0

All the corporation had to do was to receive the rent, and probably in his lifetime Harpur did this and transmitted it. However, already there were the seeds of later confusion, for Bacon sub-let to a tenant who occupied "all the rest of Lyon Field" by leases from other owners.

When Bacon's lease ran out, there was some delay in negotiating a new one. No corporation minute-book exists for this period, but probably now as later three or four members were deputed to arrange it. In 1607 they let a small fragment separately to John Tomes, a yard 80 ft. by 100 ft. with barn and stable in High Holborn, for 19 years at £2 p.a. And in 1611 they let the rest to William Langhorne for 41 years at £48 p.a. together with the reversion of Tomes' lease. Thus in 1626 the property was again under one lessee at a total rent of £50.

The system of long leases has the drawback that changes of tenancy are likely to come by death or other means. This seems to explain the Widow Plunket paying £50 in 1629 mentioned in a note at New College. Later, according to a summary at Bedford, the lease came to Henry Fetherston of the Three Cups inn and was inherited by his daughter Grace.[12]

Sub-letting had continued, by now not merely to one under-tenant, but to several. Micklow's land now belonged to Sir Thomas Fisher. Other adjoining property (probably the houses along the road) belonged to institutions such as the Bridewell hospital and the parish of St. Clement Dane,[13] and these let to tenants. The result was that the pattern of occupation became different from that of ownership; and, in the absence of frequent perambulations, the occupiers neglected boundary marks and suited their own convenience. A messuage and bowling alley were built on the smallest of the Harpur plots, the more westward of the two in Little Conduit shot. When the expiry of the lease was approaching, the corporation realised their difficulty, and in 1649 began a suit in Chancery for a commission to investigate, and to set out the Harpur lands.

After preliminary hearings, the court of Chancery in 1651 nominated a commission,[14] and the corporation on 27 October gave authority to three members of their council to give any necessary consent on their behalf. The dispute was mainly between Bedford and Sir Thomas Fisher, each owning four intermingled plots – the other owners cited seem to be those of houses and gardens along the Holborn road, whose tenants had probably encroached. Bedford claimed 13 a. 3 r., Fisher 16 a. 3 r., a total of 30½ a. But though two surveyors twice measured the land, they were unable to find more than 27 a. which could be identified with certainty. It was therefore recommended on 1 March 1653 that the loss be shared in proportion, Bedford receiving 11 a. 3 r. 27 p. and Fisher 15 a. 0 r. 13 p., and detailed bounds were drawn up accordingly. To avoid further trouble in future, an exchange was effected on 3 December, so that each party would have one continuous block. This exchange was ratified by Chancery decree of 16 February 1654. Thus the Harpur estate took its present shape. The eastern part, comprising

Emerald Street and Bedford Row are part of Harpur's original purchase, but the stretch north of Theobald's Road to the west formerly belonged to Fisher, Harpur's plots being south and west of it respectively.[15]

Meanwhile in 1652 four members of the council had been appointed to negotiate a new lease or leases, and the mayor was empowered to appoint a bailiff.[16] This seems to have been an uncertain time, complicated probably by the uncertainties of the commonwealth (in 1656 Cromwell's major-general removed the mayor and four members of the council and substituted his own nominees). There was more than one tenant; Grace Fetherston had part on a 21-year lease in 1652 at £30 p.a., and often put the chamberlains to great trouble and cost in the collection of her rent; in 1654 Adkin paid his arrears of 13s. 4d.; and in 1656 another tenant, William Tubb, wanted a licence to dig clay and make bricks, and also to sub-let a small area. It must have been with relief that in 1668 the whole property was let to a single tenant, William Thompson, for 41 years at the improved rent of £99 p.a., and with a covenant to maintain fences and boundaries. There was also a fine of £100 on the renewal of the lease; the accounts do not survive, and it is not known whether this sum was treated as endowment income or paid into the town chest.

The corporation's troubles were not over. Thompson had difficulty in securing lands detained by Barker and Brownlow, and in 1670 wanted to withdraw; the difference went to Chancery;[17] and four members were appointed to treat with Thompson. As late as 1675 he demanded a rebatement of his rent for land which had been so detained. Then there was trouble with the New River Company in connection with building along Theobald's Way, and in 1683 the corporation was involved in another suit.[18] Matters were not smooth, either for Thompson or for the corporation.

By this time the main battle over town government was over. The freemen had begun to be restive as long ago as 1425 and continued in 1597 and 1610, at which last date they secured the right to 13 representatives on the council, not necessarily freemen, and elections were held only when a vacancy occurred. The civil war gave them their chance, and in 1650 they even abolished the distinction between burgess and freeman. (It was in this very year, as part of the ferment of the time, that an Independent congregation came into being in Bedford.) At the restoration, the distinction was restored, but one positive gain remained to the freemen: though only burgesses were eligible for the council, there were to be annual elections. The right of every burgess to attend the council lapsed, and so the 13 elected burgesses were, with mayor, bailiffs and aldermen, the council. This council, under the act of uniformity, was Anglican; members of the Independent meeting could no longer hold office.

Town government however did not greatly concern the average townsman, for the council had few duties. Street repair concerned it only as regards the great bridge and a limited part of High Street: the rest was the responsibility of adjoining occupiers. Street lighting too was the duty of inhabitants, and was compulsory only in High Street and this from 1649. A town scavenger was first appointed in 1667 at £3 p.a. Probably to most town-dwellers the parish to which they belonged was the more obvious unit.

There were soon to be more complications over the London lease. The great fire of 1666 set in motion a tide of building in London. One of the most active developers was Nicholas Barbon,[19] who had qualified as a physician, but who had speculative interests which included setting up in 1681 an office for fire insurance. A contemporary[20] says "the trade of medicine failing, he fell into that of building, and the fire of London gave him means of doing and knowing much of that kind . . . All his aim was profit". By 1683 he had contributed to development in the Strand, Soho and elsewhere. Another contemporary notes in his diary in 1684 on 11 June "Dr. Barebone, the great builder, having some time since bought the Red Lyon fields near Gray's Inn to build on . . . the gentlemen of Gray's Inn . . . thinking it an injury to them, went with a considerable body of 100 persons, upon which the workmen assaulted the gentlemen and flung bricks at them".[21] Red Lyon Field, now Red Lion Square, adjoined the revised Harpur land on the southwest; between it and Gray's Inn were trees and open space, now Bedford Row. The case came before the Privy Council, where it was said that Barbon marched about the fields at the head of his workmen, shouting and halloing.

It was incidentally at this time that municipal corporations generally again came under government attack, this time by Charles II insisting on the renewal of municipal charters. The negotiations for Bedford's new charter were undertaken by Paul Cobb, mayor 1683–4 and 1684–5, himself an attorney. The new charter was issued on 11 July 1684, and the government took the opportunity of substituting for the existing recorder one more favourable to its policy. The town clerk was dismissed and there follows a period of uncertainty in the minutes. The charter had to be paid for, and the council on 15 September appointed members to assess contributions to raise the sum of £100.

It was at this time that Barbon established contact with Bedford. He was a man of grandiose schemes, and notwithstanding that the building boom was overreaching itself, the Harpur land adjoining his own was tempting. So also was the Rugby land which he leased in 1686 somewhat later. The usual practice at Bedford, when business was to be transacted, was to nominate three or four members. In this case normal practice appears not to have been followed, but it seems likely that Cobb reported at Bedford to at least some colleagues Barbon's offers before he accepted a down payment of a £250 fine for a reversionary lease of the Harpur property. This lease was issued on 9 December 1684.[22] It was not, however, till 8 January 1686 that Cobb presented his accounts at a meeting of the council, which is when Barbon's name first appears in the minutes. On 15 January 1687

Barbon was accepted by the corporation as tenant in place of Thompson for the residue of the latter's lease, though in fact Thompson did not formally assign this to him until 16 February 1687. Barbon thus had the residue of Thompson's term of 41 years from 1668 to 1709 at £99 p.a., and his own reversionary lease of 51 years from 1709 to 1760 at £150 p.a.

The question remains whether Barbon's £250 fine went into the municipal coffers at this time of extra expense, or was used for trust purposes. The £100 tax for the charter ordered on 15 September 1684 (and not rescinded) was presumably already collected when Cobb presented his account in January 1686, but it would not cover all expenses for the charter, which Cobb gives as £144 11s. 6d. Fines on the renewal of trust leases, though strictly trust income, were sometimes treated as perquisites much later than this in other places than Bedford (see ch. 3). It would seem that the council felt that their coffers had been opportunely replenished, and that the mayor, William Faldo, was overruled. He took the unusual step of insisting that his protest was entered in the minutes: "I do protest against the allowing of any of the money given or coming to the town for charitable uses to any other use or purpose".[23] Some members were shamefaced about it, and there was uneasy discussion in the town afterwards, for some months later, on 1 November, the council resolved: "We at this council here present do unanimously declare the same to be our protestation". But they did not formally resolve that the £250 should be restored to the trust funds. Since the accounts do not survive, we cannot discover whether this was done.

Barbon did not live long, but long enough for the corporation to have difficulty in getting his rent in 1687 and to consider between 1689 and 1691 voiding his lease; and long enough also to propose in 1692 what would have been for Bedford an unsatisfactory exchange of the Harpur land for two farms, site unknown. Rugby also found him an unsatisfactory tenant. He died in 1698.

Exactly how much development Barbon achieved in the Harpur area is hard to determine. When maps indicate streets, this need not necessarily mean that building has begun, or if begun that it is finished, let alone occupied. John Strype in 1720 speaks of "a row of good new built houses which runs up to Lamb's Conduit, the east side being not yet begun to be built, but the street laid out".[24] But nearby, he says, is "another designed street . . . like the ruins of Troy, some of the houses carried up to covering, others about a story, and others only the foundations"; that matters had been so "for some years", and there seemed "no likelihood of finishing". We know from the corporation minutes that there was building along what is now Theobald's Road before Barbon took over. Morden's map of 1700 shows continuous building from Red Lion Square, which adjoins the Harpur estate, up to and including the west side of Bedford Row, which is on the estate; indeed 36 Bedford Row has a lead cistern dated 1691. The conclusion of Greater London County's Department of Architectural and Civic Design is that Barbon left the area in an embroyonic state of development, but he also left most of its plan and much of its character; and that most of the Harpur estate north of Theobald's Road was built by 1710.

After his death his leases reverted to various individual mortgagees. Those for the Harpur estate were Richard Webb and Richard Chiswell.[25] The rent appears to have been paid to Bedford; and in the surviving accounts it is simply entered as paid by "Barbon's executors or assigns". Gradually the confusion of Barbon's day was sorted out. The first surviving ratebook in 1729 shows all houses occupied.

A short distance to the west of the Harpur area there were still one or two great houses, including one which in 1669 had come by marriage to the Russells of Woburn and was now known as Bedford House. To the north were still open fields.

Meanwhile the Bedford of the period 1709–60, when the rent of £150 was being paid, had over 2,000 inhabitants. Trade was becoming concentrated in the towns, small though they were, and craftsmen less and less found it profitable to operate from a village. Brewing was developing at Bedford. Here also, since this was from 1689 the highest navigable point on the river Ouse, was the main centre for coal distribution for the country round. By now the town clerk was a townsman, though the recorder was an aristocratic patron. For the annual election for mayor and bailiffs, a complicated system of nomination had grown up: the aldermen nominated three candidates, and the council three candidates, and the freemen could only vote for these nominees. For the council only aldermen could nominate, and the freemen chose 13 from a list supplied by the aldermen. Thus the main power lay with the aldermen. The freemen were quiescent. The disputes of this century were mainly party political at times of parliamentary elections, and the parties did not divide on social lines. At these elections the 3rd Duke of Bedford began to intervene. By law it was still obligatory to take the Anglican sacrament.

The accounts, where they survive, show how the corporation employed the £150 rent. They were slow to raise the salaries of master and usher; this was eventually done to £40 and £20, but these sums were still too low. From time to time a delegation went to London for a procession or perambulation of the estate; thus in 1733–4 £10 10s. was spent for seven persons to go to London; their expenses there came to £25 19s. 8d., and their dinners to a further £4 10s.; hence Goldsmith's remarks, much later, in *She Stoops to Conquer*, "Sir, do you think we have brought down . . . the corporation of Bedford to eat up such a supper?" The total London expenses on this occasion were over £40 and thus more than the master's annual salary. They began to put into effect some of the welfare provisions Harpur had laid down; thus in 1733–4 they gave 30s. each to three poor maidens as dowries. In the same year they distributed £34 18s 6d. to the poor on St. Thomas' day; and in 1751 £37 15s. But then the distribution began to rise, and by 1758 it had reached £72, about 400 persons benefiting from sums of up to 13s. each, about half the recipients being in St. Paul's parish. The cause of this rise no doubt was that in 1747 the corporation's administration had been challenged in a Chancery suit. The origin of this suit mainly concerned the school.

NEW COLLEGE

A word may be said as to the part played by the Warden and Fellows of New College. New College was entitled merely to appoint the master and usher. Here it neither could nor would necessarily always seek the best man available. The posts at its disposal, which included the patronage of about 30 livings, were regarded as a trust to provide for its graduates, more particularly for Fellows who resigned in order to marry. In those days the poor graduate in search of a position had to depend either on his college or on noble patronage. Examples of the grovelling letters which such people or their relatives were forced to write may be found in the correspondence of almost any aristocratic family (for instance, that at Wrest Park); and it is probable that in general a college exercised patronage more wisely than an aristocratic individual.

However, the master was not always a graduate of New College; sometimes there was not one available, and so occasionally one was appointed who was not even an Oxonian. One of the best of the pre-Trust masters was Nicholas Aspinall (1683–1718) who came from Cambridge – his was at first a temporary appointment, later made permanent.

As to the appropriate salaries for teaching staff, the college would be better informed than the corporation, but could only recommend increases, not order them.

Moreover, the college had no general oversight of the school. Such oversight would scarcely have been practicable. There were the estates of the college's endowment to administer. Roads were bad until the arrival of turnpike trusts in the 18th century, and the road from Oxford to Bedford was one of the last in the area to be dealt with in this way. However, the Warden did occasionally visit Bedford, for a letter of 1718 refers to his having stayed at the Swan.

What the Warden and Fellows clearly would do was resist any infringement of their legal rights or those of the school. They would both have good legal advice available, and would have the resources to make good their claim. Hence they must eventually be successful in resisting ill-advised or untoward action by the corporation, but the process might be slow.

THE SCHOOL

The periodic repair of the school building and the master's house came under the corporation. It was ordered for instance in 1682, but it was not always done thoroughly. When the Trust took over in 1764 the school building was out of repair and the master's house had to be rebuilt. In this period no alterations or extentions are to be expected, for until the 19th century the custom of teaching all classes in a single open hall remained general.

Nor was the curriculum subject to change. Up to Tudor times, when so many schools were founded or refounded, nearly all books, religious and secular, were in Latin, as were business transactions. Churchmen were frequently nominated to public office. Thus Latin was a necessity for the able boy who hoped to rise. From Tudor times Latin, now with the addition of Greek and with more emphasis on classical literature, was still the gateway to the university and was needed by the accomplished gentleman; but Latin was less and less used for business purposes and the holders of public office were more usually laymen. Yet the endowed schools were bound to Latin and Greek by the rules of their foundation, and could not experiment. Hence parents would sometimes prefer to pay a small sum to send their boys to learn reading, writing and arithmetic from a local schoolmaster who set up privately, as did Benjamin Chesterton at Bedford in 1708;[26] while some more prosperous parents in this century patronised the private boarding school at Aspley Guise, where the curriculum was less restricted and even included map-making.

Numbers at the free school in Bedford were thus not likely to grow from Bedford boys, although the only charge was a small entrance fee and the quarterly payment of a few pence. But there was the possibility of attracting boarders from the sons of country gentry or clergy.[27] Some of these at least there were. A few have been traced as going from the school at Bedford to Cambridge university: Francis Betterton from Leicestershire in 1575, George Reeve from Hertfordshire in 1640, and two others in 1670 and 1675. There seem to have been several boarders in the period 1656–60. There were apparently also at the school some boys from Bedfordshire, such as Thomas and William Orlebar in 1690, whose bill includes their entry money, two inkhorns, a phrase-book, a *Corderius*, and a horse and cart to bring over their bedding. The boarders seem to have lived with the usher over the school. Among them were sometimes children of Bedford freemen living in London. In 1724 the Lord Chancellor decreed that only Bedford children should be taught free, and this probably discouraged boarders. In 1731 that somewhat unreliable master, Priaulx, said that his usher "never had but two boarders", but in 1735 he wrote that there were "daily prospects of additions".[28] The worst period at the school was apparently 1649, when it was "quite desolate". For other years occasional numbers are quoted ranging from nine to twenty. The largest total number of boys on record seems to be 26 in 1717, when Aspinall, after long service, was about to retire; the lowest three in 1739.[29]

Staff had a bearing on the varying numbers at the school, and here salaries were a vital point. The first known figures are £20 p.a. for the master and £10 p.a. for the usher in 1629. In 1669 New College was urging £40 and £20, and the corporation began paying temporary additions (£5 and £4 in 1670). The Chancery decree of 1725 ordered £30 and £20. Eventually the figures of £40 for the master and £20 for the usher were reached, for they occur in the accounts for 1733–4. The entrance fee at this time was 12d. and the quarterly fee 2d., hence these additions were negligible. The net result was either that the staff changed constantly or that they augmented their incomes from other sources and occupied their time in other ways.

The period of rapidly changing staff lasted for more than a century from the death or resignation of Green in 1573 to the coming of Aspinall in 1683. In this period there were 13 masters, of whom only two stayed any length of time. Some were able or active men who left for other fields of endeavour. William Smyth (1573–7) left to practise law; Francis White, his immediate successor, eventually became Bishop of Norwich; John Allanson (1664–5) departed to be a chaplain at sea; and John Longworth (appointed 1672) emigrated in 1677 to the American colonies where he died in 1692. Richard Butcher, appointed 1597, soon left Bedford to teach at Thame. Richard Butler (1665–72) appears to have resigned because of delay in raising his salary.

However, some other causes operated. Henry Whitaker was elderly when appointed and died in 1601, soon after appointment. Political reasons were responsible for the departure of Thomas Butler, who briefly held office (1656–60) in the commonwealth and was later said to have taught "many gentlemen's children"; he was expelled at the restoration. And at least one master, William Willis (1681–3), seems to have been unsuitable, and had already been removed from his New College fellowship for non-residence; the corporation paid a substitute, John Rewse, and a delegation went to Oxford to acquaint New College with the state of the school and ask for a new appointment.

Masters who stayed longer usually provided themselves with other employment and consequently income, though we have no explicit information on Daniel Gardener (1610–36) who seems to have left the school mainly to his usher, and eventually departed to become vicar of Godmanchester, remarking "I know not whether any of the Fellows will leave his hopes in the college for so mean a place as I rashly did". William Verney (1636–56, 1660–3) held the living of St. Peter's parish, Bedford, and neglected his duties at the school so that it became quite desolate. Nicholas Aspinall (1683–1718), first appointed temporarily in Longworth's absence and later confirmed in his post on the latter's death, also became incumbent of St. Peter's, but he "discharged his trust with great vigilance and applause". However, the most extraordinary master was Matthew Priaulx (1718–39). He, so he says, "married a woman of fortune", became a proctor in the ecclesiastical courts for the dioceses of Lincoln and Peterborough, and town clerk of Bedford. He adds nonchalantly "My house adjoins the school, and when I teach, I teach young gentlemen there". The operative word would seem to be "when".

In such circumstances the usher had little supervision, and there was constantly trouble, either because he was inefficient, or because he resented the position in which he was put. When there was contention, both parties put their case to New College, and their accounts conflict so much that all that can safely be deduced is that often both were at fault. Gardner said that his usher, Giles James, never came to school before 9 a.m., seldom till 10 a.m., and sometimes was not there at all in the afternoon; and that his discipline was so severe that the whole street resounded with sudden yells and outcries, and one boy's life was endangered. Discipline in those days was always severe, but it may be that that of James was excessive even for his time. Many signed a testimonial for him, but he was dismissed. Aspinall's usher from 1707 was Benjamin Rogers, later vicar of Stagsden and rector of Carlton; this seems to have been a happy and fruitful partnership; on Aspinall's death Rogers noted sadly in his diary "the best friend I ever had". Under Priaulx there was again trouble. Rogers left in 1721; Beedles stayed only a short time; so did John Betts, who said that when he came, Priaulx told him he was much confined by business and could not perform his mastership, and so desired Betts to take over the whole management of the school. According to the account of the next usher, John Gamble,[30] Priaulx scarcely taught one day, and Gamble's petition to New College was supported by 26 signatories, including some of repute, such as John Orlebar, Denis Farrer and Henry Horton. But Priaulx dismissed Gamble, locked the school against him, and counter-attacked with superb aplomb: "I never could determine whether impudence or ignorance was his (Gamble's) superior quality", and enclosed to the Warden a certificate signed by 36 supporters, also reputable. The Warden must have found it difficult to know what to believe. None of this can have helped the school.

Still worse for the school, however, were disagreements between the corporation and New College. There was bound to be some friction when the appointing body was over 50 miles distant, while the corporation was not entitled to intervene in the running of the school. Hence either the school was left to its own devices, or sometimes the corporation exceeded its responsibility. As early as 1603 a resolution was passed at the court leet that from time to time from two to four learned men should "oversee the school" and "take trial and proof of the schoolmaster, his ability, aptness and diligence". In fact this seldom seems to have been done; neglect was more usual; but the claim was to be renewed at intervals long after this in the time of the Trust. On the other hand, the corporation resented admonitions from New College to raise staff stipends, as when the Warden of New College wrote in 1668 "what man of parts will come among you?" Finally, on the resignation of Aspinall as master in 1718, the corporation resolved to make the next appointment, and padlocked the school against Priaulx. The usher, Rogers, let in Priaulx at the back door, but the corporation "appointed" Benjamin Holloway, who began to teach in the gildhall. They withheld Priaulx's salary, which for the time being was paid by New College, until a Chancery suit in 1725 pronounced in favour of the college. Incidentally it must be remarked that, whatever Priaulx's other qualities, he certainly became accepted in Bedford as few other masters did, and it was no small achievement to arrive to find that the corporation claimed to have appointed another master, and eventually to become town clerk.

The worst instance of inadequate cooperation between corporation and college and of the master supplementing his income in an unsatisfactory way came on Priaulx's death, and this it was which set in train the events which led to the setting up of the Trust in 1764. The college appointed as master and usher George Bridle and William Bowles. The latter never came to Bedford and the former received the salaries of both. It may even be, as the eventual judgement in the case implies, that there was actual collusion: that it was a device to give the master a better income. If so, it was certainly irregular, but it was by no means a flagrant case if the standards of public life in 18th century England are borne in mind. At all events, the corporation was now challenged. The absenteeism of the usher, the fact that there were in 1747 only 11 boys at the school, the question whether the welfare payments laid down by Harpur were sufficiently put into force combined to bring matters to a head.

The state of affairs at Bedford was not uncommon. Troubles of this kind beset all small endowed schools in country towns. What was uncommon was the prospective vast increase in the Harpur endowment, and this must have been in everyone's mind. In 1760 the Holborn lease would fall in, and the consequent rise in income from £150 p.a. was expected to be anywhere between £2,000 and £3,000 p.a. The magnitude of the change from Bedford's point of view is realised if it is remembered that the corporation disposed of only small sums, and so also did the various parishes who raised rates for poor relief. In the largest parish, St. Paul's, a shilling rate at this time would produce £119.

THE COMING OF THE TRUST

Only a substantial man could challenge the corporation, and such a man was likely to be found only among the members of the Independent meeting. Since 1660 these had held aloof from municipal affairs, at first necessarily under national legislation. Latterly parliament had passed an annual act indemnifying nonconformists who had held office, but in Bedford nonconformists were slow to take advantage of this. The man who made the challenge was a prosperous brewer, who lived in St. Paul's Square beside his brewery. His name was Thomas Woodward, and his father – a deacon of the Independent meeting – had been administrator for John Bunyan in 1688. He had also a connection of another kind with Bunyan, for his wife Frances, a convert to Independency, was daughter of that Francis Wingate of Harlington who as magistrate arrested Bunyan. Living, as he did, next door to the school, he was well aware that there was no usher and that there were very few boys. Woodward, with his relative Francis Jennings and seven others, brought a case in Chancery in 1747. Sentence was not given till 1754, and it may be noted that the Lord Chancellor, Lord Hardwicke, able man and sound lawyer as he was, had in this case some private knowledge of the background. When in London he lived at Powis House in the open country slightly to the north of the Harpur estate; and once a year he normally came to Bedfordshire to visit his daughter-in-law at Wrest Park. He ruled that the master, Bridle, must refund the usher's salary for the last 15 years. "It is said this account will ruin the master. I cannot help that. I must do it for the sake of justice and precedent".[31] And he further directed that, on the expiry of the lease in 1760, a new scheme of administration should be laid before the court. Thus the way was prepared for a new system.

There now emerges from the background the figure of John, 4th Duke of Bedford, who had a double interest in the issue.[32] Living as he did when in London at Bedford House in its large grounds, a short distance from the Harpur estate, he was concerned for the amenities of the area. Ambitious politically, he had for long been trying to influence Bedford, a mainly Whig borough, but one concerned to keep its independence. He was extending his park and estate in Bedfordshire, and had recently given 500 guineas towards a Sessions House in Bedford. Though dictatorial, he was willing to be helpful; to put the Harpur charity on a good footing would advance his interest in Bedford, while ensuring better management for London property so near his own.

There was a brief duel. The corporation in August 1759 circulated a printed letter urging non-resident freemen and burgesses "to support men who by steady and uniform conduct for years past have been proved worthy". A reply appeared in the *London Chronicle* in September, and was reprinted as a booklet in 1761, signed Justus; probably commissioned by the Duke, it argues in general terms the case for a charitable and educational trust which, if properly administered, would promote industry, increase population, enhance the value of property, and ease poor rates; and asks "What has Whigism or Toryism to do with this?"

But the Duke obtained a key position. In 1761 a Chancery decree appointed a committee to act as referees for the new leases until the new act was passed. The five members were the Duke, his son the Marquess of Tavistock, his agent Robert Butcher, and (as a conciliatory gesture) two county gentlemen of differing political views, R. H. Ongley and John Orlebar. And it also appointed a receiver for the Harpur estate, William Waller. Incidentally in this same year the Duke had succeeded in getting his brother-in-law Richard Vernon accepted as one of the borough members of parliament.

In any new system the corporation must obviously still play a major part. Since the corporation was an oligarchy, the way to introduce a democratic element would be to have elected representatives from the five parishes. To get members' consent to a draft bill on these lines was not easy, and Butcher wrote to the Duke that they were "insolent and treacherous". But on 30 December 1763 he could at last inform the Duke, writing from Bedford, that the draft was signed, even by persons heretofore inveterate against the Duke's interest, and they "submit all to your Grace". In 1764 the bill became an act. By the act, mayor, recorder, bailiffs, chamberlains, aldermen and the 13 members of the common council were indeed on the Trust, but they were to be assisted by the ministers of the five parishes (not in fact always resident), and by 12 representatives elected by these parishes in proportion to their population and not at once re-elegible. When trustees went to London, their expenses were limited to a guinea for coach hire and 10s. 6d. a day subsistence.

Further, the act laid down guidelines for the Trust's policy. The main needs were seen as the improvement of the school by means of salaries (now £200 and £100), a new appointment (writingmaster, £60), premises and staff accommodation; and the channelling of surplus funds into what would now be called welfare of various kinds (ch. 8). The salaries and improved accommodation should attract able men who could build up the school by means of boarders; while the provision for non-classical teaching should bring in more Bedford boys. On the showing of the act, one would expect Bedford to have had a decade's start of Rugby, which began to develop in 1778. But one vital factor was unaffected. The master at Bedford was still Bridle, under whom the number of boys had sunk to three. Little improvement could be expected in his lifetime.

2 *The Endowment 1764–1973*

The year 1761 opened a new era for the endowment. After the uncertainties of transition from farmland to a built-up area, there was now on the administrative side professional management. As regards the area itself, there were to be three phases: in the 18th century residential; in the 19th century small-scale commercial, till the road system was improved; in the present century the introduction of high-rise buildings and great office blocks.

ADMINISTRATION

A residential officer was essential, and the Chancery decree of 1761 nominated William Waller, whose appointment was later confirmed by the Trust at a salary of £250 p.a. Waller remained in office till he died in 1786. He was followed by a Holborn man with Bedford connections, a one time mayor of Bedford, John Heaven (1786–94);[1] then came one who was also employed by the Duke of Bedford, John Gotobed (1795–1804), followed by the latter's son Thomas (1804–42). For this long period the Trust was served by a series of dependable men. Strict accounts were kept, and almost from the first they were printed. A surveyor, paid on the basis of work done, was needed to supervise repairs and alterations, or mark out sites if there was to be new building. The first was Thomas Lewis.

THE AREA

The area which in 1761 Waller began to administer was residential in character, small in scale, and on the edge of London. To the north, building petered out almost at once; beyond Powis House, residence of Lord Hardwicke, was the spreading open space of Lamb's Conduit Fields, broken into only by the Foundling Hospital. To the east lay Gray's Inn with extensive grounds. To the west, Bloomsbury was built up south of Gt. Russell Street, but north of this street stood the aristocratic Montagu House and Bedford House in large gardens. Thus the Harpur estate was near stately homes and the quiet precincts of lawyers. But to the south-west were the slums of the parish of St. Giles, whose inhabitants on Sunday wandered through our area to the open spaces beyond.

Local government outside the city proper was mainly by parish vestry. The Harpur estate was originally in the parish of St. Andrew. In 1706 the church of St. George the Martyr was built, and this area took in for church purposes most of the Harpur estate. For civil purposes however the two acted as one parish. In 1771 the joint vestry, meeting as usual in the workhouse in the lane by Gray's Inn, set up commissioners for paving and lighting; the lamps were to be 20 yards apart, and the number varied from 38 in Lamb's Conduit Street to two in Richbell

Court.[2] Street names were put up in this year. Piped water, where available, was supplied by companies, of which the most important was the New River Company. The wealthier houses had individual supplies, but otherwise the supply was to standcocks, and only available for certain hours each day. There had been some commissioners of sewers since 1531, but the division of Holborn and Finsbury is not mentioned till 1699.

THE RESIDENTIAL PHASE

Till 1760 there had been a single payment of £150 for the whole estate. The new leases which Waller negotiated were, according to the London system, long leases. They were either building leases for a long period such as 60 years, when the existing property was unsatisfactory or in bad repair, and the incoming tenant undertook to erect a new building; or repairing leases, usually for 30 years, when only repairs were thought necessary. The flexibility of this system thus allowed outmoded buildings to be replaced or modernised.

South of Theobald's Road, in the Bedford Row area which from its proximity to Gray's Inn was occupied by lawyers, mainly repairing leases were negotiated.

North of Theobald's Road (then a backwater), there were more building leases. Here the role of the developer appeared again. Richard Norris, bricklayer, and John Scott, carpenter, took over a block extending from Lamb's Conduit Street to East (now Dombey) Street at a peppercorn rent for two years, after which they would pay £670 p.a. They were helped by other tradesmen in what seems to have been a loose ad hoc consortium. Some of their houses still survive in the area. Barbon's street plan of course continued, but the Trust's surveyor, Lewis, may have prepared the house plans and elevations. There was a troublesome dispute over this redevelopment; one cause of trouble seems to have been the old one of getting possession of the land, as existing occupiers would not quit the property; another was Lewis' unreliability. The dispute was referred to arbitration; the arbitrator's award was thought unfair; and the affair was not ended till 1776 when seven trustees went to London to settle the disputed ground and put an end to the suit. Lewis' bill was at last paid and he was dismissed. He was followed by Robert Leave.

Incidentally it may be noted that on the Rugby estate nearby, where the long lease expired in 1779, the houses seem generally to have been in better condition, and in almost all cases repairing leases were granted.

From time to time a committee went to London to perambulate the estate and check the boundary stones. During the early years the Trust had no bank – there was of course no bank in Bedford then. The periodic transmission from the receiver of sums varying from £300 to £1,200 is recorded in the minutes, and presumably the cash was kept in a safe in the clerk's office till paid out. In 1771 an iron chest was bought for leases. In 1803 Joseph Barnard set up a bank in Bedford in addition to his coal business there, and arrangements were made with Barnard. The Trust's income during the first 30 years was £2,337 p.a.

Meanwhile London was growing. To the north of the estate a broad turnpike road (now the Euston Road) was begun as long ago as 1756. Powis House had long been pulled down, while Montagu House was the British Museum. The Foundling estate developed in the 1790s. Camden Town to the north (estate of Earl Camden) was being built. To the west the development of north Bloomsbury on spacious and dignified lines was intended by the young 5th Duke of Bedford, and Bedford House was demolished in 1800, but war delayed much of his plans. It was his brother, the 6th Duke, who eventually carried them out.[3]

After 30 years most of the Harpur Trust leases were due to expire, and once more an increase of revenue could be expected as new ones were negotiated. On 5 December 1790 a list of about 70 tenants was submitted to the Trust; these tenants were to carry out repairs varying in amount from £15 to £600, and their rents varied from £5 to £59. Further lists followed at intervals. When the various renewals were completed, the income had risen to over £6,000.

THE COMMERCIAL PHASE

But the former residential character of the neighbourhood was changing. There arose a demand from Harpur tenants to use their holdings commercially. The first hint is in 1801 when several "respectable inhabitants" complained of a "nuisance" in Green (now Emerald) Street by Joseph Hodgett. Hodgett was directed to give his neighbours as little trouble as the nature of his business permitted, but what that business was is not specified. The following year applications for a forge in Theobald's Road and a fishmonger's shop in New North Street were turned down. But the change was coming. A butcher's shop was allowed in 1806 in Lamb's Conduit Street, but slaughter was not to take place there.

It is not always easy to see on what principles this "planning permission" was accorded. Thus in 1806 John Rose was allowed to act as wine, brandy and liquor merchant in Boswell Court, if not disagreeable to the adjacent occupiers, and provided he had no door into New North Street. A shop window was allowed in Theobald's Road in 1810. But Moss the tailor in East (now Dombey) Street was not permitted in 1800 to have a high workshop – it would be a palpable annoyance to the whole neighbourhood; and in 1812 in Bedford Row an attorney was not to build behind his house offices for his clerks. This was at no. 37; no. 34 had recently been taken over by another attorney, T. H. Budd.[4]

In 1824 the then receiver, Thomas Gotobed, apparently concerned at the turn of events, urged the Trust to emulate the Duke of Bedford and get more respectable tenants. But the Duke's estate was laid out on more spacious lines than those of Barbon's small-scale plan, and the latter could hardly be discarded at this stage. It is doubtful that the trend could have been diverted. More and more licences were granted; for a surgeon in Bedford Row (provided no night-light was shown); for a goldsmith and silversmith (but not pawnbroker) in Lamb's Conduit Street – both in 1829; though in the latter street in 1831 auction rooms were forbidden, and in 1834 the introduction of a billiard room and cigar shop caused offence locally. As late as 1844 a greengrocer's shop was forbidden at 55 Theobald' Road.

In fact the changes were not merely local changes but were related to the outward thrust of London in all directions. As London grew, the functions of different areas changed; all areas were part of a developing whole.

The financial effect of the change from a residential to a commercial area did not become apparent at once. By about 1830 the leases were due to fall in once more, and a rise in revenue was achieved. A list of 19 May 1831 shows that where old rents had ranged from £5 to £59, new ones were from £16 to £120. The total rose to about £12,000, that is to say it had doubled. What should have been a warning cloud on the horizon was that between 1801 and 1831 the population of Bedford had doubled, and educational demand was beginning to be on a far wider scale than before. But it appeared to the trustees that they had the resources to meet this demand; and they planned and erected at Bedford a splendid complex of buildings, to include headquarters for themselves. It seemed like a golden age, but it was not to last.

CRISIS IN MID-CENTURY

By 1841 the position was becoming clear. North of the estate the first railway terminus had arrived in 1838, and this area was developing. The eligible neighbourhood for residential purposes was now far to the west. The perambulating committee reported sadly "Everyone in London is now gradually moving westward . . . Houses now occupied by an inferior description of trade were formerly inhabited by judges and first merchants. Unless care is taken to improve and to prevent nuisance, they (i.e., everyone) will leave that part of London to other tenants of a more inferior grade still . . . so strong is the rage for residing at the west end entertained by all classes". "The property", they said, "is a tender plant, and requires infinite care in management . . . the least additional nuisance or want of respectable exterior in adjacent houses may drive away good and desirable tenants". Yet demand was falling off so much that the perambulating committee of 1850 recommended that stringent clauses in leases relative to trades be relaxed. Some new leases could only be had for lower rents; thus in 1847 one of £70 was reduced to £68 and one of £66 to £63. The tide had ceased to rise.

Rugby found the same result. "The better class of inhabitants of the private houses has ceased in a great measure to reside in the neighbourhood . . . The surveyor to the estates gives it as his opinion that the property has depreciated since 1821 probably 30%."[5]

For Bedford the revenue was first to remain static, and then to rise so slowly that it reached £15,000 only towards the end of the century. Yet between 1831 and 1871 Bedford's population again more than doubled (6,959–16,850), and the demands of education continued to multiply (chs. 4–5).

It was a difficult time. It also happened that the steady succession of receivers was interrupted. These were now Bedford men: G. P. Nash (1842–4) and John Elger (1844–50). An economy drive was launched at Bedford (ch. 3). Meanwhile the need was acute. Already in 1847 Barnard's bank had stated that the overdraft was too large.

Quarterly (instead of half-yearly) payment of rent was resolved in 1850; but out of 215 lessees, only half responded promptly; one said it was tyrannical; and others threatened to leave.

In this serious situation the touchy receiver, John Elger, offered his resignation (not for the first time); it was now accepted, and command was taken over by the gallant Captain William Jones of Bedford, who for ten years devoted his energies to the estate. He was helped at first by nine trustees, who went to London at their own expense to help with collecting. After Jones came T. J. Green (1850–8) and another G. P. Nash (1868–83).

It is in Jones' time that we hear of the growing practice of sub-letting. Tenements let to house-farmers were over-occupied and under-maintained. It was in the period 1841–61 that Holborn's population reached its peak, with 94,000 persons; thereafter numbers began to fall. Jones found that he had to allow exceptions to the rule for quarterly payment where the lessee had let apartments to tenants, who themselves paid half-yearly.

"Judicious management" gradually effected the transfer to quarterly payments of rent, and in 1853 the perambulating committee found that, though some buildings needed much repair, the general state was better than six years previously, and that the receiver had done much to restore good feeling. The Trust now viewed their assets more soberly, and in 1856 were only modestly hopeful, "considering the fluctuating value of London property, as fashion advances or recedes from the locality".

HEALTH AND COMMUNICATIONS

A new factor now arose in a vigorous health policy in London. Health hazards in growing towns were only gradually realised in Victorian England, in London as well as elsewhere. There was a Holborn and Finsbury commission of sewers, but the area they covered was limited, and so were their powers. For water, the poorest houses still relied on public standpipes. Burial grounds were congested. However, in 1847 the Metropolitan Commission of Sewers was set up. An act of 1848 compelled provision of a water cistern in a new house, and provided that a house could be certified unwholesome by the medical officer. Sometimes the Trust was liable for the necessary improvements, sometimes the lessee; thus we hear in 1856 of foul or offensive cesspools in Devonshire Street (now Boswell), Lamb's Conduit Street, and Theobald's Road.

By the 1870s there is a slightly improved outlook, and very slowly growth resumed. The continuing expansion of London meant also the expansion of London's heart, and the time was approaching when the term central London would cover an area extending to Holborn. As long ago as 1866 the Trust even contemplated an active forward policy to meet the changing situation. The perambulating committee reported that, after all, the estate was only a short distance from the most valuable sites in London, and should be susceptible of great improvement; at the renewal of leases, care should be taken that one block should have one terminal date; then the Trust could lay it out to advantage.[6] The view was far-seeing, but the immediate difficulties proved too great. Two years later the committee ruefully recognised that such a policy would mean an immediate sacrifice of income, while the advantage would accrue only at a future period; and the Trust could not afford temporary reduction. The idea was dropped, and the surveyor in 1877 gave his opinion strongly against it, for it would "seriously diminish the rental".

However, some improvement came from outside authority. In 1855 there had been set up a Metropolitan Board of Works, elected by parish vestries; it had a Holborn Board of 49 members. The Board in 1870 resolved to make a "great thoroughfare" which would run westward through the Harpur estate and take in Theobald's Road. On the Harpur property 25 houses, principally in Theobald's Road itself, were affected, and sold to the Board in 1875 for £26,000. This new road opened up the area. London School Board bought a school site in Princes (now Princeton) Street for £11,250. Other improvements began. Harpur Mews, originally stables, were converted to dwellings by 1886. There were still over-occupied and unhealthy tenements; in 1895 Emerald Street was said to be a source of trouble on this account; but by 1901 Holborn's population fell to 59,000.

INTO THE MODERN AGE

Soon after the revision of the Harpur Trust in 1873 the administration of the estate was changed. When in 1883 A. H. Allen became clerk, the collection of rents was entrusted to him, and since then the receivership has been merged in the clerk's office, held at Bedford.

A London surveyor was still needed. From 1882 this has been the responsibility of the same firm, originally Lander and Bedells, later Lander, Bedells and Crompton, now once more Lander Bedells. Three generations of one family acted in succession: C. K. Bedells, C. H. Bedells and H. S. G. Bedells covering the period 1892–1956.

At the end of the century there came a new local government structure for London. In 1888 London County Council was set up to cover the area of the old

Metropolitan Board of Works, and in 1899 28 metropolitan boroughs were created, among them Holborn. The first mayor of Holborn was the 11th Duke of Bedford. Holborn Borough Council made purchases for housing: in 1930 in New North Street and Boswell Court (£17,750): in 1937 in Dombey Street (£19,655); and in the same area in 1946 (£37,000).

Meanwhile there had been the effect of war. The 1914–18 war, though it meant stagnation for the estate, brought only slight damage from a 1915 air raid. The 1939–45 war was far worse. The first consequence was the dislocation of London life which caused rent arrears to mount sharply. The 1938–9 income was £35,527; by October 1940 rent arrears had reached £3,650. Still worse was the damage from the air. In April 1941 9 houses in Bedford Row and Featherstone Buildings were totally destroyed, while 20 were damaged in the area, and heavy bombing continued in May. Rent arrears in July 1941 were £5,128 or 14%, and only gradually, as confidence returned, did they drop to the £2,000 mark, while some had to be written off. The actual rent roll fell by about two-thirds to £12,447 in 1942–3, i.e. to the level of 1825–67 in the previous century. But for the generous gift of £40,000 from an anonymous donor between 1943 and 1945, it would have been difficult for the Trust to continue. After the war, it took some years to recover payments for war damage; these were completed in 1954.

In urgent need of money, the Trust in 1947 let land in Theobald's Road on a building lease, on which Adastral House and Lacon House were built, at a ground rent of £9,572. Then came an offer to purchase the freehold for a large sum. There was anguished debate. Some land had been lost in the 17th century; some had since been sold for road-widening, for housing and for a school; to accept this offer meant a more sizeable reduction than any previous one. The voting in 1954 was at first to accept; at the next meeting the resolution was rescinded; finally the sale went through in 1962 for £222,000.

By this time rents exceeded £60,000, and in 1966 for the first time they topped £100,000. The estimated rent income from the London estate for 1972–3 was £230,000.

By recent reorganisation of London government, the estate now falls in the London borough of Camden in the county of Greater London. Its gross area is now 6.08 acres, the net area (less the roads) 3.77 acres. The former farmland conveyed by Sir William Harpur in 1566 is bisected by the broad traffic artery of Theobald's Road, along which rise the great blocks of Mercury House, Adastral House, Lacon House (at present, Ministry of Defence), and a towering police station. North of Theobald's Road is a roughly rectangular area from Boswell Street to Emerald Street. To the northeast are small streets with buildings going back to 1800 or before, once residential, but now with shop fronts. Here and there patches of recent building have replaced the war damage of 1940–1. To the northwest the network of paths and ramps round modern high-rise blocks recall former small-scale piecemeal building now swept away. South of Theobald's Road a long narrow strip of the estate runs nearly to High Holborn; it includes the dignified west side of Bedford Row, where war damage has been skilfully made good. Here four of the early 18th century houses have been rehabilitated with original fenestration. Since national policy is now attempting to protect buildings listed as of architectural merit, the Trust's policy especially during the last decade has been to preserve what is good that survives from earlier days.

A BEDFORDSHIRE ADDITION

In 1971 there came to Bedford School a local addition to the endowment under the will of the late Colonel G. H. Wells (d. 1952). By a pleasant coincidence this property, Ickwell Bury, is in the next parish to Southill, where the Harper family is first known, and a Joseph Harper was living in Ickwell about 1220.[7]

3 *The Trustees 1764–1973*

THE TRUST'S FIRST YEARS

Under the 1764 act the trustees consisted not only of mayor, recorder, bailiffs, chamberlains, 13 aldermen and 13 members of the common council (30 persons in all), but also of the ministers of the five parishes and 12 representatives of these parishes (i.e., a maximum addition of 17 persons). On the face of things it was clear that the corporate trustees, in a majority, used to acting together, and drawn from the more substantial inhabitants would continue to be the main force, especially since the mayor acted as chairman. As late as 1790 it was said that the corporate trustees "act in close and inseparable conjunction".[1]

The first minute-book covers the period 1764–73, and in this period aldermen were the most frequent attenders. Gidney Phillips, surgeon and apothecary, mayor three times, put in 106 attendances. Other aldermen were John Howard (74), John Cawne (71), William Palmer (69), and the Methodist William Parker (71).

The newcomers on the Trust made as yet little impact. The Anglican incumbents, theoretically five but in practice four, since St. Cuthbert and St. Mary went together, each attended once only. The twelve representatives elected by the parishes came seldom and were probably overawed. They were not eligible for re-election, though in 1790 18 electors in the tiny parish of St. John tried to renew Thomas Stone's term (Stone was a surveyor and author of a county agricultural survey), while 8 supported John Purser. The trustees by 19 votes to 3 declared Purser elected. Stone forced his way into the next Trust meeting, which had to be adjourned. The only identifiable Independent was Stephen Odell (58), an active member and deacon of the Independent meeting. It would seem that he must somehow have got himself elected by an Anglican vestry.

Notice of meetings was given in the various parish churches. Not still 1797 did each trustee receive a formal notice. The meeting place – as soon as the hospital (children's home) was acquired in 1771 – was the boardroom there. Attendance at meetings varied; on one occasion (6 July 1803) it sank to two; more usually it was from 10 to 20, and could rise to 30. In 1800 standing orders were framed and hung in the boardroom, but no copy has survived. A committee structure emerged only slowly and uncertainly, the first being (by 1781) a committee of three appointed quarterly to manage the children's home. However, this did not work very well; costs rose with war inflation; and in 1793 one of the trustees undertook to attend the market personally and order the meat required. It is not clear how long this arrangement continued. After the Stone fracas the trustees paid one of the constables a shilling a time to keep the door with his staff. They had other interruptions, for they speak of "persons breaking in", "interrupting and insulting" them. Very soon poor people with any kind of request or supposed grievance learnt to try to get access to meetings.

What were these early trustees like? One of them, Richard Cave, in 1769 wrote to the Warden of New College that there were "a few honest men, some half-friends, some direct enemies without cause, others of too low notions to be concerned in a public trust, and others so poor and ignorant that they are both rogues and fools".[2] Translating this, it seems that there were a few professional men anxious to forward the grammar school, partly on account of their own sons; some half-hearted towards the grammar school and suspicious of New College; and several small tradesmen for whose sons tuition by the writing-master (ch. 5) represented the utmost required. The last named, in so far as they understood the provisions of the act, would be more concerned with the welfare side than with education. Ignorant they no doubt were, but they had had little chance to be otherwise; and it is a function of democracy that the local citizen, sometimes through painful mistakes, slowly learns by attempting tasks to some extent beyond him. For the first 30 years of the Trust's history, the humbler trustees were mainly overruled by their more substantial colleagues.

The small tradesmen, and indeed probably all the trustees thought it appropriate that some profit from Trust contracts should accrue to the town, but they tried to be fair in sharing them out. Thus, when in 1770 the master's house was rebuilt, they divided the work into 13 lots – small wonder that later they had to give notice to the contractors to finish by September or be sued. Though in 1778 a proposal to make a rota of tradesmen who had lived in the town five years to supply the hospital (poor children's home) with provisions, clothes and repairs, was lost by one vote, yet in the 1780s clothes were provided successively by Webb, Clements, Savage, Hodgkins, and John Cave; shoemending by Field, Woolston, Johnston; and so on. In 1807 James Webb and John Barns are to alternate quarterly with stationery and printing. In a small town, with so large a Trust, it was inevitable that trustees would be those most suited to carry out contracts. On 8 February 1774, out of 29 bills to be paid, 14 were presented by trustees.

New College's right to appoint master and usher of the grammar school was confirmed by the 1764 act. Here was a definite link with the world of learning, which might counteract narrow views at home. But in practice it was an uneasy partnership. In the 18th century the distance (over 50 miles of unturnpiked road) was just too great for easy intercourse. When an occasional deputation of trustees went from Bedford, as in 1769, they were inclined to be on their guard; and in the latter half of this century no Warden is known to have visited Bedford. Education in the grammar schools was at this time, with rare exceptions, a shrinking service, not a dynamic and expanding one; so the master and usher in writing to New College were not concerned to raise educational issues. On the contrary, they looked on New College as securing their salaries, their coals and candles, their houses and stables, and generally acting as their protector against the Trust; and, instead of building up good relations at Bedford, they directed complaining letters to the Warden.

The Trust needed two main officers, clerk and receiver. The latter has already been mentioned. The position of clerk was of central importance, and the superb series of minute-books and of printed accounts, all of high standard, bear witness to a long succession of clerks giving faithful service, sometimes in periods of extreme difficulty. The first, Thomas Cave, held the post only four years; his successors, Richard Wakefield (1768–91) and Edward Chapman (1791–1807) nearly 40 years between them. By 1815 when John Whitehouse was clerk (1809–34) it was decided to build him a house on St. Peter's green (the site is now occupied by the Gas Board offices).

Meanwhile, there had come a change in the Trust, in its constitution, in the character of its personnel, and in some of its guidelines.

Criticism of the 1764 act had arisen in 1769 and 1790. Its allocation of specific sums to the welfare side, intended to prevent irregularity, meant difficulty for the trustees when they had to meet capital expenditure on buildings. But the general agreement needed for a new act was hard to secure without the backing of a determined individual or individuals. By the time such backing was forthcoming, there was in prospect a doubling of rental by the falling-in of leases from midsummer 1793 onwards (ch. 2); so that not merely were financial difficulties not expected, but once more there was a preoccupation to lay down rules for the anticipated increase. This increase was a spur to bring matters to a head.

THE TRUSTEES IN 1793

The 1793 act widened the membership of the Trust and altered the method of election. Behind it one of the main figures discernible is Samuel Whitbread the younger, Whig M.P. for Bedford 1790–1815, energetic and concerned for education, for social conditions, and for political liberty, but as yet young. His father, Samuel Whitbread the elder, the previous member, a shrewd and determined individualist, was still a force to be reckoned with, and was alive to the existence of progressive schools elsewhere. His friend and ally was the young 5th Duke of Bedford.

Most intriguing, however, is the younger Whitbread's trusty lieutenant, William Belsham who, as long as he himself lived in Bedford, kept Whitbread constantly in touch with events there. Belsham was the grandson of the Independent brewer Thomas Woodward, whose action in bringing a suit against the corporation in 1747 had led eventually to the setting up of the Trust (ch. 1). Woodward's daughter Ann married James Belsham, and he, though pastor of the Independent church at Newport Pagnell, lived in Bedford. They had two sons:

Thomas, the unitarian minister, and William, who inherited the St. Paul's Square brewery. Ann Belsham became unhappy with the Old Meeting (Bunyan) when its pastor developed a belief in adult baptism, and she and her son William were founder members of the New Meeting (since known by its most prominent founder member, John Howard the philanthropist), set up in 1772.[3] By the 1790s William Belsham was making a name by political and philosophical writings, and before long he sold the brewery.

The alert spirit now perceptible in Bedford was mobilised in the politically active Independent Society (political, not religious), founded in 1789, whose secretary was the solicitor Theed Pearse, soon (1798) to become clerk of the peace for the county and later town clerk. This society in 1790 made various suggestions for the new act.

This spirited team was not an easy one to drive.[4] Further, the agreement of the corporation and of New College must also be secured. The younger Whitbread wanted 12 county trustees (both Rugby and Manchester had county trustees). The corporation saw this as a possible opening for political influence, and refused; the inclusion of the lord lieutenant and of the two borough members of parliament (then always county gentry) was as far as they would go. Whitbread urged that no trustee should hold a contract, but the corporation and the society both thought this need not apply to regular supplies for the hospital (children's home). It was probably Belsham who secured an increase in the elected trustees from 12 to 18 and their election by a new method. As the terminal date of leases approached, tension mounted. But by May 1792 fairly general agreement had been reached.

But the bill did not secure a place in the 1792 session. A mild panic set in that there would be confusion over the first lease renewals. In December 1792 the Duke casually gave directions that no lease should be renewed without consultation with his surveyor. Bedford opinion was up in arms, and the Independent Society prepared to file a bill in Chancery to secure an injunction against renewals before the act. It required all the ingenuity of Belsham and the personal influence of Whitbread with the Duke to smooth matters over, but he did so. On 18 December Belsham wrote "the result of your conference with the Duke will give universal satisfaction".

But the sturdy old Samuel Whitbread the elder was not prepared to be swayed from what he thought right by dukes or anyone else. He proposed to clinch matters and instructed his solicitor to proceed with a Chancery bill. Belsham wrote urgently to inform the son of this "most unpleasant embarrassment . . . I hope you will be able to dissuade him". The younger Whitbread cleared this last obstacle, and in 1793 the bill was passed.

The 1793 act endured for a generation, and in many ways this period was a golden age for the Trust. What then was achieved? First, it was something that an act had been passed; the alternative, as was found later when positions had become more entrenched, was a lawsuit, and that spelt disaster to all concerned.

It was a pity that the inclusion of county trustees was not carried. The corporation's resistance to this proposal is understandable in view of the ingrained opposition to outside influence which they had learnt during their 18th century resistance to the Duke. In this instance, however, the past was not a good guide for the future; there was to be less and less risk of attempted ducal domination. The addition of the lord lieutenant and of the borough members of parliament was ineffectual, as they did not attend. (The 5th Duke, in his capacity as President, attended once in 1795.)

However, the increase in the number of elective trustees to 18, and the alteration in the method of their election provided a notable change. Hitherto they had been elected in the five parish vestries, and therefore were almost always Anglican. Now they were elected at a meeting presided over by the mayor, held at the Sessions House. (The Sessions House, built in the 1750s when the old gildhall was pulled down, served for both town and county meetings.) The electors were £10 householders or £15 leaseholders. Now it was easier for Independents to take part.

Chief of the elected members was William Belsham: Abbot (then usher) calls him "the regulator of these fellows", and Hook (master) writes to the Warden of New College of him as "the chief instigator". Another was the Rev. Samuel Hillyard, minister of the Old Meeting since 1788, "amiable and exemplary, mild and discreet . . . the cause of harmony in Bedford".[5] The able attorney, Theed Pearse, secretary of the Independent Society, himself an Anglican, was a third.

It happened also that during the period of the 1793 act there was an active and intelligent Anglican incumbent at St. Peter's who took his trusteeship seriously, the Rev. Philip Hunt. In the latter part of the period the aldermen included Sir William Long, the brewer who acquired from Belsham the St. Paul's Square brewery, and who was four times mayor. There was a high standard generally.

The other interests of some of the men who were trustees at this time indicate their outlook. Some joined in a movement to set up an improvement commission for the town in 1803. At this time, when municipal corporations had few powers, there was a widespread desire to improve towns by sweeping away squalid little streets, centuries old, and by replanning on more spacious lines. In Bedford the commissioners cleared St. Paul's Square and rebuilt the bridge.

Part of this impetus no doubt came from the borough member, Samuel Whitbread. He, as executor of his father, was largely responsible for the new infirmary, and as county justice was behind the new gaol and the asylum.

It was the trustees of this period who at last in 1811 secured for the grammar school a dynamic headmaster (see below and also ch. 4). They initiated in Bedford what later came to be called elementary education. It was they who, long before the idea of public housing had been conceived nationally, built 40 houses for the town after the fire of 1802 (ch. 8).[6] They helped other charities hit by inflation: that of Christie in 1810 (similar help was given to Hawes charity in 1835).

They would have been prepared to show an enlightened attitude towards the rights of Jewish children. A few Jewish families had settled in the town, and the question arose of the right of their children to participate in Trust benefits. Unfortunately, after advice had been sought in 1817, the Lord Chancellor, the reactionary Lord Eldon, in 1819 ruled against allowing Jews to share, and thus Jewish participation was held up for the time being.

THE TRUSTEES IN 1826

As the time once more drew near for repairing leases to fall in, it was decided to obtain a new act to regulate Trust affairs (1826). There was no leading figure in the background to make a fresh assessment of the changing situation and advise accordingly. Samuel Whitbread was dead. The 6th Duke of Bedford was not inclined to interfere. Belsham was no longer in Bedford. Some of those leading Bedfordians who had led the Trust for years were still trustees, but were growing elderly, and were perhaps lulled into false security because all had gone well for so long. Among more recent trustees, we find the main attenders include J. and F. Green, Joseph Okely, G. P. Nash, John Pheasant, William Smith – some of these names are indeed known in Bedford, but rather as business men than as associated with wider interests. No new thinking was done. It was taken for granted that the revenue would continue to rise; and the expected increases were alloted to existing activities in similar proportions to those of 33 years previously, without consideration being given as to whether alterations should be made and priorities revised.

As regards the appointment or election of the trustees themselves, no changes were made in existing arrangements. Not even the disallowance of all trustees from holding contracts was achieved; but this did come by a resolution of 1831.[7]

Most important was the fact that the trustees of 1826 did not make a new assessment of the London situation on which all their activities depended. As London expanded, the eligible residential area moved to the westward outskirts (ch. 2). The Harpur estate was losing the pleasant character it once had, but the time was yet far ahead when it would gain in value as being near to London's centre. Income was ceasing to rise, and would soon remain stationary for a long period. But the trustees supposed that they had funds to spare for which an outlet must be found. A belief had become general in Bedford that the Harpur estate was an inexhaustible gold-mine. Perhaps this belief has still not entirely disappeared – there is a traditional saying "The Harpur Trust will never bust!"[8]

Ironically the 1826 act helped to make litigation easier. Its care in this respect may have been partly due to the firm of Pearse, who acted for the Trust (Theed Pearse, as well as being town clerk and clerk of the peace for the county – both of course part-time occupations – carried on a private practice with his son's help).

Mainly, however, it was probably due to increased public vigilance as regards charities, since Brougham had set up the Charities Commission in 1818. The 1826 act provided that eight trustees might petition the Lord Chancellor (who could make orders accordingly); further that the Attorney General (or anyone with his consent) might do so; and that these costs could be met out of the estate.

Staff salaries were increased: the receiver in 1826 to £400 p.a., the clerk in 1830 to £150 p.a.

In order to appreciate the (on the whole) successful guidelines both for education and welfare laid down by the 1793 act, and their dangerous enlargement, without revision of priorities or need, and in a quite different financial situation, in the 1826 act, policies in these two spheres need to be traced over the period.

EDUCATIONAL POLICY IN 1793 AND 1826

Educationally the 1793 act made useful improvements, but the 1826 act misjudged the situation.

The 1793 act planned to stimulate the grammar school. One way was to give the master and usher, in addition to their salary, a capitation fee of £3 for each boy up to 20 boys; i.e., there was a ceiling of £60. This would also give the staff a better income, since their salaries were not raised by the act. The proposal came from New College. On the suggestion of the Independent Society, the act also provided that the grammar school boys should be examined annually by two visitors from Oxford; and at the instigation of New College the further provision was made that a university exhibition of £40 should be awarded on the result of the examination (there were not to be more than three exhibitioners in residence in any one year). It had been proposed that the visitors should receive a fee for their trouble. The college politely declined this, accepting only expenses; but when in 1799 the expenses came to £22 the trustees somewhat ungraciously objected. Neither capitation fee nor university exhibitions affected numbers in the time of the then master, Hook. When he died in 1810, the trustees realised that the appointment of the new master was vital, and it was after this new appointment that at last the grammar school began to grow. The recipe for development had been found: the right headmaster.

By a rare and fortunate chance, the mayor this year was an Oxford man, G. D. Yeats, a physician at the new infirmary. He, Theed Pearse and Dr. Philip Hunt went on a deputation to New College. Their reception was "such as to augur most happy results; the Warden and Fellows were anxiously desirous of contributing all their aid to ameliorate the grammar school, to remedy errors and prevent their recurrence; and seemed to hail the deputation instead or deprecating it". It happened that an able young graduate of New College, in fact a son of the rector of St. Andrew's, Holborn, was a teaching assistant at Blundells school, Tiverton, John Brereton, and he was appointed by New College.[9]

By the time of the 1826 act, numbers at the grammar school under Brereton had risen to 40. At this stage it was probably hard to imagine that the rise might continue indefinitely. The trustees in effect signed a blank cheque. Although a needful rise was secured to master and usher by increasing their salaries to £250 and £140 respectively, the capitation fee was raised to 5 guineas and 4 guineas, and its £60 ceiling was removed. As numbers continued to rise, the capitation fees eventually soared to £1,000 for the master and £800 for the usher, when the school was sorely needing better premises, more staff, and a playing field. The whole finances of the school were (to modern eyes) distorted.

That the university exhibitions were raised in 1826 to £80 and their number increased was a provision both more useful and less costly. Eight exhibitions could now be held at any one time, six of them by Bedford boys.

At the writing school there is a happier picture. Here the grammar school's late start had a fortunate side effect. Had a dynamic master come earlier to the grammar school, that school would have needed increased funds – funds which would not then have been available for other purposes. The outcome might have been a Rugby. But just as a plant which is checked branches out, the other side of the foundation, the writing or English school had developed, and, though of inferior status, was larger. The salary of the writing master was raised in 1826 from £80 to £200. The trustees came to have particular sympathy for this school, which was their own creation, and the management of which was under their control and not shared with New College. Besides it clearly met a need. The eventual outcome was that within a century there were to be two important boys' schools instead of one.

With regard to what was later to be called elementary education, perception of the need for this was still everywhere at an early stage when the 1793 act was passed. But soon in the country generally some such education began to spread, partly by teaching on Sundays, and partly by day schools established by religious bodies or by private individuals. In the county Whitbread was one of the most active in this respect – indeed in 1807 he unsuccessfully proposed in parliament a state system. But for many years such education was to depend on voluntary effort. In Bedford it was felt to be clearly the responsibility of the Trust: why attempt to raise money by subscriptions when the trustees had it at command? From 1815 the Trust provided what was called a "national" school (the method of teaching being the monitorial system used by the National Society – see ch. 5). It was as yet small, but as it was to provide a general service it would inevitably grow. Some teaching would soon be thought necessary for all boys, and later for girls and infants too.

These problems would be intensified by the rise in Bedford's population. In 1826 the population was about 6,000, and it was to rise by about 2,000 in each decade. Three census reports had now appeared: 1801, 1811 and 1821; and the

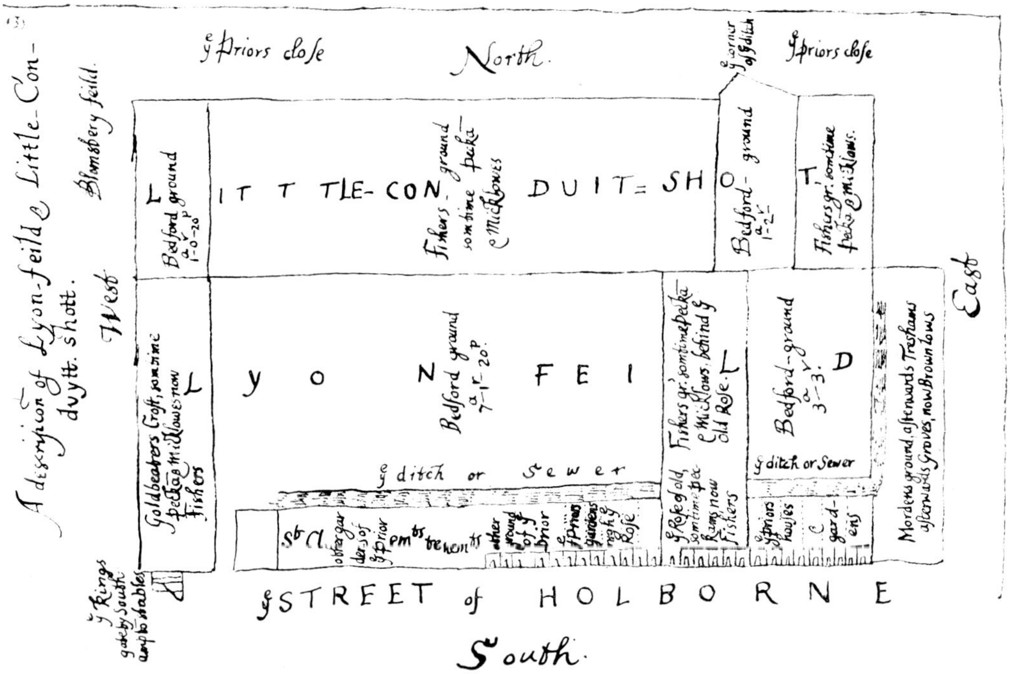

1a Sketch plan of Holborn estate, 1650 (farmland)

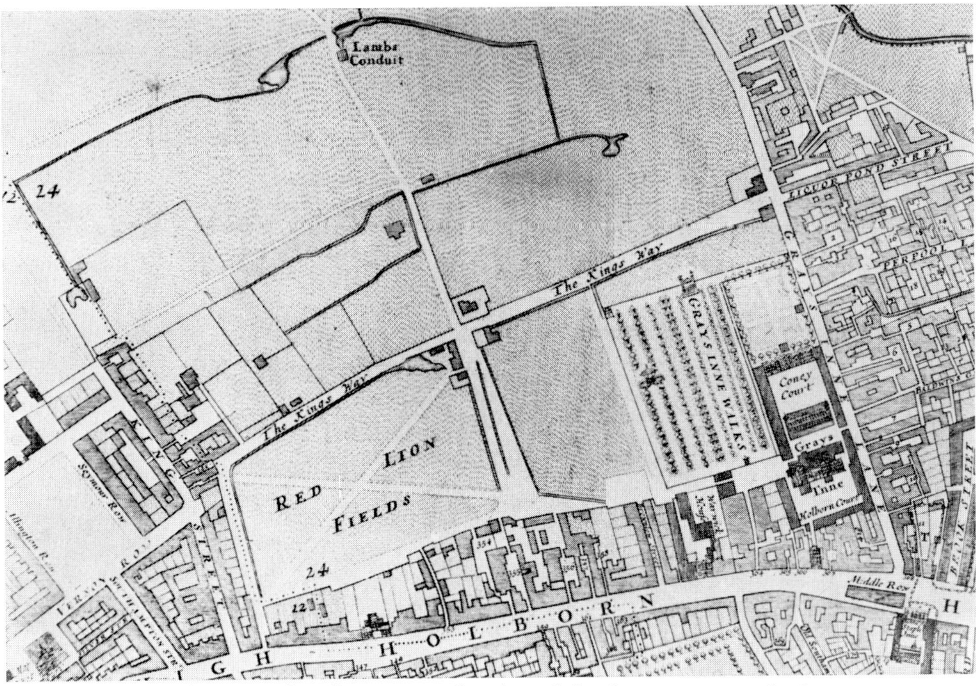

1b Map of Holborn, 1682 (residential development approaches)

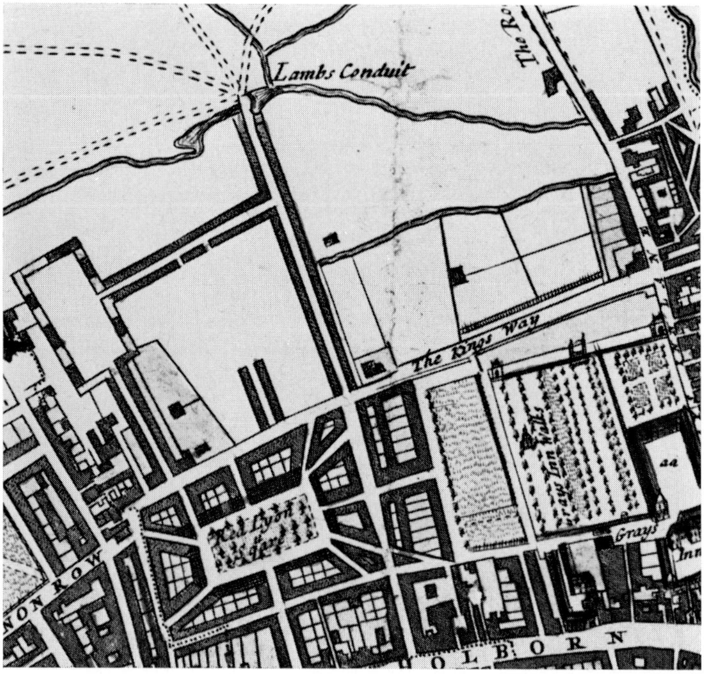

2a Map of Holborn, 1700 (residential development in progress)

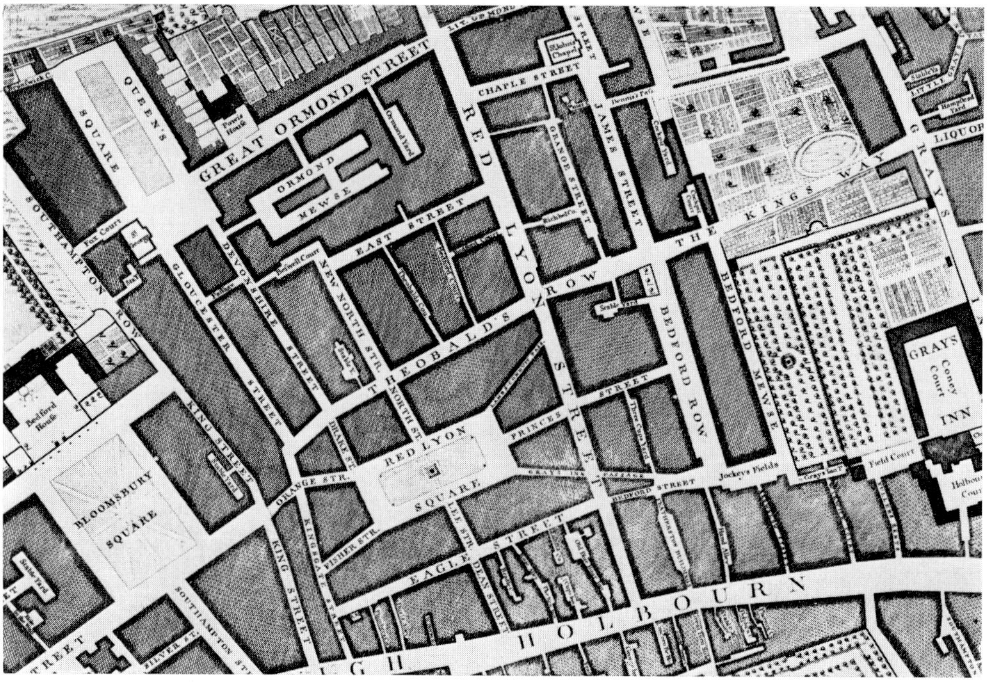

2b Map of Holborn, 1746 (residential development complete)

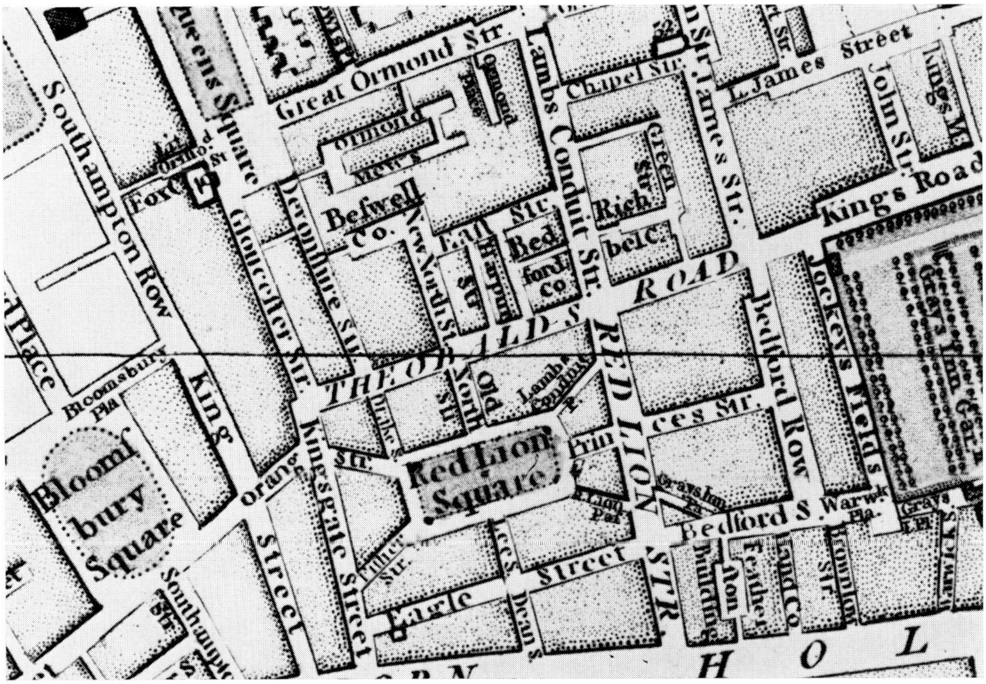

3a Map of Holborn, 1803 (commercial phase approaches)

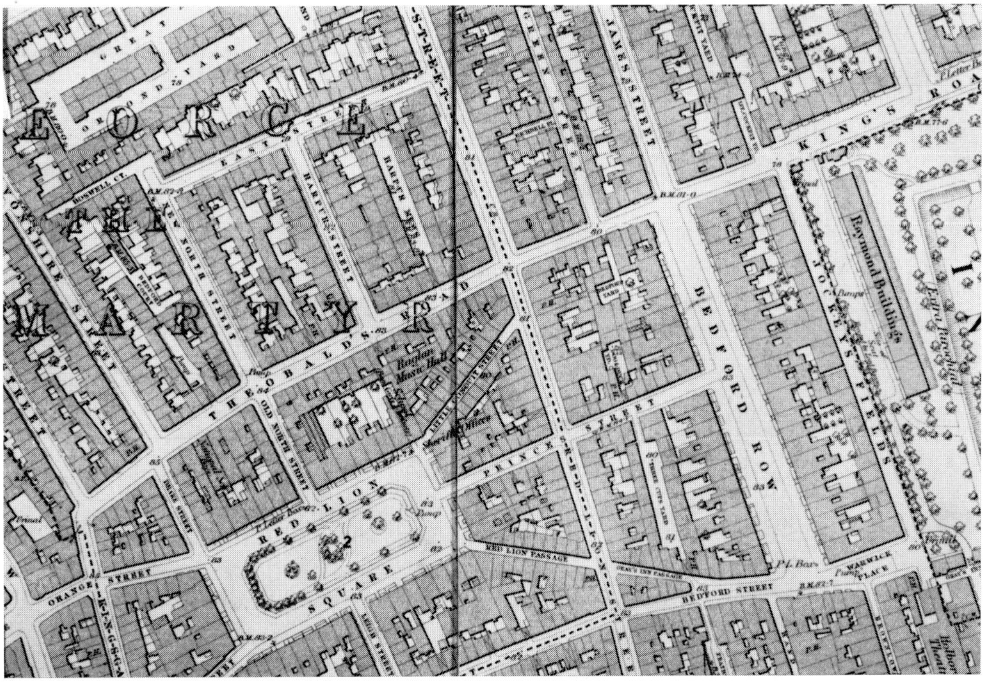

3b Map of Holborn, 1878 (Theobalds Road widened)

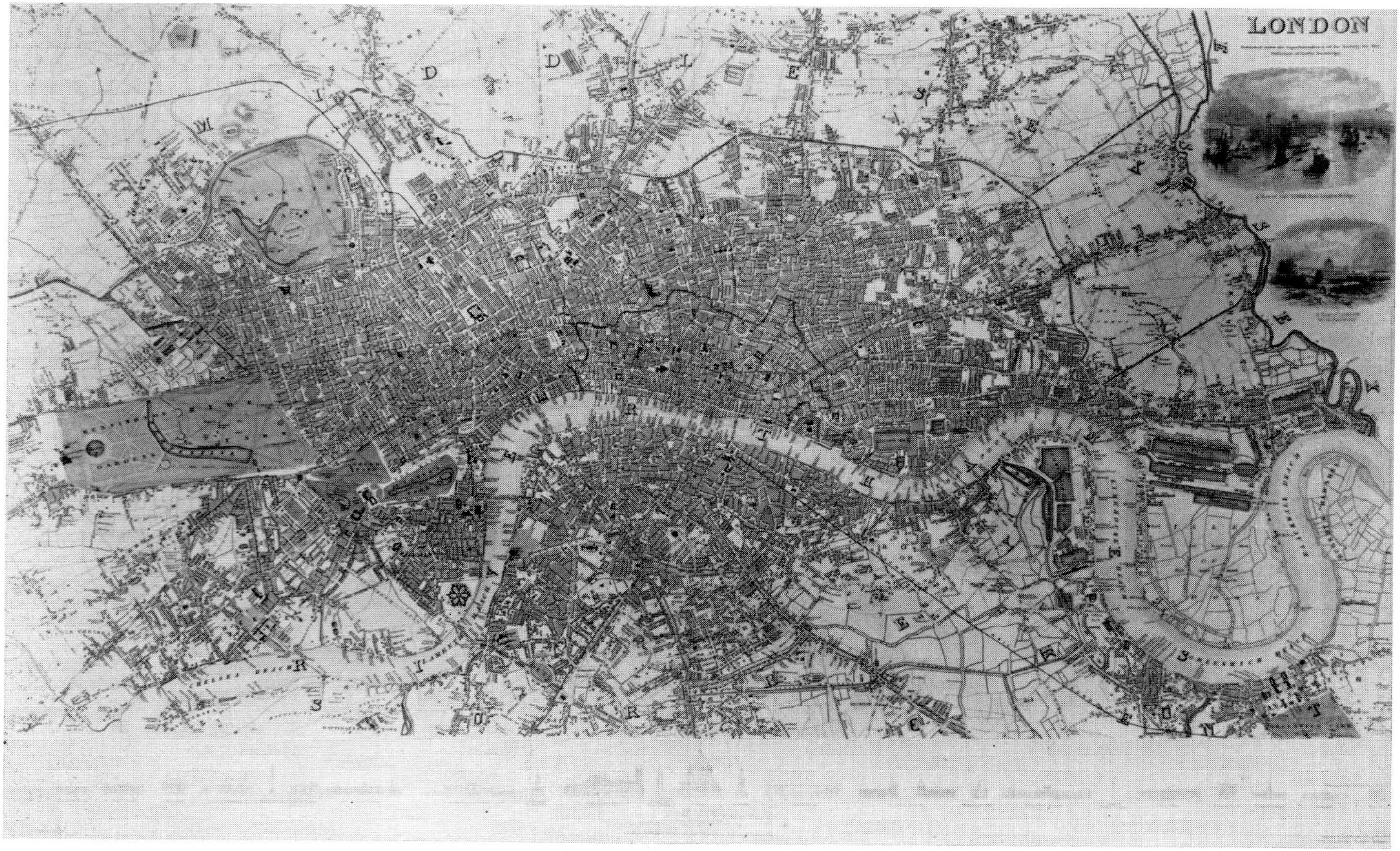

4 *Map of London, 1835 (residential area has moved west)*

5a Blitz on Theobalds Road, 1941

5b Bedford Row restoration

6a Harpur's brass in St. Paul's church, Bedford, 1574

6b Boy from the children's home, c. 1840, by Bradford Rudge

7 Central Bedford, 1833, by William Dawson, OB

Above: Grammar school with headmaster's house and boarders' premises; on left, brewer's residence once occupied by Thomas Woodward, later by William Belsham.

Below: Children's home, elementary ("National") school, and English or commercial school.

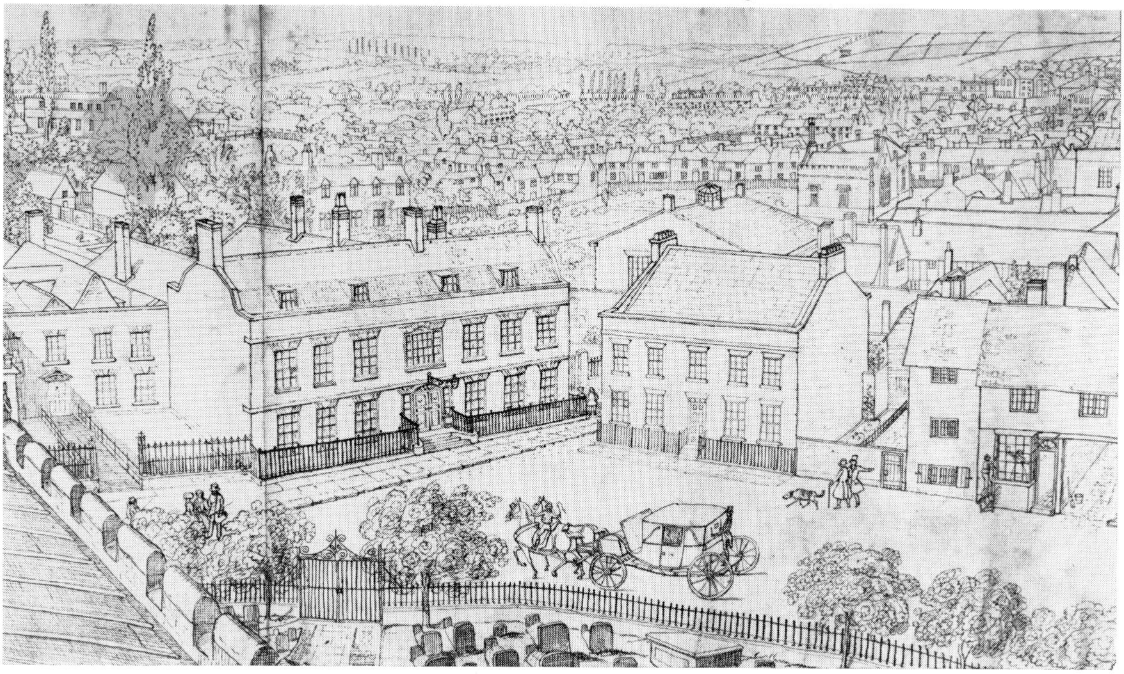

8a Sir William Long, Trust chairman, 1803, 1813, 1822, 1829

8b John Howard, Trust chairman, 1858–61

8c George Hurst, Trust chairman, 1855

8d Samuel Whitbread, Trust chairman, 1873–95

trend might have been perceived. But the framers of the 1826 act completely failed to see both the expansion of elementary education that would be required, and the rate at which Bedford's population was growing.

WELFARE POLICY, 1764–1826

We turn to the welfare side. Its history is given in ch. 8, but an outline must be added here because of its relation to the problems which the trustees faced.

Harpur, as was to be expected of a well-to-do, public-spirited man of his day – a day in which national policy for the poor was in process of being shaped – was concerned not only for education but for the welfare of the less fortunate in Bedford.

Already when the 1764 act was being prepared, there was hesitation in translating the terms of his endowment into the spirit of contemporary requirements, in that marriage portions for poor girls, created by Harpur himself, were retained. The 1764 act did, however, initiate provision for the apprenticeship of poor boys and girls. In the 18th century the system of apprenticeship was general. For those in real need it was normally carried out by the overseers of the poor, but the Harpur Trust was able to apply it more widely. Then there was to be a home for poor children (the medieval term hospital was retained). Surplus funds were to be distributed in alms. The 1793 act, on the suggestion of the Independent Society, added almshouses, again an advantage when the usual refuge of the aged pauper was the workhouse. Thus some useful changes had been made, though possibly they did not go far enough.

Some of the provisions of 1764 were extended in 1793 and 1826, but (apart from the useful addition of almshouses) they were not rethought. By 1826 the system of apprenticeship was declining, yet the allocation for this was increased from £600 in 1764 to £700 in 1793 and £1,500 in 1826, plus benefactions on completing the required term. Marriage portions for poor girls were by 1826 anachronistic, if they had not been so before. The 19th century needs of the young people who received these payments would progressively be better served by education – that education which in fact the Trust increasingly set itself to provide (ch. 5). At least marriage portions were not raised, but remained constant at £800, and so in fact were fewer in proportion to the population. The children's home, in the main catering for about 20 children, was allowed by the 1826 act to go up to 50 children, though this remained inoperative. The almshouses, of which 20 were authorised in 1793, had before the 1826 act been increased to 66; the extra ones were originally public housing after a fire in 1802 and were later converted to almshouses. The hall money, or distribution of alms (in mid-winter), laid down originally by Harpur for disposing of any residue, became a fixed sum of £300 in the 1793 act and £500 in the 1826 act.

Deceived by the grammar school's late start, not realising that their predecessors had laid the foundation for expanding elementary education, and unaware of financial stringency approaching, the trustees of 1826 continued and extended the statutory commitment to welfare provisions, some of which were more appropriate to an earlier age. They were like men standing on a cliff edge with a hurricane blowing up. A particular disadvantage of extending and fixing the welfare commitment was that, as in the 19th century the power of the voter made itself increasingly felt, it became more and more difficult politically to curtail, alter, or discontinue the welfare payments. The way was prepared for a violent struggle in the mid-19th century between opposing claims.

Before this struggle broke out, however, there are two pleasant features to record in a kind of sunset-glow of the Trust's golden age. One was that the Lord Chancellor's ruling against Jewish children was tacitly allowed to lapse. A son of Godfrey Levi was admitted into the "national" school in 1833; and in 1842 a resolution, proposed by Alexander Sharman and seconded by William Rogers, was carried: "It being doubtful whether the decree applies under the present act of parliament (1826), the trustees do not consider themselves called upon to exclude the children of Godfrey Levi and Joseph Lyon from the benefit of this charity".

THE HARPUR COMPLEX, 1833

The other feature at the end of this period is the creation of the splendid Harpur complex of buildings. It was planned from 1828 onwards by those very trustees responsible for the 1826 act. They had failed to see the trends of the times in education, in population, and in the London situation. They bequeathed to their successors the causes of a struggle that would convulse Bedford for years. But one thing they saw clearly: that Bedford had a great heritage from Harpur, and that this should be worthily housed. So they gave Bedford a building which has graced it for nearly 150 years, and of which the façade will still be preserved in the forthcoming redevelopment, and should endure long after the troubles of 1850 have been forgotten. All honour to them for this!

The site of the complex is now known as Harpur Street. In the 18th century it was Angel Street, and here in 1771 a house with a certain amount of ground had been bought for use as the children's home. As opportunity offered, other purchases were made between 1804 and 1831, in particular the manse of the Old Meeting in 1829; so that by 1831 the Trust owned the whole west side of what is now the south section of Harpur Street (except for a house at the southwest corner where Horne Lane now runs). Here the trustees proposed to build from north to south premises for the writing or commercial school (thus leaving the now growing grammar school in complete occupation of the original school building); the children's home; a house and offices for the clerk, with a boardroom for themselves; and premises for the "national" or, as it was sometimes called "general preparatory" school; i.e., four buildings in all in similar style.

The first plans prepared by John Elger in 1828 disappointed them. The four separate buildings seemed functionally adequate, but the general effect was unpretentious and unimpressive. They wanted something in "a more ornamental and architectural style", something impressive and beautiful. They resolved that that style should be the increasingly popular Gothic. In April 1829 they offered a premium of £50 for the best plan, though they did not pledge themselves to use the winning entry. The competitors included young Lewis Vulliamy, a pupil of Smirke. The premium was adjudged to Wing, but the Bedford architect John Wing (designer of the bridge) had always inclined to a classical style, and they were not willing actually to use his entry. They decided to submit the plans of both Elger and Wing to the rising architect, Edward Blore, who had been employed by the Duke of Bedford for Woburn town hall, and who was also architect for the Pitt Press at Cambridge.[10] The 32 trustees present on this occasion on 29 March 1830 included both well-known elderly trustees like Theed Pearse, G. D. Yeats, and Dr. Philip Hunt, and more recent ones like Thomas Barnard, the Greens and the Nashes. In the chair was the mayor, Sir William Long.

In June 1830 Blore, using Elger's internal plans, provided an "improved exterior elevation", combining the four buildings behind a single impressive Gothic façade with a central tower. The contract for the building was for £13,730 – more than a year's income; and was given to the firm of Wing, who himself had lately died. The street was levelled and macadamised, in consultation with the improvement commissioners. In 1833 the first part of the work, the commercial school, was completed, and £10 was spent on a Christmas eve supper for the workmen. Samuel Bailey (1834–42) was the first clerk to occupy the new official residence, and when he took office the Trust was already overdrawn at Barnard's bank. The remainder of the building seems not to have been completed till 1837.

A feature of it was the boardroom. This was found in September of that year to be cold. A coffered ceiling was ordered in December, and in August 1838 a design was chosen for an inner enclosure with specially carved furniture. Unfortunately the sub-contractor, Kensit of London, lost on this, for the contractor, Barry, failed. Search was made in vain for a portrait of Harpur to adorn the room.

So proud were the trustees of their contribution to Bedford's appearance that, when Assembly Rooms were planned in 1835, they gave £100 to help the subscribers secure the opposite site for their proposed "large and handsome public building".

Incidentally, the new Harpur premises were built just before the somewhat similar ones in New Street, Birmingham, for King Edward's School, opened in 1838. Here an enlightened headmaster, Jeune, persuaded the trustees to combine the two schools (grammar and writing) in the same premises under one overall direction.[11]

CHANGES IN THE CORPORATION, 1828, 1835

There now came through national legislation two changes in the corporation, and these therefore affected the Trust.

The first was the removal in 1828 of legal obstacles to public service by nonconformists. At the restoration in 1660 the Independents had had to withdraw from municipal life, and though for most of the 18th century parliament had passed an annual indemnifying act, the Bedford Independents had been slow to take advantage of this. As has been shown above, they were already elective trustees. Now there was no obstacle to their serving on the common council, members of which were also members of the Trust. The first time a member of the Old Meeting was mayor was in 1856. Methodists were less affected by the change. In their early decades they were still part of the Anglican church, and during this period the Parker family was particularly active in municipal life: Wesley himself had commended William Parker, senior, twice mayor. In the 19th century their main representatives were the industrialist family of Howard, John being mayor four times and his son James twice.

One consequence of the strong nonconformist representation on the Trust was the policy of non-sectarian teaching in Trust schools. When some years later there was an attempt to ensure that teaching staff at the grammar school were Anglican, William White (father of "Mark Rutherford") vigorously opposed it, and in 1844 wrote a pamphlet *The Bedford Charity not sectarian.*

The other change came by the municipal corporations act of 1835, which everywhere swept away oligarchic systems in favour of town councils elected by ratepaying householders of three years' standing. Thus the Trust was henceforward composed partly of an elected town council and partly of elected trustees. The revolution in the management of Harpur's endowment within a century, initiated by public-spirited nonconformists and helped by whig leaders, was completed as a side-effect of national legislation for municipal reform.

The special position at Bedford, as compared with educational endowments elsewhere of comparable importance, may be realised by comparison with that at the opposite end of the spectrum at King Edward's School, Birmingham.[12] Here the governors were a self-perpetuating body. Though Birmingham was incorporated in 1838, and was to a large extent radical and nonconformist, yet when in 1866 a royal commission came to enquire into the endowment, no town councillor nor nonconformist had been a governor.

It is one thing to introduce democratic procedures, but another thing for them to operate effectively by the fair registration of opinion. It was to be years before bribery was eliminated from Victorian political life, and years before the ballot-box safeguarded voters from pressure. With the increased political awareness which accompanied the parliamentary reform of 1832, elections to the Trust, like those to the town council, could become almost entirely political; indeed to many voters the former was of more interest than the latter. The town clerk, Theed Pearse (son of the former Theed Pearse and more conservative than his father), in giving evidence in 1835 for the municipal corporations enquiry, said that one or two recent Trust elections had produced great strife, excitement and animosity, and that it was common knowledge that the rates of poor ratepayers (tenements were rated from £2 upwards) had been paid to secure their votes, though he would not commit himself as to who had done so.[13]

Besides, there were opportunities for interested pressure from the electors on candidates for the Trust. Theed Pearse in his evidence above had said that if almost the entire Trust were elected, the effect would be "most injurious", and that the people elected would not be fitted to execute so large and important a trust. When financial difficulties came, as soon as welfare provisions were threatened, poorer members of the community were up in arms at election time.

The years 1838 and 1839 show the effect of politics. At this time there were growing conservative hopes that, after many years of whig government, their rising leader Peel would come to power. The numbers who polled in Trust elections reached 752 and 913 respectively.[14] All conservative candidates were returned, including Captains Leech and Smyth and the banker Benjamin Trapp; while the defeated whigs included Thomas Kilpin, Isaac Wale and the Greens. How far this was achieved by paying the rates of poorer voters it is impossible to tell.

In the 1840s and 1850s there is little to distinguish trustees elected directly to the Trust, or sitting on the Trust after being elected to the town council. Some names, such as that of the solicitor William Rogers, appear now on one list, now on the other.

With 51 members in a town of about 7,000 population, professional men (more informed about grammar school education and interested in promoting it) were in a minority; and there were not, as in such a body today, co-opted members with special educational knowledge. Charles Brereton, the headmaster's son, writing in 1851, thought it would be better if management reverted to the corporation: "if the 18 elective trustees were removed, there would still be enough of the popular element".[15]

Thus it was that, as a major crisis approached, with difficulties on a scale which the Trust had not yet experienced, practically all the large body of trustees were elected, and the whole of Bedford was convulsed by the struggle.

THE ALIGNMENT OF GROUPS

The professional men included the solicitor, Alexander Sharman, mayor in 1846. His son won an exhibition to the university in 1847; and until 1850 he acted professionally for New College. With the professional men were allied several substantial or "respectable" inhabitants. Among 70 signatories of an undated petition to New College of about this time are John Bull the silversmith, Charles

Deane the coach-builder, George Higgins the brewer, the Rev. John Jukes of Bunyan Meeting, and James and Frederick Howard the industrialists.[16]

Reinforcement came from the squatters. These were generally retired service men, or the wives of active service men, or widows, all anxious to educate their families cheaply. They said later in a petition to parliament that they had "at considerable cost become settled inhabitants of Bedford" and "erected or purchased houses". The parents' column in Brereton's admission register is revealing. First comes in 1822 Captain G. B. Trollope, R.N., and no wonder, for in due course appear six young Trollopes. In 1831 Captain Trollope managed to get himself elected a trustee. Captains follow thick and fast, though apparently not always naval: Griffith, Leech, Mitford, Home and so on. Their addresses reflect the growing residential area: the Crescent, Adelaide Square, Priory Terrace. One of the most active was Commander Charles Hutchinson; and others like Captains W. H. Smyth and Henry Leech became trustees.

The professional men, the substantial business men, and the squatters, though in a minority, had in the background a powerful ally in New College.[17] It was not the province of the Warden and Fellows to look at the situation as a whole, and to consider the impossible situation the trustees were in; but simply to insist that the letter of the law must be carried out as regards the grammar school; and they could safely do this because their legal costs would be recoverable against the well-meaning but ill-informed trustees who formed the majority on the Trust. It was to the college that the "respectable" Bedfordians appealed. Commander Hutchinson urged in 1849 that the trustees were "wholly unfit"; Isaac Elger, the surgeon, in the same year still hoped to prevent the "sad consequences of legal conflict"; but T. J. Green the coal merchant in 1850 wrote "New College alone can rescue our noble charity".

The "respectable" inhabitants realised the value of grammar school education; those among them who were Bedfordians saw that the squatters both developed the town and helped to improve the grammar school. These views were no doubt genuinely held. At the same time, as parents they expected to derive benefits in free education for their sons. They derived two other advantages from the Trust. In any other town of comparable size they would have been called on to subscribe for voluntary or National schools for poorer children, since many years were to pass before education became a national service; but in Bedford these schools were provided by the Trust (ch. 5). They also had low poor rates. Though by the poor law reorganisation of 1834 Bedford was combined with 40 rural parishes in the Bedford Union, a union which had one-third of the county's population in 1841 (33,043 out of 107,936), yet the amount spent in poor relief in 1837 was only a quarter of the county's total (£9,896 out of £39,024);[18] and this difference would seem to be due to the Trust's welfare work in Bedford. The squatters did well in Bedford, and it hardly became them to complain so bitterly when trouble arose.

On the other side were mainly small tradesmen: men like the liberal draper, George Hurst, several times mayor; the hairdresser John Mantel; the veterinary surgeon, Charles Dines; and William Rogers, described by Green as "a clever and not very scrupulous lawyer". These did, it is true, have a local and somewhat limited outlook; that is, they thought in terms of Bedford (though Hurst came only in 1826), and yet did not take into account that the squatters made a contribution to the town's development. They also supported the welfare provisions of the Trust's acts. In doing so, they retained some of the community feeling for the less fortunate, felt by public-spirited men of Harpur's day, but less fashionable in Victorian times as the concept of self-help gained ground. Some of them, like Samuel Cooper, William Walker, and N. W. Small, campaigned for a girls' (elementary) school, which was opposed in 1834 by Brereton, Hunt and Barnard, but achieved in 1836 (ch. 5). They were acutely aware that there was a differential rate of spending per head in the Trust's schools. In 1852–3 the grammar school of about 140 boys (some boarders and some the sons of squatters) absorbed over £3,000, of which £1,901 represented capitation fees for master and usher; while the other schools put together (and by this time there were five, taking about 1,260 Bedfordian children) cost £1,865. The addition of books and stationery brought the educational total for this year to £5,523. The rate per head was over £20 for the grammar school boy and about £1 10s. for other children.

In this year the welfare total was £5,607. Here was the real difficulty; yet the welfare side had the same legal authority as the grammar school. It was not the doing of the existing trustees that it was so; but that of their predecessors who framed the 1826 act. To solve the problem was impossible without a new act or scheme; but how to get agreement on its provisions? A lawsuit could only make further inroads on those funds of which the inadequacy was the cause of trouble. Yet there was no statesmanlike figure to bring parties together.

When Brereton first came as an eager young man, he got on well with the then trustees; in 1812 he wrote "I have found the trustees ever desirous of promoting the good of the school in everything I have suggested". But with the years, though he would support local activities such as concerts or the Horticultural Society, he became more Olympian, and no doubt the changing character of the trustees encouraged this withdrawal. It was characteristic of his position that, while the master of the English school collected his salary from the clerk's office, the clerk was instructed to wait on Dr. Brereton with his.

There was not a good atmosphere between the Trust and New College. To the master and usher it was natural to go over to Oxford (in this period it became possible by train), or to call there en route for somewhere else; but such easy intercourse did not come naturally to the trustees; and once when a deputation went in 1828 to discuss modernising the grammar school curriculum, the Warden was away and there were few Fellows. Further, college responsibility for teaching appointments meant that, when Brereton needed increased staff, he wrote to New College, and the Warden endorsed this in writing to the Trust. It was a pity, however, that New College also endorsed his alarm at possible rivalry from the other boys' school when the teaching of Latin was introduced there in 1837. A perennial source of irritation was the annual examination of the grammar school by two visitors; the trustees felt that they should be present, and that a report should be sent to them; the college withstood these claims as possibly interfering with their academic freedom and that of the master; but it would have been good if some way could have been found of keeping the trustees' interest. As it was, the annual visit, instead of leading to friendly intercourse and keeping communications open, often exacerbated both sides. When in 1836 a committee appointed to confer with the examiners explained that, because funds were so liberally bestowed, they needed to ask if the present mode of education was good, the examiners replied that it was not their duty to discuss management. It was a rare occasion when in 1847 the Warden, the Rev. Dr. D. Williams, came in person, and was brought by Dr. Brereton to the boardroom.

During this critical period there were three clerks: Samuel Bailey (1834–42); Henry Francis Leech (1842–9); and William Jones (1849–58). The post cannot have been enviable.

CRISIS, 1848–53

Such were the alignments when increasing financial difficulty brought matters to a head. Since the main buildings were put up in 1833, the trustees had added to them a girls' and an infants' school (ch. 5). All schools were growing, and the capitation fees mounting, and income was stationary. In 1843 there was a debt of £9,000. The trustees attempted an economy drive, but small economies like discontinuing two lamps in front of the school and reducing the Bedford surveyor's salary from £30 to £20 could effect little, and others (like closing the infants' school or discontinuing French at the grammar school) were hotly opposed by one side or the other. In 1848 cuts in capitation fees and in welfare payments were proposed, but counsel's opinion doubted their legal validity. Now Barnard declared that his bank could no longer make advances. The trustees decided to apply for an act of parliament (for which the Lord Chancellor's approval was required). There followed five years of strife, culminating in the new scheme of 1853. Of the uproar in Bedford during this period, and of the various twists and turns in the legal processes involved, it is impossible to give here a full account; an attempt is merely made to indicate the two sides and the outcome.

Positions were hardening in 1848. On the grammar school side Brereton wrote to the Warden that the trouble was "all these schools not contemplated by the founder". But he was not the main protagonist; he had, as he said, "devoted 38

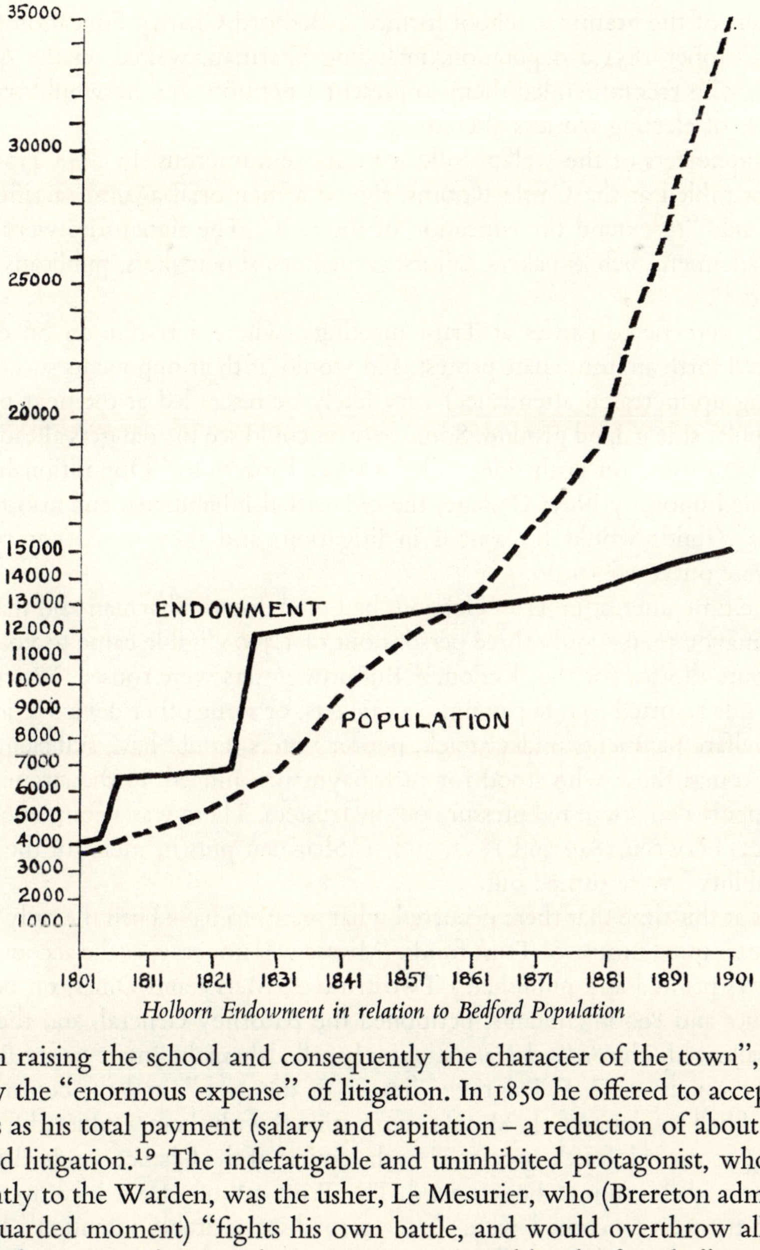

Holborn Endowment in relation to Bedford Population

years in raising the school and consequently the character of the town", and he foresaw the "enormous expense" of litigation. In 1850 he offered to accept 1,000 guineas as his total payment (salary and capitation – a reduction of about £250), to avoid litigation.[19] The indefatigable and uninhibited protagonist, who wrote constantly to the Warden, was the usher, Le Mesurier, who (Brereton admitted in an unguarded moment) "fights his own battle, and would overthrow all claims of the other masters because they are not mentioned by the founder". Brereton's son Charles, in a private letter to the Warden in 1851, thought the usher should not be a trustee; "he can thwart the views of his superior, whom he could not oppose in school".[20] Le Mesurier (next to Brereton who was nearing retirement) stood to lose most by reduction of numbers and of capitation. In the town, supporters of the grammar school formed a Bedford Charity Education Society, and in October 1851 a deputation, including Sharman, waited on the Attorney General, who recommended them to present a petition, and he would try to get the mode of electing trustees altered.

The supporters of the welfare side were more numerous. In 1848 430 inhabitants, assembled at the Castle Rooms, signed a memorial against sacrificing the welfare side "to extend the education of the rich". The signatories were mainly small tradesmen, such as bakers, tailors, carpenters, shoemakers, publicans, and 16 labourers.[21]

There were fierce battles at Trust meetings, where a resolution on one side would call forth an immediate protest, and would (if their opponents succeeded in whipping up increased attendance) very likely be rescinded at the next meeting. The popular side gained ground. Some trustees could see the dangers ahead, and in March 1849 some on both sides called a special meeting. "Opposition has been determined upon by New College, the old settled inhabitants, and also the new residents", funds would be wasted in litigation, and they urged compromise. They were outvoted 10:20.

At one time interest in Trust elections had died down. Sharman said that when he was mayor 1846–7 only three persons out of 1,300 eligible came to vote in the three hours allotted for the election.[22] But now voters were roused. Whether the welfare side resorted to rate paying, beer tickets, or some other device is not clear. With welfare payments under attack, poorer voters would have sufficient reason to rally round those who stood for such payments. Indeed, in the circumstances their support was interested pressure on the trustees. There was a complete change of trustees between 1849 and 1852, and, as Sharman puts it, men "of the highest respectability" were turned out.

It was at this time that there occurred what seems to have been the only specific case of attempted misuse of Trust funds. (Misuse was not easy, as the accounts were from 1764 printed and published.) Two trustees, Merry and Dines, on behalf of themselves and 800 inhabitants, petitioned the Attorney General, and their costs were disallowed. The *Bedford Times* stingingly called them the "martyrs" of Bedford. In 1850 the mayor, C. F. Palgrave, "leader of the mob", and the committee in charge of hall money (see ch. 8), who sympathised with them, deducted from hall money £100 2s. 7d. for these costs.[23] In the course of the Chancery suit, the Chancellor ordered this sum to be refunded. The Trust minutes for 1 July 1852 record that the trustees concerned were "free from dishonourable intention" but had made "an error of judgement". To see this incident in the perspective of the day, it must be borne in mind that at this very time at Eton the fines on college leases were distributed among provost and fellows, and that in the 20 years before the Clarendon commission the sums so disbursed amounted to £120,000.[24]

With financial difficulties growing, the new and inexperienced trustees, ill informed as to the legal dangers they were incurring, in February 1850 ordered a 10% reduction all round. The legal conduct of the proposed new scheme was taken away from the firm of Pearse and entrusted to Rogers. Rogers devoted himself to Trust affairs to such an extent that in 1852, after presenting a bill for £250, he was "in pecuniary difficulties", and his appointment was rescinded.

The trustees' draft scheme, printed while Rogers was in charge, provided for larger salaries but reduced capitation (with the then number of about 150 boys, Brereton would have had £800 and Le Mesurier £565); and there were to be no boarders, which would have abolished an auxiliary source of income. (Only Brereton took boarders, but according to Winchester fashion he paid Le Mesurier four guineas for each.)[25] The Attorney General's proposals discarded altogether the system of elective trustees, and proposed that the Lord Chancellor should nominate 24. It was at this late stage that the town and county members of parliament were drawn in, though one – Hastings Russell – said that he did not know enough about it!

As finally passed by Chancery order of 12 March 1853, the scheme was an inevitable compromise. Capitation fees at the grammar school remained at the same rate, but were to cease with 167 boys (189 boys in 1848 was the previous highest number reached); and the 10% deduction from salaries was to be made good; boarders were limited and could no longer hold exhibitions (for further details, and for the provisions for change on Brereton's retirement, see ch. 4). The welfare side was reduced: apprenticeship from £1,500 to £1,200; marriage portions from £800 to £600; and hall money was to cease.

There was still to be fought the battle over the Trust's constitution, for the Attorney General was preparing to introduce a bill into parliament. The local members in 1854 suggested a compromise: while the Chancellor should nominate 18 trustees, the mayor and corporation should still be on the Trust; but nomination was the one point which all trustees were determined to resist; and by June 1855 the bill was dropped altogether.

There came the inevitable costs of the whole process, both those of the Chancery suit and of the Attorney General's proceedings. It was hoped at least to avoid the latter, and the local members, Samuel Whitbread and Captain Stuart did their best; but all had to be paid; and the total legal costs as finally reported on 18 December 1865 were nearly £7,000.

After this period of stress, it seems hardly surprising that the then clerk, poor William Jones (1849–58) was worn out, and trustees commented in 1856 on his "age and decline of human powers". Yet assistance was supplied, and he was allowed to hold the post till he died in 1858.

CALMER WATERS, 1853–73

Now ensued some years of calm, during which a sadder and wiser Trust set itself to achieve solvency with an income which, even with the welfare commitment reduced, was still not adequate for an expanding educational service. It now had the power (with Chancery sanction) to borrow up to £10,000, and it had to do so to pay costs. Moreover there were two urgent needs for capital expenditure: a new building for the junior department of the English or commercial school, in order to let the latter expand into the whole of the northeast wing; and enlarged premises for the grammar school to provide classrooms instead of the old open hall system (ch. 4). One problem was that, to gain room for expansion, the trustees needed to buy the last remaining house at the south end of its Harpur Street site, and this purchase, which had long been negotiated, at last took place in 1859.

Plans were prepared for both new school buildings by the local surveyor, James Horsford. Many trustees, including Dines and Mantel, conscious of precarious finances, felt that the proposals for the grammar school were lavish; for its numbers, though they had recovered from a brief drop to 48 in 1854, had only recovered so far as to average 100 1855–60. In these circumstances New College in 1858 made representations to the Charity Commissioners, indicating that they were again prepared to take legal action. Prudence prevailed, and on 15 November Horsford's plans were carried by the casting vote of the then mayor, the elderly industrialist John Howard (21:20), and in 1859 the tenders of £2,450 for the grammar school and £1,238 for the preparatory commercial school were accepted. The finances were still balanced on a knife edge; teaching staff, long waiting for increases (there were not then rising scales), were told that applications must be postponed; and an economy committee managed to save £400 by small retrenchments, which included prizes, the cricket ground (£22), and in 1862 the ringing of St. Paul's bell for the schools (£6).

Meanwhile important staff changes had taken place at the schools, the chief being new headmasters at the grammar (1855) and the commercial school (1860).

When the grammar school vacancy occurred, George Hurst who, as mayor, was chairman, signed an official letter to New College. The wording was perhaps formulated by the clerk, but the opinions may be presumed to be endorsed by Hurst. "We want a man who as a teacher is fully up to the times . . . The old curriculum of the grammar school is much too narrow; all honour to Latin and Greek, but let them not stand alone . . . mathematics, natural philosophy, the modern languages and English literature should all be likewise taught . . . We want a man as a master who, like the late Dr. Arnold, can rule and yet be loved." Perhaps the Warden and Fellows received this letter with a smile. No New College man was available; still it must be someone from Oxford; Fanshawe of Exeter was reported to be anxious to give up his fellowship and marry, and he was a Wykehamist – would not Bedford be the thing for him?

When the headmaster of the commercial school was appointed, the mayor and chairman was John Howard. There were no fewer than 126 applications. Of these, three were short-listed: one from Frome, one from Beaumaris, and Moore's faithful deputy, Finlinson. Their testimonials were read, and on the proposition of the Rev. R. Fitzpatrick, seconded by Colonel Mellor, Finlinson was appointed.[26]

By 1870 the two main boys' schools were about the same size: the grammar school 274, and the commercial school 289. Together they cost the Trust over £6,000 a year (the grammar school taking the larger share). The cost of the elementary schools was under £1,000; and more accommodation was urgently needed. The welfare side (mainly almshouses) cost over £3,000.

The invariably high standard of the Trust's record-keeping is thrown into relief in 1876. The clerk who succeeded Jones, D. H. Francis (1858–76) at last found the task too much and resigned. The extensive accounts had been his particular worry. It was found that in fact he had left himself £14 out of pocket.

Some years before this (about 1840) the private boarding school so long kept at Aspley Guise by the Wright family had come to an end. Since the grammar school's extension on its restricted central site came about only slowly, and since the limitation of boarders and capitation marked a policy of non-expansion, some leading figures in the county thought that an alternative must be found. Thus was formed in 1869 the Bedfordshire Middle Class Public School company, which built at Kempston the County School, later known as Elstow School.

THE BEGINNING OF NATIONAL POLICY

And now Bedford, instead of working out its own educational provision, subject only to the remote control of New College and the occasional discipline of the Lord Chancellor or the Charities Commission, was brought into the national vortex. At last a national educational policy was being worked out, both for secondary and for elementary education. Secondary education came first. Two commissions reported. The Clarendon commission dealt with the nine great public schools: Charterhouse, Eton, Harrow, Merchant Taylors', Rugby, St. Paul's, Shrewsbury, Westminster, Winchester; and the result of their work was the public schools act of 1868. The Taunton commission reported on the many endowed grammar schools, with special details for the eight best endowed:

	gross income	educational spending
	£	£
Christ's Hospital	56,000	48,000
Dulwich College	16,829	3,034
Bedford	13,121	7,046
Birmingham	12,218	9,506
St. Olave's	4,605	2,413
Tonbridge	3,614	2,643
Manchester	2,994	2,480
Monmouth	2,925	2,191

Both sets of commissioners approached their task in the belief that the founders of endowed schools had only a subordinate interest in their own neighbourhood – their general object was education. The commissioners also shared the contemporary acceptance of a class basis: that is to say, they believed that secondary education was (with few exceptions) for the minority, and that the best educational instrument so far produced in England was the boys' boarding-school. Further they had the contemporary predisposition to look critically at the use of funds of old endowments, and rather to expect to find misuse. Real misuse in some cases there certainly was, especially at the public schools. It has been said by a recent historian that "no headmaster came out of the revelations of the public schools commission (Clarendon) with the honour of his school intact".[27] (For humbler charities, the Charities Commission had exercised a growing surveillance.)

The commissioner who visited Bedford in 1866 was R. S. Wright. With regard to the Trust, he thought that the elective system produced trustees associated with the prejudices and mental condition of the town. Accepting this, the commission thought that dual control of the grammar school with New College should cease, and that there should be 21 trustees, of whom only eight would be members of the town council, and the direct election of others would cease.

On the schools he produced an objective factual report. He noted, for instance, that at the grammar school out of 194 boys, 130 learnt French and 83 mathematics, and there was no history. There were 40 boarders. At the commercial school, which with its junior department had 751 boys, 220 learnt French and German: their arithmetic was rapid and accurate; and 80 boys learnt drawing voluntarily on their half-holiday. At the "national" (boys' elementary) school, which had 370 boys, the average number to a master was 123, the master being helped by young monitors. At the girls' school (490), the average number to a teacher was 70; and at the infants' school (250), 83. This last building, he pointed out, was ill-placed and destitute of all conveniences for teaching.

After this factual analysis, he launched into comments prompted by the educational outlook of his day. He thought fees should be introduced, and that this would allow of education for middle-class girls. Yet he also had great expectations from the endowment. Bedford did nothing for the county, nothing for the country at large. That class of boy (the pick of wide districts) which maintains the standard of public schools was practically excluded – and this was detrimental to Bedford itself, which might have become one of the greatest places of liberal education in the country. In short, Wright's view was that which the commission's final report endorsed. The commissioners even thought with him that the Trust could maintain day schools in convenient places within the county and affiliated to the boarding-school. This proposal for activity in the county was dropped, but the vision Wright saw for Bedford itself was that which, under governmental pressure, came to pass.

As regards elementary education (ch. 5), the deficiencies which Wright noted do not seem to have weighed heavily with him, nor did they with the commission. To make proposals for elementary education was not in their brief. They did say that the Trust should maintain in full efficiency the schools needed for Bedford, but they did not rate Bedford's needs highly. "The population is but 15,000 and can hardly increase very much more." Perhaps they were aware that there was likely to be before long legislation dealing with this side of education. In 1870 an education act at last aimed to make coverage nation wide, by providing that in all areas where there were not sufficient schools, school boards should be set up, empowered to build schools from rates.

On the welfare side (ch. 8), the climate of opinion of the day was bound to produce an unfavourable report. More than a generation was to pass before the introduction of legislation for old age pensions, and for insurance for sickness and unemployment; nearly a century before an act for the care of children. Compassion for the unfortunate was not much in evidence: Samual Smiles' *Self-help* (1859) was at the height of its vogue. Old endowments were in any case suspect, and this attitude is reflected in the fiction of the day, as in Trollope's *The Warden* (1855).

Wright correctly stated that marriage portions were an anachronism and that apprenticeship was being artificially kept alive. He also alleged that the "almshouses were jobbed for political purposes". It may be that in allotting a vacancy, trustees would favour a political supporter, but all 60 almshouses did not become vacant at the same time, nor was the same political party always in power, so the political effect cannot have been great. It is hard to see what is meant by "injurious doles", since hall money (alms in mid-winter), gradually phased out since 1853, came to an end in 1868. Wright summed up his conclusion in words adopted by the commission: the use of part of Bedford's endowment for purposes other than education illustrated the "unrestrained application of local and indiscriminate lavishness".

The commission recommended the abolition of all the welfare side, except for a reduced number of almshouses.

The commission's report, published in 1868, gave the Trust a shock. The trustees disputed the assumption that Harpur had intended to make "an upper-class boarding-school for All England". When the endowed schools act of 1869, the result of the commission's work, called for such schools to prepare for approval new schemes of management, the trustees tried to make common cause with other trustees affected. In May 1872 they asked the local M.P.s to help the member for Leeds to defeat a scheme for Ripon grammar school – the "objectional system of a large boarding-school for the sons of the wealthy". They affirmed with some justice that "no charitable endowment in the kingdom has suffered less from bad management or misapplication of its funds than the Bedford Charity". None the less, they were obliged under the act to submit a new scheme. This, to have any chance of acceptance, had to approximate to the commission's recommendations.

Again there was long, drawn out wrestling with clauses; again there were rear-guard actions in defence of Bedford's rights. A deputation (accompanied by three members of parliament, Samuel Whitbread, James Howard and Colonel Gilpin) waited on the Vice-President for Education – in particular the first of these gave constant advice and support. Under duress a new scheme was agreed on 6 March 1873 and approved 4 August.

Other endowed schools were also obliged to submit new schemes. At Birmingham less change was demanded; there was no point in requiring boarders in a city developing so rapidly. However, the old self-perpetuating governing body gave place in 1883 to one similar to that introduced at Bedford in 1873.

THE SCHEME OF 1873

The Trust was reduced from 51 to 27 members and was reconstituted. Bedford remained the core, with the mayor and representatives of the town council. There were special educational members: the universities of Cambridge and London each appointed one and New College two. (In the present century a notable representative of New College was H. W. B. Joseph, 1900–35). There were ex-officio governors: the members of parliament and the lord lieutenant. One member was appointed by the Lord Chancellor. An elected representative for the elementary side was added in 1893.

For the first time, there was continuity in chairmanship. Samuel Whitbread became the first chairman, and held office till 1895. To a lesser extent there was also continuity with the committees for the various schools: Thomas Barnard, the banker, was chairman of the elementary committee till 1894.

Some trustees were nervous lest girls' schools should mean women members. "Will they really join us at meetings?" queried the elderly industrialist, John Howard, making a speech to the Trust in 1871. "Oh, how delicate! Oh, how feminine! . . and the Oxford lady can attend all your meetings, for, she being a spinster, there are no children's stockings to mend." At first, however, all that happened in this direction was that five women were co-opted on to the committee which was to plan the girls' schools. They included Miss Mary Ewart, a benefactor of Newnham College, Cambridge, and Miss Smith of Oxford.

A dedicated clerk, young enough to adapt to the new trend and able to serve the Trust adequately, was above all required. It was at this time that D. H. Francis (1858–76) retired. No more appropriate successor could be found than A. H. Allen (1876–1922), who had begun life as a junior master at the commercial school. He stands alone for long service (46 years), and at the end of his life his knowledge, financial grasp, and "devotion to everything that was Harpur" were acclaimed by all. He was the first clerk to be also receiver, and the last to live in the Harpur complex.

Whatever reservations we may have today as to the Taunton commission's views of Harpur's intentions, whatever uncertainties there are as to the role of boarding schools today, the commission correctly gauged the national requirements of its day and the part Harpur's endowment could play in relation to them. As early as 31 August 1883 the *Daily News* said that Bedford was rapidly becoming the metropolis of education in England, while in 1894 the Bryce commission reported that Bedfordshire, "though a small county, is probably unique". Like Cheltenham, Bedford became a centre for professional and service families (see also ch. 6). The town was small and pleasant, with little industry, but with a river and parks. School fees were low and there were no school rates to pay, because there was till 1897 no school board. One who remembered those days wrote that High Street every morning saw a procession of the *haut ton*, all well turned out, but wretchedly poor, for pensions were small and families large. "In one form of 30 boys of which I was a member, 17 had been born in India".[28] It was said in a Bedford brochure of 1913 that "society in Bedford is just what Anglo-Indians have been accustomed to".

Incidentally, these developments at Bedford meant that the newly-founded so-called County School never in fact became such. In 1894, out of 104 boys, only five boarders came from Bedfordshire, and three day boys.

Secondary education (for a fuller account see chs. 6–7) was now entitled to 8/11 of revenue, and benefited slightly by the introduction of modest fees. The grammar school moved into new buildings in 1891. The commercial (now modern) school expanded into that part of the central buildings left vacant by the children's home which had been closed. For girls' secondary education, hitherto left to the Moravians or to private schools, two schools corresponding to the boys' schools were opened in one building in 1882, and grew so quickly that soon one of them had to move into other quarters.

Elementary education (for more detail see ch. 5) was now to take 2/11 of income. Even this proportion was secured by the Trust only after a struggle – the government thought that a fixed sum of £2,000 yearly would be sufficient. The education act of 1870 had no effect at all in Bedford, and for nearly 30 years the Trust continued to provide most of the town's elementary education, and built two new schools in 1876 and 1894. Yet rising population and rising standards in even this service (still regarded as subsidiary) strained resources. In 1895 there were 3,868 children in buildings planned for 3,500; and in the boys' school on the central site there were 918 boys in a school built for 700. There was also urgent need to improve staff salaries. Efforts by the churches to supplement the Trust's work proved inadequate. In 1897 a school board became inevitable. Then under the 1902 act this responsibility was transferred to the town council. The Trust, however, continued to devote 2/11 of its income to this purpose, mainly to those elementary schools on the site of the Harpur complex, which were now voluntary schools.

The welfare proportion of revenue under the scheme of 1873 was 1/11. It was limited to almshouses. The twenty almshouses on the Harpur Green site, known as the best ones, were in due course pulled down, and the site appropriated for a building for the two secondary schools for girls opened in 1882. The almshouses in Dame Alice Street were continued.

THE PRESENT CENTURY

During the present century certain changes have been made in the composition of the Trust, mainly in 1919, and all with the object of securing wider participation. That of the county council was desirable when that body became responsible in 1902 for secondary education (see below); first introduced in 1919, it was extended until the county council, like the town council, now appoints six members. Parents and staffs of each school were given one representative each in the same year.

One new feature is that it has been increasingly possible to call on the services of distinguished old boys who can combine intimate knowledge of the schools with experience gained in other fields. To single out by name any among the number who have thus contributed would seem to be invidious, but the longest serving present member (since 1953) is A. A. Jones, M.P., O.B.M. Another feature is that since 1919 there have been women members – in fact the representatives of staff and parents at the girls' schools must be women. Among the first of these were Miss Katherine Jex-Blake and Lady Ampthill in 1919, and Lady Jaqueta Williams was appointed in 1926. Dr. Agnes Towers served 1951–71 as a representative of parents. There are also sometimes women among the representatives of town and county councils.

No chairman has equalled Samuel Whitbread's term, but Sir Richard Wells (1938–56) was chairman for 18 years, and Geoffrey Howard (1906–21) 15 years. The clerkship, on the retirement of A. H. Allen in 1922, was held briefly by E. D. Hay Currie (1922–8), and then for a devoted period by R. L. Elgie (1929–64), who with 35 years, which included the difficult time of the second world war, comes second in respect of long service in this office, and whose knowledge was encyclopaedic. His successor held the post for less than two years, and it was in 1966 that R. N. Hutchins took over.

The endowment (ch. 2) has produced problems during this century. Holborn, once on the fringe of London, now belongs to its heart, and therefore a rise of revenue was to be hoped for. The damage caused by the 1914–18 war was slight, but that of 1939–45 far more serious, and revenue sank in proportion. Since then there has been a problem of how to administer the estate to maximum advantage. Developers on the large scale required today have desired to purchase part of the freehold, and part was sold in 1962. The present policy, however, is to allow no further diminution. The Trust has also aimed at preserving the best buildings, and for 25 years had the benefit of the advice of Sir Albert Richardson (governor 1939–64). In Bedford the Trust, adopting a forward policy, is itself initiating development on its central site, but even here it is preserving Blore's façade (ch. 9).

CHANGES IN SECONDARY EDUCATION

Well adapted as the 1873 scheme was to the England of the day, it was no more possible that national conditions and requirements should remain unchanged than it had been in Bedford in 1764, 1793, 1826 and 1853, for commissions and governments are no more able than are ordinary townsfolk to see long-term trends far ahead. The first change came with the act of 1902, which meant expansion with local and national help. This act made county councils responsible for secondary education: thus the Trust must work in harmony with the county council as part of a system for the county, while yet at the same time it was fulfilling that wider function towards which the government had propelled it.

From the Trust's point of view a proposed further intake of children from the area round Bedford posed problems. The income from the London estate (ch. 2) was rising only slowly. Fees were minimal, and the consent of the Board of Education was required before they could be raised. (Increasing control had replaced the former freedom – which was freedom to develop or to stagnate as the case might be.) School extensions were needed, especially for laboratories. An increased intake of free-placers (of whom there were already some) was only feasible if their cost was met by other means, in short if the county council paid their fees.

The county council was faced with an almost complete lack of provision in Luton (population then 36,000), and with inadequate provision in Dunstable, Leighton Buzzard and Biggleswade. That the Trust schools existed in Bedford was of immense help. It was calculated in 1923 that, whereas the average county council expenditure throughout England per head of day scholar for secondary education was then £17, and in Durham as high as £26, in Bedfordshire it was only £6.

It took a little time to achieve the new relationship, but co-operation was gradually established, and county council support in 1924–5 reached £7,000, the total Trust educational expenditure in that year being £13,687. There was county council representation on the Trust from 1919. As the years passed, and national policy favoured increasing extension of secondary education, so the Local Education Authority's participation increased.

There was also a national source of help, namely by direct grant. A higher scale of grant could be obtained directly from the Board of Education, provided the proportion of free places was sufficiently high – usually 25%, though a lower proportion was allowed in some cases. Application for the Modern School in 1907 was rejected because the required proportion was not reached. At last in 1916 the Board agreed to a direct grant for this school if free places were raised in that year to 20% and in five years to 25%. Subsequently all four schools became direct grant, the modern schools taking 25% of free-placers and the other two schools 10%. For the year ending March 1925 the total income including national and local grants was as follows:

	government	county council	fees and other income
	£	£	£
Bedford School	5,500	2,340	24,473
High School	3,763	1,622	14,742
Modern School	3,899	1,884	12,031
Girls' Modern School	2,444	1,150	5,673
	15,606	6,996	56,919

The Trust endowment included in the last column was £13,687.

The 1944 act took national policy a stage further, by providing for universal secondary education in some form. Clearly the four Trust schools could no longer meet all the requirements, not only of Bedford, but also of north, east and mid-Bedfordshire. Local authority secondary schools were at last put in hand.

But still the Trust was faced with a problem, for direct grant schools could now be required to take a higher proportion of free-placers. In 70 years the Trust schools had built up a special character, and men and women from them had filled many professional positions at home and overseas. This very development over the whole period had been undertaken in response to government stimulus, and now the order seemed to be "About turn!" The Trust hesitated, and Bedford School and the High School resumed their independence, though still taking 10% free-placers, whose fees were paid by the county council. At the Modern School and Dame Alice School (former Girls' Modern), the proportion of free-placers rose to 50%.

In 1971–2 the total income including grants for the schools was:

	government	county council	fees and other income
	£	£	£
Bedford School	—	30,761	288,098
High School	—	17,878	176,169
Modern School	55,322	96,680	123,972
Dame Alice	44,117	82,045	84,159
	99,439	227,364	672,398

The Trust endowment to the schools included in the last column was £95,516. The price was high. Fees had to be progressively increased. The decision of the county council to adopt a policy for comprehensive education added a further factor. After long negotiation, an agreement was worked out between the Trust and the county council as to co-operation. For this agreement and for the Trust today, see ch. 9.

ELEMENTARY EDUCATION

In this field, responsibility diminished. From 1902 Bedford town council became the LEA in Bedford, The Trust elementary education committee was dissolved, though the Trust appointed managers for the elementary schools on the site of the Harpur complex and continued to carry out repairs. Under the 1918 act this school became a central school; in 1944 secondary modern; and in 1965 was removed by the LEA to a new site under the name of Westfield School (ch. 5).

The Trust, however, is still bound to apply 2/11 of revenue to a purpose connected with elementary education, and this sum began to accumulate, owing to the difficulty of finding enough suitable purposes. Bedford opinion has lost none of its vigilance, and anxiety grew lest this money be diverted. In 1956 an amending scheme was approved by the minister of education, laying down the purposes for which it was to be used (ch. 5).

WELFARE

Meanwhile, on the welfare side, this century has seen the remodelling of national policy, the introduction of retirement pensions and of insurance for sickness and unemployment, of family allowances and of arrangements for the care of children in need. In particular we have become increasingly aware of the need to provide suitable care and housing for the old. This one function which remained to the Trust has been well discharged by the modernisation and extension of its almshouses in 1970 (ch. 8).

4 *The Boys' Schools 1764—1873*

THE GRAMMAR SCHOOL, 1764–1811

The grammar school in 1764 was housed in the Tudor building in St. Paul's Square erected for it by Sir William Harpur. This building of two floors, with a room 49×20 ft. on each, was now in bad disrepair. Still worse was the state of the master's house adjoining, in which only one room was secure against wind, rain and snow, as the result of which the master had "a continued cold".[1] No house was provided for the usher, who at one time lived above the school. Their salaries had recently been at the unrealistic rates of £40 and £20 p.a. respectively,[2] so that they had been obliged to find supplementary sources of income, but were now £200 and £100. Their appointment had been in 1725 confirmed to New College, and the present incumbents were George Bridle (1739) and Edward Towersey (1755).

Education was given in Latin and Greek "grammar", the normal education of Harpur's day, when almost all records were still kept in Latin. Now a classical education was mainly a requirement for the university, the church and the law, and for the culture of a gentleman; but it was of limited use to the generality of boys in Bedford. It was probably as much due to this as to quality and diligence (or lack of it) of the teaching staff that numbers were few and fluctuating, and in 1747 were 11. To extend the range of provision, the act of 1764 required that an alternative education of more general use – reading, writing and arithmetic – was to be given by a writing-master (salary £60) in a separate room. The practice adopted was that the writing school had the lower room of the building, and the grammar school the upper room.

The 1764 act therefore offered two hopeful prospects for the future. At a restored grammar school, an energetic master and usher, with good salaries and both re-housed, might have begun a new chapter, as Thomas James did at Rugby in 1778; while the writing school might prepare the way for more modern education. The second chance was taken, but as regards the first, no improvement could be expected till death or retirement made possible a change of staff.

Boarding, an essential element in the growth of an endowed grammar school, seems to have ceased at Bedford some years before 1764. Boarding arose as no part of a cultural ethos, but as a practical answer for a contemporary need. For the sons of gentry, of better-off clergy or solicitors, a classical education was still appropriate, and these often needed to board. For some years this did not become obvious to the townsmen who were Harpur trustees (Manchester grammar school at this date took boarders, but there the trustees were county gentry).

Moreover their attention was not called to it by local demand, because this was met by a modern boarding school at Aspley Guise. Boarding served another purpose, because the profit on boarders eased the financial difficulties of a master on a fixed small salary. At Bedford, even if this aspect had been appreciated, it would have been thought unnecessary, with the relatively high salaries for master and usher in 1764.

The building operations required by the 1764 act were carried out by the trustees, though somewhat slowly. They repaired the school house, according to Uriah Clayson's plan, with a classic refronting of Portland stone; and added a statue of Harpur in 18th century dress, by a Holborn stonemason, Benjamin Palmer. They had a new desk made for ten boys, put in two lamps, and paid St. Paul's parish clerk 50s. p.a. to ring a church bell to summon the boys to school; while 25s. p.a. was allotted for sweeping the school on Saturday afternoons. By 1771 (but only after one of their number had privately sent a moving appeal to the Warden of New College), they spent over £800 on a new house for the master, with a wainscoted study and parlour, and a water supply conveyed by a cistern and pipes. Later still (1776) they resolved to build two adjoining houses for usher and writing-master on the site of the late John Marsh's house in Horne Lane, which they bought and pulled down. These were smaller and were always to give trouble. Their occupants were not friendly neighbours. The drainage was defective: a later usher (1803) complained that for 11 months of the year his cellar was a foot deep in water, and (he used it as pantry, having no other) that meat kept there was tainted in summer and sodden in winter, while in the parlour above a fog rose when the fire was lit.[3] By the time these buildings were complete, Bridle and Towersey were dead.

A new start might have seemed possible with the next master. What Bedford grammar school needed was a man with the urge to teach and the ambition to make a successful career, boarders being the key to both aims. But that man was not to be appointed yet. Even today, with the widespread advertising of vacancies and with interviews for those short-listed, it is not always certain that the most appropriate man for a post will be chosen. If it happened in the 18th century it was by good fortune rather than good management.

When a vacancy occurred in 1773, Bedford narrowly missed having James Woodforde, since famous as a diarist. On 1 September he wrote in his diary "the third best thing in the gift of New College – a new built house with an exceeding handsome garden . . . an usher also found and paid . . . about 12 boys to teach . . . The only bad thing belonging to it is being a borough town, and there is no such thing as being neuter. Upon the whole I like it very well, and I believe shall accept of it, if it comes to me". But apparently it did not.

The next master was John Hook, previously master at Thame. The usher, after one man had stayed a few years only, was Charles Abbot, 1787. Both were

Winchester and New College men, and in early middle life. Hook was not ambitious or exceptional. Years later (in 1792) he wrote without any apparent compunction "The number of boys has not amounted to more than 6 or 7 at a time, I believe, in general for these 20 years or more".[4] As the years passed he grew feebler; and was "quite a cripple, with an obstinate sciatica", taking "80 drops of laudanum nightly".[5] In the days before pensions it was necessary to wait for death before a replacement could be made. Hook died in 1810.

Abbot was able – but not as a teacher. He was a notable botanist, and in 1798 produced the county's first *Flora*. The school he seems to have regarded simply as one source of his livelihood (he held more than one local living also). He was not particularly happy at Bedford, where he thought the trustees, if not the inhabitants, "a set of mean wretches". When the time came, with the next master, for a real new beginning, he was disgruntled and unco-operative, and at first refused to teach the first boarder.

A committee of three – the mayor, G. D. Yeats (physician and Oxford graduate), Theed Pearse (county clerk of peace and town clerk), and Dr. Philip Hunt (a local incumbent) considered the position. They were knowledgeable men, and they did not take as a standard of comparison other endowed grammar schools nearby, such as Northampton where the master had been totally blind for some years; or even Hertford or Huntingdon, which each had about 40 boys plus a number of boarders.[6] (These masters were paid sums ranging from £20 to £33 p.a. – it was the profit on boarders that enabled them to make a living.) But the Harpur Trust were paying master and usher £200 and £100 p.a. respectively, plus a £3 capitation fee; and there were in 1811 5 boys. They simply were not getting value for money. They looked a little farther afield to Rugby, where the salaries for master and usher were £113 and £80 respectively, plus the same capitation fee as at Bedford. They reflected that "that school is admirably conducted, but the school of this foundation is nearly useless". In fact "the children of this town do not derive those benefits from its establishment that were so evidently intended by the founders and the legislature, and . . . instead of having a classical education gratis, are in fact sent to other schools at a considerable expense to their parents". The writing school, providing a more modern education, had at this time over a hundred boys, and it certainly seemed as if there ought to be more than five boys in Bedford destined for professional life.

Yeats wrote privately to the Warden of New College, and also on 26 Nov. 1810 formally as chairman of the Trust. The prime need was to appoint a master who should be "zealous, ardent and indefatigable". The trustees begged "to observe with all delicacy that the appointment has been considered more in the light of a sinecure than a high trust with great and important duties" – this was perhaps hardly fair, for the dynamic conception of a master was, it might almost be said, only now emerging. On 6 Dec. the committee went by appointment to

Oxford to consult with the Warden and Fellows, who "seemed to hail the deputation instead of deprecating it". They were "anxiously desirous of contributing all their aid to ameliorate the grammar school". On 24 January 1811 John Brereton was appointed.

THE WRITING SCHOOL, 1764–1831

Meanwhile the growth of the writing side of the school had shown that a real need was being met. The salary of this master was £60. The first appointed, clearly unsuitable, resigned in 3 months, and was followed by George Jackson of Hampton, aged 29, who had taught in the free grammar school at Highgate, the master of which recommended him as honest, sober, diligent, and extremely capable.[7] He remained at Bedford till he died in 1803. He taught in the lower room of the school building (Hook and Abbot dealt with their handful in the room above); five desks and nine forms were bought for him "as cheap as possible", and some years later seven more benches. By 1775 it was necessary for him to have an assistant, Bolney, (£20) – an undated report in Jackson's hand specifies 74 boys, about half of whom learned reading, writing and accounts, and a few reading only.[8] The hours were then 7 a.m. – 5 p.m. in summer, with two breaks, and 9 a.m. – 4 p.m. in winter with one break; holidays were few, and he was directed to keep the school open in harvest time.

After about 30 satisfactory years, the writing school had an equal period of trouble. This began with the ageing of the master and usher, Jackson and Bolney. Bolney was the first to decline; after 25 faithful years he was in 1797 "incapable" owing to "age and infirmity", and the trustees "discontinued" him; he died the following year. They did not feel they could dismiss Jackson, but in 1799 his "advanced age and growing infirmities" made it "impossible for any person of respectability to act jointly with him"; so they "discharged him from active concern"; they continued to pay his salary, while recognising the usher as in real charge. Jackson died in 1803.

From the time of Jackson and Bolney till the coming of John Moore in 1831 the school was served by unsatisfactory staff. No doubt Jackson's last years made it difficult for the assistants, of whom since 1797 there were at least two. But none of the four masters who taught in quick succession 1803–31 was able to pull the school up. Inflation fostered by the French wars diminished the value of the master's salary (the 1793 act had raised it only to £80), and John Whitehouse (1803–9) eked out his salary by other means, and had to be reminded that trustees expected strict attention to the business of the school and punctual attendance in school hours, and that he should not enter into any engagement inconsistent with this. A few years later he resigned. Robert Ruffhead (1809–14) died. The trustees now got round the difficulty of legal limitation of salary by giving his successor, William Massey, a gratuity of £25; but Massey seems either to have had no vocation, or to have been generally incompetent. The worried visiting trustees drew up rules for his guidance, but he paid "very little attention" to them. After a warning in 1819, he was given notice, when he pathetically asked for a chance to try again; but this was refused. W. H. White (1821–31) was no more successful; he was seriously warned in 1828; in 1829 the trustees thought that perhaps he was depressed by his prospects, and raised his salary (£120 under the 1826 act), and held out hope of a further small increase if his exertions warranted it; but nothing availed; in 1830 he shut up the school to spend a day in London; and in 1831 he was dismissed.

An ineffective head does not bring out the best in his staff. In this period the school's run of bad luck applied also to the assistants. The only one who emerges with any credit is William Swepson (1797–1821); when he retired – his salary then being £40 plus £10 because a house was not provided – he received a pension of £40; he was then described as "faithful but incompetent". Swepson was the junior assistant, and must have found it difficult in Jackson's last years, when he had to take orders from the senior assistant, James Stimson (1794–9), who was dismissed for flagrant misconduct and negligence. John Jeffrey, a boy promoted from within the school, for whose services from 1801 a small annual sum was paid to his father, had little chance in these circumstances; he was finally discarded in 1820. Mainwaring (1821–2) "absented himself". Thomas Wagstaff (1822–8) developed "mental infirmity". Most difficult of all, perhaps, was J. H. Matthiason (appointed 1821), able, erratic, and impossible to work with; author of *Bedford and its environs*. When dismissed, he brought a suit against the Trust, and ended a debtor in gaol, where the number of his visitors embarrassed the gaoler.

In spite of staff failings at the writing school from 1797 to 1831, numbers continued to increase. In 1810 room was found for two additional desks in the ground floor room by removing to the outside of the building, at the southwest corner, the stairs which led to the upper room where the grammar school functioned. In 1817 there were said to be about 140 boys. Even at the then rate of 6 sq. ft. per child (130) there was overcrowding.

As regards the curriculum, emphasis was still laid on writing. Prizes were given for this: one of the prizewinners in 1803 was the future industrialist, John Howard, whose later success seems attributable rather to his own capacity than to his school training. In 1819 the visiting committee urged an extension of the curriculum. In order to qualify boys for trade, commerce, navigation and agriculture, they advised the introduction of algebra, geometry, geography, practical mensuration and French. French was in fact introduced in 1820, and was taught out of school hours by M. Dupont, who also taught at the grammar school. Books and maps were bought for the library in 1821; and a pair of globes in 1823. In 1828 the committee found ignorance among "a considerable portion of the scholars"; the master did not examine the whole school (as he should do, at least once a week); and a lot of time was spent by boys "entering arithmetical exercises in ciphering books".

Discipline was not severe. The holidays allowed by the master were in the Trust's view too many; they should not be given for saints' days (perhaps a lingering medieval survival derived from the grammar school), for fairs or assizes, but only for the royal birthday, Good Friday, Easter Monday and Tuesday, Whitmonday and Christmas; with a total of eight weeks' vacation in spring, at harvest and at Christmas. Truancy should be punished by "extraordinary tasks", in the view of the 1817 committee, who found the ushers themselves insubordinate. Even numbers fell off: in 1831 there were 124 boys. There were expulsions in 1827 and 1830 – on the latter occasion of nine incorrigible boys.

In 1831 the examining committee's report strikes a note of despair. Few if any of the boys leaving school at 14, when their education should be complete, were qualified to become articled clerks for professional practitioners, assistants in banking houses, or apprentices in the higher departments of trade; and very few had a foundation of religious knowledge. Though the members trusted they had shown no intimidating severity of manner, they had found a most disgraceful state of ignorance which must have arisen from gross negligence. The Trust must not leave the sons of the numerous and most important class of fellow townsmen in such a degraded state. What was required was not merely a man of attainments, but one qualified to teach with success and to govern a school with firmness. Perhaps such a man might be found by personal appeal to the master of a well-known school, such as Christ's Hospital. Meanwhile the school was closed for a few weeks. It was from Christ's Hospital that John Moore came in 1831.

TWO NOTABLE HEADMASTERS, 1811–55 AND 1831–60

Two men made what are now Bedford School (then the grammar school) and Bedford Modern School (then the English or commercial school) their lifework respectively, John Brereton and John Moore. Their lives and their tasks were different, but each set his school on the forward path.

John Brereton came from what might now be called the side of the establishment. Son of the rector of St. Andrew's church, Holborn, he had been educated at Winchester and New College, and at the time of his appointment was a teaching assistant at Blundells School, Tiverton.[9] John Moore had come up the hard way. Educated at Christ's Hospital, where he went at the age of 9, at 17 he became an assistant there, and later second master; he was, wrote the Rev. J. H. Alt, "thoroughly conversant with our system", and in his then post "decidedly below his level"; and he was "in every way calculated by his talents, disposition and experience" to fill the vacant post. Brereton was a firm adherent of the old school of classical education, in which he exacted proficiency; he had also the wider interests of a cultured gentleman of the day – astronomy, archaeology, music and gardening. Moore was a Latinist, but his qualifications in commercial arithmetic and the use of the globes were stressed. Brereton is said to have been short and dapper, with black silk stockings and ruffled shirt front; his portrait in oils shows an erect and challenging Romneyesque figure. Moore's photograph shows a human but somewhat tired-looking man in plain black suit and heavy Victorian bow tie. Neither was apt to speak much of his religious faith, though Brereton once in 1848 in a letter to the Warden of New College wrote "our present system has, I thank God, made the pupils well informed in the Bible, in religion, and in those qualifications which fit them for any profession".[10] Brereton had at his back the Warden and Fellows of New College, to whom he could send a message by old pupils, or through whom he could signify to the Trust his requirements for staff.[11] Moore was subject to directives from the Trust in their boardroom a few yards away. Brereton had an income which, though it began at £260 (£200 salary and £60 capitation at £3 a head up to 20 boys under the 1793 act), at its peak was about £1,300; indeed it is possible that he was then the richest man in Bedford.[12] When he retired, he had a pension of £500 p.a.; and he was then presented by an old pupil to the living of Grayne in Kent, where he died in 1862 at the age of 80. Moore had a salary of £200, and had a small additional amount from about 20 paying pupils; he was medically advised to retire in 1847, but the outcry in the town against the Trust's paying him a pension obliged him to carry on till 1860; when he retired on a pension of £200, and died – his life no doubt shortened by overwork – in 1863, aged 61.

The two men lived a short distance from each other and within a few yards of their respective school buildings, though Brereton's house was approached from St. Paul's Square and Moore's from Horne Lane. Brereton's which stood till the present century, was large. An inventory of his fixtures in 1855 mentions his library with five mahogany bookcases (one 10 ft. high), drawing-room, dining-room, store-room, housekeeper's room, kitchen, larder, butler's pantry, scullery, brewhouse (with 120 gallon copper), 7 bedrooms, and an observatory which he built himself. Moore and the usher of the grammar school lived in two semi-detached houses in Horne Lane of the same date as Brereton's, but presumably small since they were built on the site of one former house. A list of repairs in 1815 indicates that they had library and study, dining-room, kitchen, back kitchen, and washhouse; and four or five bedrooms. The garden was divided between the two houses, giving each access to the river. Perhaps Moore's cellar did not flood, as did the usher's; at all events complaints from him are not recorded. The privies adjoined in the garden; and when in 1838 a water-closet was installed for Moore, the usher (Le Mesurier – see below) declared himself greatly annoyed by it. It was unfortunate that the Trust economised by building in 1778 a single stable to be shared. At that time the master of the writing school did not keep a horse, and the usher bitterly resented having to surrender part of the stable in 1810; in fact the stable was a bone of contention till 1844.

BOARDERS AND DAY BOYS

Brereton and Moore faced different tasks. Brereton's was to create a school in the 19th century style out of an old grammar (day) school, which had always been tiny and had now dwindled almost to non-existence. In the twenty years to 1831 when Moore came, he had built up the numbers to a hundred, nearly half of whom were boarders. That he should be permitted to take boarders "as masters of other public schools are universally permitted to do" – he instanced Rugby and Harrow – was the first item of the new plan which he put forward on his arrival, and which he had already discussed with New College. To provide the necessary premises, the coachhouse, stable and outbuildings adjoining his house were converted by the Trust to a dining-room with dormitory over. (The new plan provided that the usher might take boarders when the Trust extended his house, but this permission remained a dead letter till 1865, when the usher at long last secured the adjoining semi-detached house as well as his own.)

The first boarder was Thomas Pearse, aged 13, son of the town and county clerk, Theed Pearse (ch. 3).[13] He had previously been boarding at Aspley Guise, and his father had long been anxious for the Bedford school to develop. At first new arrivals came slowly; two the second year; eight in 1813. A survey of grammar schools published in 1818 says that Dr. Brereton takes 30 pupils, who each had a single bed, and three changes of linen weekly (they must bring six towels); and the fees were 55 guineas, with dancing and drill as extras.[14] This fee was on the high side; Repton and Blundells at this time charged 34 and 35 guineas, Shrewsbury 50 guineas.[15] The allowance of one bed per boy was not maintained. In 1820 there were 52 boarders; and in 1830 the Warden (Dr. Shuttleworth) wrote that he was informed that the present dormitory had only 34 beds but there were 61 boarders. In 1843 the dormitory was still a single large room; the Warden, prompted by Brereton, advised division into two or three rooms; and alterations were made accordingly in the following year, when at the same time a small room was thrown out at the back to provide a master's residence.

The boarders, as Brereton's admission register shows, tended to come from neighbouring counties, Bucks., Herts., Hunts., and Northants., and were often sons of clergy.[16] Occasionally their homes were farther away, for instance, Devon. Once in 1844 a father from Newport, Mon., whose son had won an exhibition, wrote to the Trust to ask if his son must return to school until the university term, but was told this was not necessary. Sometimes a boy boarded temporarily, while his parents were settling in Bedford, as William Young did in 1832 while his mother moved into a house on St. Peter's green – where later sometimes Dr. Brereton came to call.[17] And some boys came from Bedfordshire villages, such as the Gibbards of Sharnbrook. The admission register also gives some overseas addresses: East Indies (George Boyd, 1822), or West Indies (Mrs. Mills, 1828).

These boys provided Brereton with a worth-while school to teach, and with an acceptable addition to his income. It has been estimated at Rugby under Arnold that the profit on boarders was about £15.[18] Out of his profit, Brereton, following the Winchester custom, gave four guineas a head to the usher for his trouble in teaching the boarders.[19] When the number rose to 50, it seems likely that he would still be left with about £500, double the amount of his salary (raised by the 1826 act to £250).

Boarders were well cared for. The Doctor was humane as well as stern. Food was ample, though lacking in variety. There was monastic silence at meals, but books could be read. On weekdays the usher carved. On Sundays "the rattling of gold chains and seals" heralded the approach of the Doctor, who, after a long sonorous Latin grace, "dispensed roast fillets of veal" with zest and liberality. The housekeeper, Sarah Carter, introduced a warming pan into the icy beds in winter. The Doctor also gave a free firework display at Christmas.[20]

At first, day boys outnumbered boarders; the register opens with 25 day boys. Their names include Wing, Trapp, Hillyard – the fathers who might be expected, architect, banker, nonconformist minister and so on; but at first there are also fathers with humbler occupations, such as coachman or hairdresser; these seem to be trying out the new master; but such entries decline; no doubt the boys transferred to the English school. Incidentally, one of the first boys was Nathan Joseph, a silversmith's son. In the first seven years the admissions totalled 42 boarders and 63 day boys; but as 52 had left, mainly day boys, the total in 1817 was 53.

In calculating numbers it must be remembered that they fluctuated widely in all public schools.[21] Thus at Bedford the number of day boys (ascertainable quarterly from capitation payments) was as low as 24 in October 1827, but 69 in the following August. Boys entered and left at any time, and it was long before the whole school year became the normal unit. Thus rather than attach too much importance to any particular year, it is better to take the long-term trend. Brereton opened with 25 boys; he reached his peak about 1848–50. In the latter year the school list gives 178 names.[22]

Over this period the proportion of day boys to boarders changed. By the 1820s, boarders were in a majority, and the school list of 1820 gives 33 day boys to 52 boarders. In a few years day boys were increasing, while boarders fell off. School lists show the following proportions:

	day boys	boarders	total
1835	72	43	115
1840	68	31	99
1845	116	15	131
1850	156	22	178

In this last year, 1850, Brereton's income must have been over £1,300 (£250 salary, £858 capitation, and perhaps about £200 net profit on 22 boarders).[23]

These figures are probably related. It may well be that, since Brereton had a viable school without boarders, he was no longer particularly anxious to attract them, especially as he was getting older. On the other hand, though the increase in day boys may be partly due to more Bedford parents desiring classical education for their boys, some at least of the increase is due to "squatters", who settled in Bedford in order that their sons might attend the school: and on each of these boys a capitation fee of five guineas was due to Brereton (and four to the usher) without the trouble of supervising boarders. His highest capitation fees were £924 in 1848.

Some squatters seem to be naval men, whose prospects of promotion were slow in the years of peace after Waterloo. First came in 1822 Captain G. B. Trollope, with the first of his six sons; then in the ten years 1824–34 Captains Griffith, Leech, Mitford, Home, Smyth (later Admiral), Haig, Howe, Scriven, Hasleham, Bell, Sparrow, Duval, Addington, Law. Parents' addresses in the 1830s are sometimes on the edge of the old town; for instance there were six families at St. Peter's green; but more often in the developing residential area, New Town, the Crescent, Priory Terrace, Adelaide Square; later there are Kimbolton Road, Goldington Road, Victoria Terrace, Conduit Place, Albert Terrace, Union Street. However, all the fathers were not naval; there was Colonel Hamilton, 1834; and there was H. P. Russell of Bengal whose wife came in 1836 with their four boys to live in Priory Terrace.

The number of day boys for whom capitation fees were paid never fell below 100 after June 1845; and when the Trust ran into financial difficulties (ch. 3) the squatters were foremost in clamouring for what they deemed to be their rights. An example of the squatters' viewpoint is given in a letter of 13 Feb. 1849 to the Warden of New College from Commander Charles Hutchinson, R.N., complaining that, if the then policy of economy continued, the new residents, disgusted and discouraged, would quit the place, and Bedford would be comparatively deserted, while the trustees would be only dissenters.[24]

If the parents, having lived a few years in Bedford as the Ommaneys did, withdrew for any reason, questions were asked at Trust meetings. Thus in 1851 it was asked where was now the residence of the fathers of Mackness, senior and junior, Ommaney and Souper; the boys were to be refused a free education after quarter-day "until the parents be inhabitants"; and in 1853 a check was made of parents entitled to free books for their sons.

Brereton's achievement was notable. He had obtained boarders, he had attracted squatters, and he had made a viable school and kept it firmly on the old course of classical scholarship. Much was due to the man himself. Something, however, was also due to the temper of the times. The older public schools were growing. New ones were being founded: Cheltenham 1841; Marlborough 1843; Radley 1847; Lancing 1848. Education was a growing demand.

NUMBERS AT THE ENGLISH OR COMMERCIAL SCHOOL[25]

The task which Moore faced in 1831 was quite different. He had no need to go out in search of numbers to get a chance to show that he could both teach and organise. He had, so to speak, a captive audience, for the parents of boys at the English school could not easily transfer them elsewhere and must take what was going. His increase of numbers would come inevitably with the growing population of Bedford, and would rise steadily. He said in 1843 that when he came there were 95 boys; his first report gives the number as 109; by 1842 it had reached 202; and in 1859 there were 255. In addition he was allowed to take for a small fee a few private pupils (boys who did not qualify as free entrants); their number was usually something over 20.

PREMISES

The history of the premises of both schools in this period – indeed of all the Trust schools – is one of increasing pressure on limited space, and of the emergence of a demand for classrooms instead of an open hall. Brereton, who had been in Bedford 20 years when Moore arrived in 1831, and was by then an established figure, had in 1829 secured both floors of the original school building for his hundred or so boys. When he came in 1811, he had asked for this to take place when a new building was provided for the other school; and he had pressed for it at intervals, as in 1820, when he complained of noise and interruption from the English school on the ground floor. The sharing of the building during the other school's unsatisfactory period must constantly have caused friction. In March 1829, the lower room was "appropriated to the use of the grammar school", and the necessary repairs and alterations were made.

In 1814 it occurred to Theed Pearse that the two schools ought to be under one control (as was the case later at Birmingham), but nothing came of his suggestion.[26]

In spite of the increase in numbers during the 1830s and 1840s, Brereton obtained no major extension during the rest of his career. He was hard put to it to make suitable arrangements for his staff: in 1822 he asked for a sitting-room between dormitory and school, for an assistant; and again in 1843.

Still more difficult was it to secure the privacy of classrooms for that more individual style of teaching which was slowly beginning to emerge from the mechanical drilling of earlier days. By 1838 Brereton was accommodating one class in the boarders' dining-hall. This became a permanent arrangement, and eventually in 1846 he was reimbursed the cost of fire and gas. In 1848, a peak year for numbers, he protested urgently his "great want of room"; there were then, he said, 128 boys in the lower schoolroom. (Incidentally it was a favourite diversion, in these crowded conditions, for a boy to creep under the next bench and prick another boy's leg with a pin.)[27] Brereton even looked wistfully at the imposing façade of the Harpur complex across the road, and observed that "other

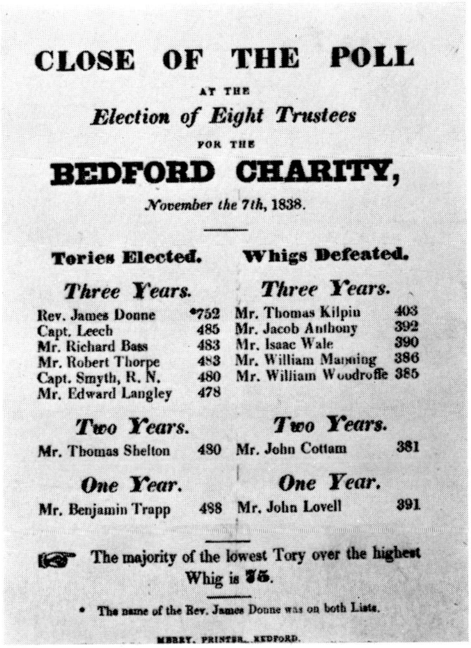

CLOSE OF THE POLL

AT THE

Election of Eight Trustees

FOR THE

BEDFORD CHARITY,

November the 7th, 1838.

Tories Elected.		**Whigs Defeated.**	
Three Years.		***Three Years.***	
Rev. James Donne	*752	Mr. Thomas Kilpin	403
Capt. Leech	485	Mr. Jacob Anthony	392
Mr. Richard Bass	483	Mr. Isaac Wale	390
Mr. Robert Thorpe	483	Mr. William Manning	386
Capt. Smyth, R. N.	480	Mr. William Woodroffe	385
Mr. Edward Langley	478		
Two Years.		***Two Years.***	
Mr. Thomas Shelton	480	Mr. John Cottam	381
One Year.		***One Year.***	
Mr. Benjamin Trapp	488	Mr. John Lovell	391

☞ The majority of the lowest Tory over the highest Whig is **75.**

* The name of the Rev. James Donne was on both Lists.

MERRY, PRINTER, BEDFORD.

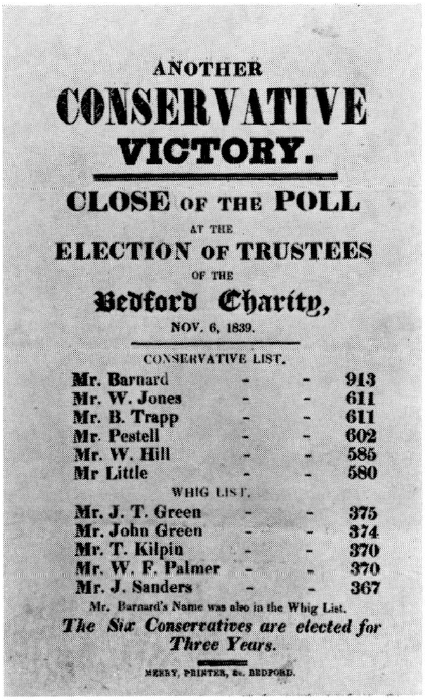

ANOTHER

CONSERVATIVE VICTORY.

CLOSE OF THE POLL

AT THE

ELECTION OF TRUSTEES

OF THE

Bedford Charity,

NOV. 6, 1839.

CONSERVATIVE LIST.	
Mr. Barnard - -	**913**
Mr. W. Jones - -	**611**
Mr. B. Trapp - -	**611**
Mr. Pestell - -	**602**
Mr. W. Hill - -	**585**
Mr Little - -	**580**
WHIG LIST.	
Mr. J. T. Green - -	**375**
Mr. John Green - -	**374**
Mr. T. Kilpin - -	**370**
Mr. W. F. Palmer - -	**370**
Mr. J. Sanders - -	**367**

Mr. Barnard's Name was also in the Whig List.

The Six Conservatives are elected for Three Years.

MERRY, PRINTER, &c. BEDFORD.

9a and b Trust elections, 1838, 1839

9c Boardroom, completed 1838

10 *Harpur complex: Elger's proposed elevation, 1828*

11 *Harpur complex: Blore's façade, 1833–7, drawn by George Moore*

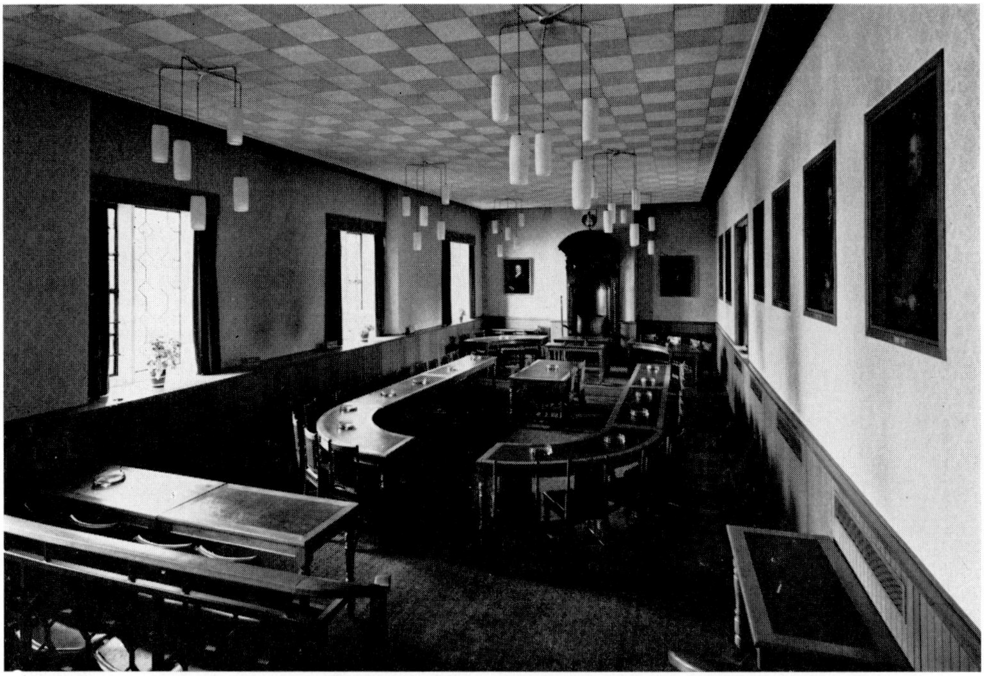

12a Grammar schoolroom (now Town Council chamber), c. 1548

12b Commercial School (northeast wing of complex), 1833 (children's home on left)

13a John Brereton, headmaster of Grammar School, 1811–55

13b John Moore, headmaster of Commercial School, 1831–60

13c J. S. Phillpotts, headmaster of Grammar School, 1874–1903

13d R. B. Poole, headmaster of Modern School, 1877–1900

14a Grammar School extension, 1861

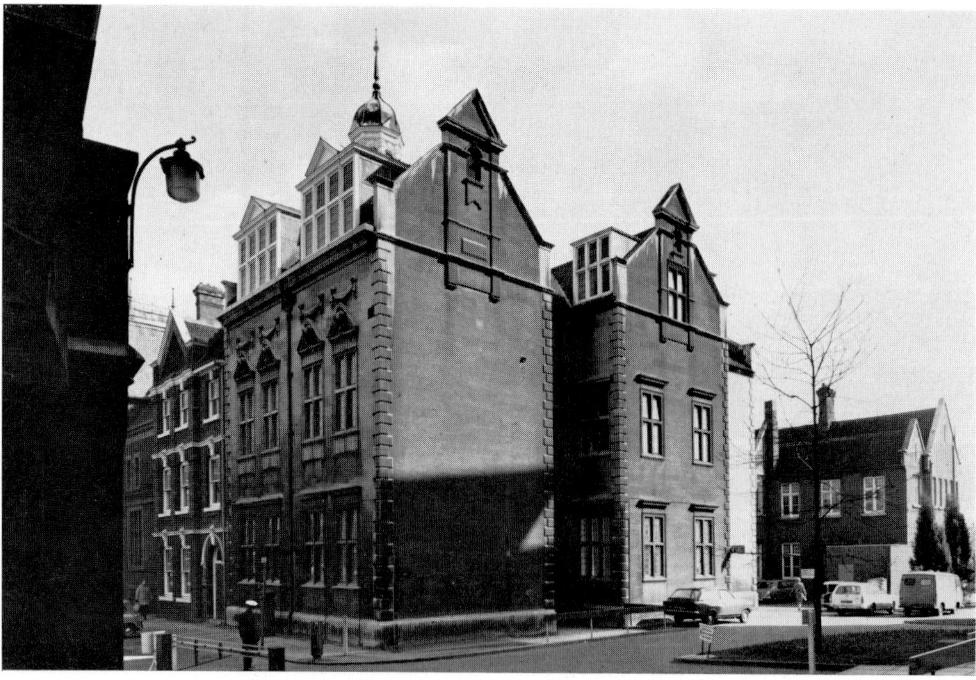

14b Grammar School extension, 1884 (Girls' Modern School, 1892)

15a Elementary ("National") school for boys, 1834

15b Elementary school for girls and infants, 1840

16a Elementary school for girls, 1879

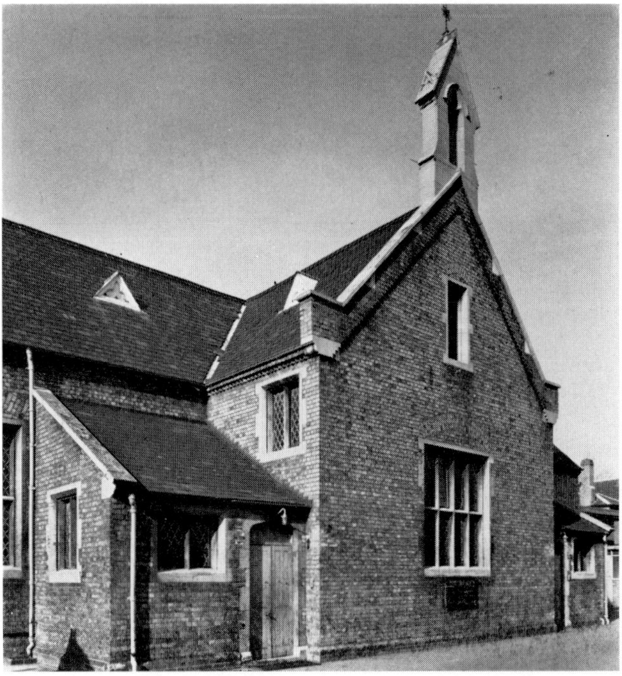

16b Junior commercial school, 1860; elementary infants, 1880

schools have ample room and a due supply of masters". Almost certainly he never went inside the schools there; and Moore, Riley, Jagg and Mrs. Furze would have been amazed at his statement. In 1851 the trustees offered Brereton the use of a room in the (largely ornamental) tower of the Harpur complex, but it does not appear that he accepted.

The English school, when Moore came, was in temporary premises.[28] This was in Angel (or Harpur) Street, but where is not clear; perhaps in the children's home or hospital; for the Assembly Rooms (pressed into service years later) were not yet built. The new building planned by the trustees was not completed till the end of 1833, so that Moore for his first two years had very difficult conditions. In 1834 his school moved into the northeast block of the complex. There was by this time a preparatory or junior department of the commercial school with about 50 boys. First thought of in 1828 for boys from the age of seven, it took effect in temporary premises in 1832 under an unsatisfactory master, Charles Whitehouse. (Canvin was an incorrigible truant.) Moore was asked to report on it, and in 1837 it was brought under his supervision. The senior and junior departments occupied different floors in the northeast block. The former had a large room or hall which (Moore says in 1843) was fitted up for 146 boys; and an "inconvenient room", where there were 42 boys; and numbers were still growing. The smaller room was enlarged in 1844 by incorporating the adjacent passage and making an outside staircase to the upper floor. Ventilation was a constant problem – two windows were added in 1844. In 1850 it was proposed that a room in the tower should be fitted up. Still numbers grew, and there is almost a note of petulance in his statement of 1853 that he really needs double the amount of room, or admissions will have to be limited. At last in 1853, having taken over two rooms in the tower, he was able to report that, though these were not as convenient as might be, still they had given great relief. Two actual new classrooms, costing £358, were planned in 1855.

By this time accommodation was urgent for the junior department, which in 1859 passed the 200 mark. Moore had reorganised this school, but his control lasted only till 1847, when his illness made it necessary for his responsibilities to be reduced, and one of his staff, James Bannister, was appointed head of it. By 1859 rooms for some of these boys had to be taken nearby in a house lately occupied by Randall. A modest new building for the junior school behind the main block of buildings was planned, and in 1859 the tender of £1,238 was accepted. Moore at once applied to take over the old schoolroom of the juniors when available, and for it to be converted to two classrooms. The new building was ready at the beginning of 1860. Thus in his last year the rooms vacated were obtained by Moore, though not refurnished till 1864. He now had the whole of the northeast block, besides his two rooms in the tower.

STAFF AND CURRICULUM

Questions of staff and curriculum at the two schools were to some extent interrelated. The grammar school held firmly to the old classical tradition, and had as prime feature the awarding (on annual examination) of exhibitions to the university; while the boys from the commercial school looked to business as a career and were later awarded premiums for articles; yet some modernisation was made at the former, and it was sometimes convenient for staff to teach at both. At both schools throughout the period it was a case of increasing numbers calling for more and more staff, with a time-lag before the extra staff were acquired.

Two major differences marked the staff of the grammar school. The status of the master and usher – or as they may soon be termed headmaster and second master – both financially and actually was far superior to that of any other staff at either school. Both had a seat on the Trust; though Brereton seldom appeared at board meetings, preferring to remain in aloof dignity. The usher could take his own line there. The other was that for the grammar school staffing appointments went through New College. The trustees had to sanction the outlay; and indeed sometimes ventured to express an opinion, as in 1828 when a deputation went to college to discuss teaching arrangements for an extended curriculum, that staff should not be limited to New College graduates, and that it might be well to have a Cambridge man to teach mathematics.

Brereton during his career increased the school's full-time staff from two to seven and added two part-time staff.

The usher, as has been said, was in a special position. When Brereton came, the usher was the elderly, unco-operative and probably ailing Abbot, who at first expected equal authority, as he had had it under Hook; he did not – so Brereton wrote to the Warden – treat him with civil attention, nor did Brereton like his general conduct to the boys. In fact, the new headmaster had "no small anxiety lest my exertions should fail of the desired effect of establishing a respectable classical school, of which I have every prospect".[29] Parents complained. By August 1817 Abbot was ill, and seems to have had a nervous breakdown; and Brereton felt he could not have him back, if the good reputation which the school had now gained was to be preserved. He therefore (with New College's approval) planned to introduce his own brother Tom, to whom he paid the teaching allowance for boarders, while Abbot would remain in receipt of his salary from the Trust. However, Abbot died in October, and Tom Brereton became usher until 1832, "assiduous, exemplary and effective" in a harmonious partnership with his elder brother.

His successor as usher, in fact as second master, was a very different man, the Rev. Henry Le Mesurier, 1832–73, also of Winchester and New College. Powerful, truculent, quick-tempered, uninhibitedly concerned for his own position, he was not an easy colleague. Though Brereton was ultimately in control at the school, there was one occasion in 1838 when a "prejudicial misunderstanding" between the two men came to the ears of the trustees. Le Mesurier even in 1850 interfered with the annual examinations of the boys by visitors from New College, "took nearly the whole of the examination of his own classes into his own hands", and, when the examiner "took exception" to a boy's construing, upheld the boy's version. It was, the visitors felt, bad taste to argue the point before the boys, but it was making the examination mere farce.[30] In the Trust boardroom he used his privileged position to the full. When financial difficulties overtook the Trust, and the trustees planned to reduce capitation fees, while Brereton tried behind the scenes to work for the good of the school, Le Mesurier unashamedly stressed his own anticipated loss; and in 1848 printed his speech in a 27-page pamphlet. In this year he received £724 in capitation fees alone while all other staff had incomes of less than £200 from the school. Yet there was a zest and a humour about him, which in spite of his fierce discipline made him accepted by the boys; he was – it was said when he was older – "like some dear old bear who took buns quite civilly as a rule"; and he is said once, after throwing into the river a bargee who jostled him, to have jumped in himself and pulled the man out.[31]

Brereton had from the first a writing-master; writing was an extra and the master was paid by himself. In 1820 French was introduced, as at the other school, and J. F. Dupont was paid 30 guineas to teach French out of school hours "so as not to interfere with the school exercises". Modernisation of the curriculum was discussed in the 1820s, and the 1826 act provided for such other masters, up to £100 p.a., as might be agreed between New College and the trustees, with a provision that there should be a mathematics master who would in addition receive a capitation fee of three guineas. A conference with New College on 24 April 1828 agreed on the need for this last; and for an assistant to teach writing, arithmetic and geography at £80 p.a.; while the French master was to have £50 p.a. The writing-master was James Bowden. For the mathematics master, New College left the trustees to make their own approaches to Cambridge, and the post went to Edward Swann.

But these innovations made little headway; modernisation was slow in gaining acceptance not only by teachers but also by parents; and this was the case at most comparable schools.[32] Swann had so few pupils that he was glad to fill up his time by helping with classics. In 1831 there were only two boys learning mathematics; then the number fluctuated between four and 13; it did not reach 20 till 1844; and gradually climbed to 29 in 1852.

No doubt parents, besides being – like teachers – influenced by tradition, bore in mind that the annual examination for university exhibitions was held in classics. Indeed in 1849 there was a complaint from C. W. N. Hyne that he had understood mathematics would have weight in the examination, but the college replied that the examination was in every respect regular and correct.

Incidentally, the custom (probably of ancient origin) still continued of the head boy writing a Latin letter to the assize judge when the latter came to Bedford, and asking for a holiday. This custom lasted into the present century.[33]

Nor did French fare better. Dupont, later Rodde, had about nine or ten boys. Drawing, introduced in 1840, was an immediate success under the talented master Bradford Rudge, who soon had 28 boys. Meanwhile Brereton had secured two more classics masters, one in 1835 and one in 1844. The latter post was more than once held by an old boy.

Yet there was some uneasiness in the town. In 1843, when it was proposed as an economy measure that the teaching of French and drawing should be dropped, a public meeting pleaded for modern subjects. Classics qualified for the university, but comparatively few went thither; "fewer still can make their way in the world by classics"; if more ordinary branches of education were added, the school would be more attractive to strangers and boys would be better qualified to meet life.

With rising costs, the limitation of salary to £100 under the 1826 act was frustrating for junior masters. Presumably they augmented their income by other means. Le Mesurier in 1848 said that when he first came (and his income from the school even in 1832 must have been nearly £400) he had to take private pupils and a curacy; but he lived in Victorian style, his household in 1848, even in his semi-detached house, comprising 14 persons. For Bowden a way was found of making some increase in 1840 by an allowance of £50 in lieu of house; he applied in vain for an assistant in 1848, and did not get one till 1853. In this year the new scheme allowed a higher maximum, varying from £150 to £250. Yet on the whole Brereton managed to keep his staff. For the general level was low – national scales were not to come till the 20th century. And it must be remembered that salaries of £30 p.a. were being paid in some of the other Trust schools.

Moore's constant trouble was that, as soon as young staff were trained into his ways, they obtained promotion elsewhere. In 1832 J. T. Hannum, who had formerly worked under him at Christ's Hospital, followed him to Bedford as his senior assistant, but in 1841 left for Christ's Hospital at Hertford. Robert Craske, 1841–3, who succeeded Hannum, after only two years became headmaster of a new school at Bury St. Edmunds. James Bannister, junior assistant 1832–47, did indeed remain in Bedford, but took over the headship of the junior school. When it was reported in 1838 that Hannum and Bannister had classes of 63 and 67 respectively, a new assistant was brought up from the junior school, William Long, but in 1844 Long took orders in order to become a missionary for the S.P.G.; and another young man was brought up from the junior school. As numbers were over 200 when Craske left in 1843, an additional appointment was made. Moore's serious illness in 1847 brought a crisis; it seems to have been gastric trouble accentuated by worry. His doctor, Dr. Witt, advised that he should retire; and at first the Trust, recording their entire satisfaction with his work and his "very high and unexceptionable character", voted him a premature pension. At once there was an outcry in the town. Moore, knowing Bedford only too well, reflected wearily that if he retired his pension would be insecure, and in a dignified letter he declined it; if given six months' leave, he would try to carry on. One advantage came out of this that, to relieve him, a deputy was appointed, Wilkinson Finlinson, who came from Stockwell school. Finlinson was no high-flier, but he was steady, loyal and reliable, and he stayed; and with his help Moore continued till 1860. By this time there were six assistants; Gutteridge (who however was absent for a time to take a degree) was appointed as sixth assistant in 1849. All these had salaries lower than those of masters of the grammar school, usually £80 or £100 (Finlinson £120 with extra allowances).

At this school too the curriculum was diversified. In 1833 Moore was already attempting to rise above the era when the "merest rudiments" were required, and to aim at "extended notions of education"; and also to build up a much better library (the existing books being few, ill-adapted, and falling apart). An early step was the introduction of Latin in January 1837. After all, some boys might want to go to the new university in London, and there would need Latin; and – the trustees said – "it could not injure our present celebrated classical school". Of course the boys must only be taught grammar, no literature. With delight the trustees found that their existing staff knew Latin, so no extra expense would be required, beyond buying some Latin grammars. Oddly enough, Dr. Brereton was unhappy about this; and the Warden of New College wrote to remonstrate, fearing the schools might clash; but Latin teaching had already begun.

French (1820) and drawing (1840) were begun at the same date as at the grammar school, and with the same staff; in fact, the need to hire a room at the Assembly Rooms for Rudge's drawing class, his requests for models and prints, and the commendation of the school's work by an examiner (greater improvement in 1844 than W. M. Watts would have thought possible) show a more marked success here than at the other school. French did less well; the difficulty was to fit in the classes, since only a certain number of boys took it. Rodde, who had succeeded Dupont, was mainly concerned to teach grammatical rules; the examiner in 1845 reported habitual carelessness among the boys, who preferred punishment to trying. So in this year a change was made: boys of the three top forms were taught French by their regular masters, who would have a small allowance for this, and Rodde was dismissed. Moore was at first not happy with the change, but by 1847 had come to the conclusion that it was beneficial. Geography he had introduced long ago. Algebra and geometry were advocated by him in 1833. History was first suggested by an examiner in 1839. German was considered in 1842, but not actually introduced till 1858 with H. Steinmetz, appointed to teach both schools. The first hint of science came in 1850 when the school committee mentioned it as a possibility; but all that happened in Moore's time was that in 1856 the senior boys were allowed the use of a classroom on holiday afternoons for "scientific investigations". Science came slowly in all schools: there were weekly lectures at Eton and Rugby in 1849, and at the latter school in 1861 about 41 boys were spending two hours a week on it.[34]

EXAMINATIONS

For the grammar school an annual examination in classics by two visitors from New College dated from 1793. At first three, after 1826 up to eight exhibitions could be held at any one time (six by Bedford boys, two by boarders). But for a time the trustees tried also to play a part. It was natural that they should feel interest and responsibility in a school where progress was only recent; yet it was understandable that the headmaster should be nervous of intervention from laymen. It was some time before the modern practice of written papers was introduced; and the old oral method in public in inexpert hands of uncertain competence could have been a farce. Besides, Brereton felt that the Trust had no responsibility for his boarders. However, in 1821 the trustees determined to examine the town boys at the hospital (children's home) in writing, arithmetic and French. But the parents of 19 (including Pearse, Nash and Pulley) shared Brereton's apprehensions, and declined to submit their boys; two others were absent; so only 11 were "examined", and were found (according to the committee) to have made satisfactory progress in writing, but not in arithmetic, algebra and geometry. The attempt to make an additional examination had failed. Even at the classical examination the trustees were not able to establish their claim to be present officially, only as individual members of the public. In 1836 an indirect attempt was made by conference with the visiting examiners: as funds were so liberally bestowed, they said, they felt the need to ask if the mode of education was consistent with the present improved state of classical knowledge. The visitors replied that it was not their duty to discuss management, but that the examination had been highly satisfactory. In 1837 and 1838 the trustees asked the college for a copy of the written report which apparently they supposed the visitors made to the college on their return. This again was refused.

In fact the college archives reveal scarcely any reports, and these are uninformative. The visitors of 1843 (while reporting Brereton's current requests for staff and premises) suggested that in future the examination had better take two days instead of one, and should include mathematics.[35] Once, in 1847, the warden, Dr. D. Williams, came himself with the Rev. J. E. Sewell, and both were brought by Dr. Brereton to the boardroom (they took the opportunity to stress the need for more staff and premises). Those of 1850, who complained of Le Mesurier's interference, simply declared themselves "much pleased" with answers to the nine printed papers (all Latin and Greek except for one on classical history and one on geometry).[36] (There is also a very brief report for 1857 – see below.)

However, the Warden did occasionally reassure the trustees (who in fact must have known it from the school's numbers) as to the school's reputation. In 1821 he wrote to Hunt that the fellows were "highly gratified by the reports which we continually receive concerning the meritorious and successful exertions of master and usher"; and in 1830 to the Trust: "New College has no other wish than to secure to Bedford the advantages of an active, well-regulated and highly respectable place of education".

Among the boys awarded exhibitions are names of prominent Bedford families in this period, including John Wing, Anthony Pulley, Benjamin Trapp, Thomas Kenworthy Brown, J. Ll. Roberts, Alexander Sharman, Henry Pearse, G. F. Maclear.

At the commercial school also the trustees at first conducted an examination themselves. Thus in 1832 the school committee examined the boys in reading, spelling, writing, grammar, arithmetic, geography, the catechism and French, and found them all much improved from 1831, and recommended an expenditure of £20 on prize books. For the future they decided to arrange for an external examiner. The first was the Rev. A. P. Kelley of Caius College, Cambridge, who examined annually till 1838, in an increasing number of subjects as the curriculum was extended. At his first visit he found the boys "remarkably well instructed", except in French. The next examiner was W. M. Watts, at whose instigation history was introduced. In 1845 T. Sansbury, of the Diocesan School, Rose Street, Soho, said that he had no greater professional pleasure than that experienced on his recent inspection of "your noble establishment", with its order, regularity and discipline, the diligence of the masters, and the pains of the boys. Then in 1846 came James Prince Lee, Headmaster of King Edward VI School, Birmingham, and was "most favourably impressed", especially with English grammar, Latin, French, and drawing – though there could be more interest in history. After this for some years two Rugby masters came – the Rev. Charles Evans and E. W. Benson (later Archbishop); and Evans continued to come, even after he had succeeded Lee as headmaster at Birmingham. Evans evidently had a very high opinion of the school, its efficient instruction, admirable discipline, and the zeal of its staff; while he praised, however, he made suggestions, such as that the Latin classes might be allowed to read Cicero and Caesar; and that history should not be limited to a meagre outline of facts; but in general he gave his "strongest approbation".

From 1853 two premiums of £50 were awarded to assist boys in their careers. The first two to receive them were both articled in London: Samuel Clarkson to a civil engineer, and William Taylor to an architect. One of Moore's boys, David Gostling, who in 1863 was one of eight candidates to pass the newly instituted R.I.B.A. examinations, wrote gratefully to the Trust: "I owe it all to my school education".

BOYS AND SPORTS

Corporal punishment was severe at both schools – indeed at schools everywhere throughout this period, and was taken for granted by parents. Indeed the stepmother of William White (b. 1807 and therefore at the grammar school under Brereton while Abbot was still usher) particularly asked for her stepson to be thrashed, so that (his son "Mark Rutherford" records) he had "dreadful recollections" of his schooldays.[37] Much later at the grammar school Le Mesurier was said to cane equally for perfect work (when a crib must have been used) or for carelessness.[38] It is also said that once when he could not find his spectacles he caned the whole class for theft; then, finding them on the top of his head, caned them again for laughing. Bowden used a large round ruler on skulls and knuckles.[39] At the commercial school Moore too had a reputation for severity and irritability, the latter probably increased by his poor health; but he told the Trust in 1847 that he only resorted to corporal punishment in extreme cases, and normally imposed extra tasks. In an enquiry into alleged severity by a junior master at the commercial school in 1856, Moore reported that only one boy was "very slightly marked on the hand" and the trustees accepted his account. Severity must have been the only way to enforce the teaching of those days, which by modern standards was dreary and mechanical. "Mark Rutherford", who went to the commercial school, says "we had to learn the Eton Latin grammar till we knew every word of it by heart".[40]

Leisure hours were precious. The majority of the 200 boys at the commercial school about 1840 were, says Rutherford, very rough, but about a dozen kept apart. The country was very near to the small Bedford of those days; "never was there a town better suited to a boy than Bedford at that time for out-of-door amusements". He loved the river. He had one of the few pleasure boats; his father got him leave to fish at Kempston and Oakley; on the preceding evening he would walk four miles to lay bait; he would wake early (having arranged for a string tied to his toe to be pulled), and spend the day fishing, sleeping away the noon hours. At dusk he went with other boys bat-fowling, with lanterns on either side of the hedge. In winter, when flooding on the Ouse had not yet been brought under control, and the meadows for miles around were a great lake, he went skating; or would shoot sparrows with an old flint musket; and on foggy half-holidays roast potatoes in a bonfire. Some boys had artistic tastes. William Dawson of the grammar school, whose brother was curate at St. Paul's, employed some leisure hours about 1833 in sketching a delightful panorama of Bedford from the roof of St. Paul's church.

Boarders, says an old boy later, casting his mind back to 1829–30 at the grammar school, were confined to the playground.[41] Space for this had been acquired in 1813 when the Trust secured the old prebendal estate where Herne chapel stood. It was surrounded by iron railings and gates, through which the boarders passed when going to church on Sunday or for a walk in winter. The only organised game for which there was room was fives, for which a brick wall on the east, 30 ft. long and 20 ft. high, was erected; and only four boys could play at a time. So the boys found other outlets. The bigger ones made the small ones fight. They also yoked them in teams to large boxes or baskets and drove them with whips at speed, as many big boys as possible getting in the box or basket; and the small boys were often rolled over or trampled on. One boy found a large bottle-crate and put small boys underneath to drive round. Broken knees, cut faces and sprained wrists were the result. There was then no tuck shop, but occasionally at night a small boy would be let down by a sheet from the dormitory window (which looked on to Horne Lane) to go and buy mutton pies, sausages and ale. (A few years later another old boy remembers a woman coming to the gate to sell pastry and sweets.)[42] Sometimes in the dormitory there was bolstering and cold-pigging. But in Tom Brereton's time as usher, a few small boys boarded with him, and there all was quiet.

A field was clearly needed when by 1841 there were in all at the two schools 300 boys. The Warden of New College – probably prompted by Brereton – brought the matter to the Trust's notice in July: the grammar school playground was insufficient; boys needed space for exercises suitable to their age. As usual it took some time before anything was done; though in March 1842, after Captain Hutchinson and other inhabitants had petitioned the mayor, the trustees resolved that it was desirable to comply. And after all, what about the commercial school? The matter was referred to a committee, and it was found that a 6-acre field to the north of the town, usually used for cattle fairs, could be rented from the House of Industry, the Trust putting up a 7 ft. fence and "taking steps to complete" it. The latter ambiguous phrase seems to mean that the ground would require levelling before it could be used as a cricket pitch. The cattle fairs would still take place at appropriate dates, and the grazing (sheep could be hurdled off) was let to tender. The levelling was overlooked until May 1844, when the boys thanked the Trust for the playground, but its roughness made it insufficient; the Trust then ordered levelling to be carried out forthwith. The work, if done, seems not to have been perfectly carried out, for in the following January an offer was accepted from St. Paul's churchwardens that the cost could be met from their fund for employing poor labourers in winter.

For a time from 1847 a local (adult) cricket club was allowed to use the ground on Mondays, on paying one-third of the rent, but this club was dissolved in 1850.

After the field was obtained, the grammar school boarders used to walk in crocodile to it. Local feeling sometimes gave rise to trouble. It was reported to the Trust in June 1846 that town boys – i.e., boys not at either school – incited others to bad conduct. In 1848 the two schools jointly complained of annoyance and interruption from persons not connected with either school.

However, really serious trouble came in 1859 after Brereton's time and was between the schools. The field seems to have been discontinued for a few years; in the late 1840s with increasing financial difficulty, relinquishing the playground was more than once put forward as an economy measure; and seems at last to have taken place. When, after agitation in 1858, it was resumed in 1859, the schools to use it on alternate days, a misunderstanding led to a riot.[43] Boys from the commercial school found grammar school boys (who had been given an extra half-holiday) in possession. A running battle ensued to St. Peter's green between forty or fifty boys. One of them, Foulkes at the grammar school, knocked Clarke of the commercial school unconscious. (These were rough times – the last public execution in Bedford was in 1868.) Feeling ran high in the town, especially next day when a warrant was served on Foulkes; a crowd gathered, and windows were broken. At the ensuing court proceedings Foulkes was fined.

MARKING TIME: 1855–74 AND 1860–77

"Marking time" is not an entirely satisfactory description of the terms of office of the next two headmasters, Fanshawe and Finlinson; for in this period both schools obtained an extension of premises; and for both the Taunton commission of 1868 and the new scheme which followed it in 1873 meant a change of direction which was to have far-reaching results. Yet for both schools the period was an interim one, after the term of an exceptional headmaster who had largely created his school – "the object of my long labours", as Brereton said, "which I pray God may flourish". At both it was followed by a century of progress, including removal to a new site: the grammar school removed in 1891; for the other school, removal is planned for 1974.

Fanshawe and Finlinson were the last headmasters to be appointed under the old régime, that is to say, Fanshawe by New College, and Finlinson by the pre-1873 Trust; and their appointment has already been discussed (ch. 3). J. F. Fanshawe[44] at the grammar school was a Wykehamist and a fellow of Exeter College, who, as he wished to marry, was obliged to seek another post. He was not, as the trustees had hoped, another Arnold, though he did institute monitors. He also introduced at St. Paul's church on Sunday afternoons a school service, a practice which continued there till 1903. And he established a speech day at the end of the summer term. He came of a military family, has been described as "conservative by temper and instinct"; precise, almost pedantic, in his scholarship; a "high churchman of the old school"; stiff and reserved, but with an inner warmth, so that those senior boys who penetrated his reserve felt a "glow of affection". He was little prepared for the situation he found at Bedford – for a small town, for old-fashioned and restricted premises, and for a Trust with extensive commitments and limited income, a Trust, moreover, which had just been through a crisis (ch. 3). He stayed 19 years; frail-looking, his health suffered and he gave up boarders about

1870; and in fact he died in 1876 two years after he retired.

Wilkinson Finlinson at the commercial school had lived with the situation there since 1847 when he came from Stockwell to be second master to help the ailing Moore. Solid and sturdy, he was no innovator, but carried on in the main the system Moore and he had worked together; and he was on the whole content to do the best he could with the conditions he inherited. Having been promoted from the staff, in 1865 he had some trouble, both with the second master, the Rev. W. Harris who had come from Chichester, and the French master Hobacq; but the trustees upheld him. Harris was replaced by W. J. Porter, promoted from within the school; and instead of Hobacq there came as language master Joseph Gostick. In 1865 the irksome proximity of Finlinson's official residence to that of Le Mesurier ended; the latter secured both houses, so that he could take boarders; but Finlinson, removing to a rented house in Albert Terrace, must have found compensations.

PREMISES

To modern eyes the grammar school premises in 1855 were really bad, but at that date old buildings on a cramped central site were not peculiar to Bedford. Charterhouse did not move from London to Godalming till 1872; Shrewsbury moved outside the town in 1888; and King Edward's School, Birmingham, moved in the present century. Fanshawe was anxious for a hall and classrooms. The most he hoped for, and what he with difficulty secured, was an extension on the existing site; and as Horne Lane ran close beside the old school building, it was necessary, in order to build on adjoining land, to divert the street northwards, as was done in 1858.

On arrival, he had the original school building with its two floors, as secured by Brereton in 1828. He had to continue to make use of the dining hall in the boarders' premises nearby, as had been done for nearly 20 years; and he also had in use a hired room in Randall's house across the way; which meant that small boys had to go through the street, where sometimes market or fair was in progress. As he put it in 1857: "While I am hearing a large class in the upper school, Mr. Hobacq has a large class so near to us that we cannot but interfere with one another; a third class is saying lessons to the assistant classics master. At the same time the second master and the writing master are both engaged with classes in the lower school; Mr. Cave in the room at Mr. Randall's house; and Mr. Swann and Mr. Brereton have their classes together in my boarders' hall." That is to say, there were three classes in the upper room of the original building, two in the lower, two in the boarders' hall, and only one class had a room to itself.

Numbers when Fanshawe came were 99; they had fallen owing to the uncertainty caused by the Chancery suit and the disputes ending in the new scheme of 1853 (ch. 3). Under this scheme boarders were limited to a total of 70, of whom the headmaster was to have 30 and the second master 20 and two other masters ten each; but Le Mesurier's house was not adapted for boarders till 1866; and in July 1855 the trustees wanted to postpone even the taking of boarders by the headmaster, till he threatened to resign at once. When he left in 1874 total numbers were nearly 300, having both recovered, and continued to rise.

Fanshawe secured a hall, 58 ft. by 30 ft., the present civic theatre. He also obtained classrooms – apparently seven in all: three in the extension, and four by division of the two floors of the original building.[45] This was after a long struggle. To him the trustees seemed obstructionist, and in fact they were not well equipped to consider training for the university and for professional careers. But the main barrier between them was that the Trust conceived their responsibility for Harpur's bequest was to Bedford as a whole; they had over 1,000 children in their five schools, with numbers growing and staff certainly not overpaid, while the Trust income was almost stationary. Thus the trustees felt no strong compulsion to enlarge the grammar school, for which families came to Bedford. If it must be enlarged, they thought it should be done on a small scale. Fanshawe's ancestors were military and not diplomatic; as he wrote to the Warden of New College on 14 February 1857 "If they declared enmity against the school, I avowed myself openly as their enemy". In June of that year, thirty parents sent a memorial to New College in which they said that the present accommodation was so confined and ill-arranged that it was prejudicial to health. New College, who had obtained the plans from the Charities Commission, in December said that these were too contracted. Yet the larger proposals were rejected in March 1858. In June the Trust was notified that the College was prepared to take legal action. Other memorialists then applied to the Attorney General in support of the more modest plan. It seemed as if the whole legal fiasco of ten years previously would be repeated, when on 15 November a further vote on the two plans was 20:20, and the mayor, John Howard, gave his casting vote for the more spacious one. The new buildings were opened in 1861.

The commercial school could call on no ally to support its claims for premises. At this time the commercial school proper (where numbers reached 300 about 1864) and the junior school were still run as separate departments, and were not reunified till 1877. The former had little hope of a planned extension. It had the two floors of the northeast block, where there seems to have been some conversion to classrooms, and two rooms in the tower. But Finlinson, reporting in 1866, could only call this "utter inadequacy". The place was built for 120; he packed in 320; there was nowhere for hats and coats. At the tower, where a hundred boys went up and down the stairs five times a day, the stairs were in bad condition. The building, in spite of its imposing exterior, was badly ventilated; the windows admitted draughts (or as Finlinson said "pernicious currents of air"). In fact the trustees planned an extension in 1869, but (probably in view of the endowed schools act of that year) the Charities Commission advised waiting. Then, with the closing of the adjoining hospital (children's home) in 1871, the school was able to take over these premises. But radical re-planning in the direction of a modern school (so far as feasible in the limited circumstances) had to wait for the next headmaster.

At the junior school Bannister remained in charge till he retired in 1869, to be followed by W. J. Porter. Here the modest new building behind the main complex was already too small by 1866, when numbers were 225; and in 1868 Bannister declared his task "utterly impossible". Arrangements were made to hire, first the Methodist Sunday school, and then the Castle rooms.

STAFF AND CURRICULUM

At both schools, though science teaching was still in the future, the curriculum became slightly more varied. At the grammar school the trustees in 1855 had put out a rather grandiose memorandum, which required in addition to a "mainly classical training", "astronomy and other sciences", civil and mechanical engineering, languages, history and geography, so as to prepare boys for naval, military, learned and scientific professions, commerce or trade, India and the colonies. Fanshawe declared himself in favour of much of this; and the annual examination by visitors from New College, though mostly classical, now also took in French, history and mathematics. In 1855 there were 50 boys learning mathematics. Fanshawe's personal predilections however were classical. To some extent also he was limited by his staff: there was for instance the aged master for writing and arithmetic, Bowden, who was too old for his work but could not afford to retire; and was at last given a pension in 1859. More English masters were appointed in the 1860s, and German was taught from 1858; but French and mathematics still had only one master each. There were several classical masters.

At the commercial school the examiners in 1862 (Charles Evans of Rugby and G. F. Maclear of King's College school, London) reported a steady improvement in arithmetic and algebra; French was idiomatic; the school was "one of the best commercial schools in the kingdom". Gradually these ad hoc examinations began to give place to general examinations which from the 1860s the universities began to set for schools who wished to enter candidates. At the first in 1861 16 out of 20 boys passed (Oxford);[46] in 1872 (Cambridge) 24 out of 29. Staff gradually increased, but salaries were low; £90 was the salary of an assistant master appointed in 1867; and when G. E. Langley became second master in 1870 his salary was £150. Incidentally, Rudge, the well-known artist, retired from teaching drawing in 1874. The junior school still relied heavily on trainee teachers at £30 p.a.

SPORTS

Sports were still a minor consideration, and handicapped by the use of a distant shared field (used also in the evenings by the Bedfordshire Rifle Corps and the

Tradesmen's Cricket Club). A Cadet Corps for both schools was formed in 1863, but seems to have lapsed. The trustees were beginning to be conscious of the need for all their schools to have playing space; as a trustee observed in 1864, over 1,000 boys assembled daily, yet playground space was very limited. This same year the external examiners at the commercial school (Evans and Arnold) pressed it; there was danger of boys overworking for the prize premiums; recreation would be most valuable; and vigorous out-of-door games could not be too much encouraged. But years were to pass before the two main boys' schools each had its own field.

5 *Elementary Schools 1815—1965*

EARLY YEARS

In the comparatively well-ordered educational world of today, with universal school attendance, teacher training colleges, local authority committees, and a ministry in charge of all, it requires an effort to visualise the conditions of 1814.[1] Nothing of this existed. As soon as children could work, they did so, either at lace-making, or farm work, or helping their parents. Those responsible parents who could manage to do so scraped together a few pence to get their children taught at a dame school to read or write. Here and there a few charity schools endowed by some past benefactor catered for a few more; in Bedford there were two such schools – Leith's and Newton's – for a total of 45 children. In the growing towns an increasing number of children ran wild. Informed public opinion began to feel responsibility, not so much as yet for equipping them to be useful citizens (for the work they would do as adults seldom needed book-learning) but for giving them moral training; or, as a Trust committee said in 1828, so that their minds might "be early formed on moral and religious principles". Individuals or churches began to make arrangements for those children who would attend to be taught on Sundays; and where in the villages it was possible to get some to come on weekdays people like Samuel Whitbread would make a small grant to a local teacher. To encourage and co-ordinate efforts in the county, the Bedfordshire Institution was formed in 1815, and was in touch with the already formed National Society which could help Anglican schools with grants. Nonconformist schools were promoted by the British and Foreign Society (1814). At Bedford the Moravians, in their settlement near St. Peter's green, taught their own children; and Isaac Anthony, minister of the New Meeting (Howard), 1801–22, kept a school for paying pupils.[2]

In normal circumstances there might have been expected in the county town, as there was beginning to be in at least some villages, a voluntary effort to provide teaching for the poorest. But this was the golden age of the Harpur Trust, whose resources were not yet under strain. Bedfordians were gladly relieved of the responsibility and expense of organising voluntary schools, and left the Trust to promote and co-ordinate a system of education for the town. So in 1814 a Trust committee was appointed to draw up a plan. Its school was opened in 1815, the first of five Trust elementary schools which in 1895 were in all educating 3,868 children.

The committee's original brief was to provide for the education of boys under eight (at which age they were eligible for the writing school); and in fact brighter boys, or boys whose parents were willing or able to spare them, did go on to this school – sometimes as many as 17 in one year (e.g. 1844 and 1858); but from the beginning the school catered for poorer boys, and in fact in 1815 it was agreed in these first years to admit them up to 14 years. In 1819 the committee pointed out that, after all, there were some "who require only a very limited education". From 1828 each child was given a Bible on leaving. Most boys went straight into work, as the master's reports show; a few were apprenticed; a few went to the workhouse or the children's home; usually some died. In 1850 out of 91 leavers, 55 went to work, 15 left the town, 14 went to the commercial school, 3 were apprenticed, 2 died of cholera, 1 went to the hospital, and 1 to sea. Always in the background is the assumption by Trust and master that it is the parents' moral duty to send their child in a neat and clean state to be taught; George Warren in 1849 was "in so disgraceful a condition" that the master sent him home; his "idle and dissolute parents allow him to wander about the town in the most forlorn state of destitution"; and in 1851 the master refused to receive Charles Smith again after Smith had been brought before the police – "the worst boy I ever knew".

As reform acts extended the franchise, the trustees became conscious of the need for educating responsible citizens, and in 1867 felt that the "great political change about to take place" made their schools "still more important".

As regards girls, the Trust's approach was slower and more hesitant. When the boys' school (variously called "National" – since the National Society's monitorial method of teaching was used; or general preparatory – since it had first been conceived as a preparatory school) was opened in 1815, it was thought that some provision should be made for girls, so from 1818 they were to attend on Tuesday and Thursday afternoons (later also on Saturdays), when the boys had a holiday. Parents "did not appreciate" the offer; attendance was very irregular; so to induce the girls to come, in 1818 weekly tickets were issued for regular attendance – 20 tickets would qualify a girl to obtain a new frock; and once a year the girls were "treated with tea and cakes". In 1828 most trustees were beginning to admit defeat; they deplored "the mercenary conduct of parents"; there were so few girls that the school did not "answer any useful purpose" but impeded the education of boys; and in 1831 it was discontinued. But a minority of trustees, including W. F. Palmer, Joseph Brown, Edward Langley, Isaac Wale and N. Small, seem to have realised that parents' apathy was perhaps not the whole explanation of this early failure, and were determined to establish a proper school for girls. After fierce battles on party political lines in the boardroom, where (as finances were becoming straitened) the reactionaries declared that the Trust could not afford to reopen a girls' school, a new and full-time girls' school was opened in 1836. The trustees reflected that it would promote "virtuous and moral habits among females generally" and hoped that it would be "for ever a blessing to the town".

Meanwhile it was already clear that only for a very small proportion of boys did the preparatory school in fact serve as such; that it was what a later generation would call a boys' elementary school; and that therefore there were grounds for setting up for all very young children a separate infants' school. This idea was first conceived in 1826 when the perambulating committee took the opportunity in London to visit "two schools lately established for infant education . . . likely to produce very great moral improvement to the labouring classes", where children were taken care of during the busy hours when their parents were at daily labour and their first impressions would thus set them on the right path. It at last took shape in 1839. Thus were established on the central site of the Harpur complex the three schools which, almost unaided, were catering for elementary education in Bedford when the education act of 1870 was passed.

PREMISES 1815–73

For the first building for the general preparatory school a plan was made by Wing in 1815, and till it could be erected the magistrates were asked for the use of the Sessions House. It adjoined the hospital (children's home), and was in fact built in the latter's grounds – its roof can be seen on Dawson's panorama (Pl. 7). The original plan (90 ft. × 40 ft.) was intended for 600 children – this allowance of 6 sq. ft. per child was to be the general standard for many years; and it was to be divided into two rooms for boys and girls. The division was somewhat advanced for its day, when even at public schools classes were taught on the open hall system. But second thoughts reduced the building to be of a size for 250 children, the girls coming only when the boys had a half-holiday. It was hardly built when the adjoining owner, Gurney, complained of being overlooked, so that the west windows had to be blocked up; and he also objected that the privies were a nuisance. Till 1829 the boys had to clean the building after school; but in that year the grammar school caretaker, T. Gammons, was told to clean the preparatory school also.

This first building was replaced when plans took shape for a whole complex of buildings on the Angel (now Harpur) Street site, as the trustees gradually secured ownership of it. Since in 1831 efforts to teach girls were for the time being given up, only the boys' school was built as the south wing of the complex. The old school was taken down in 1834, and the materials stored for possible future use. When the move was made on 21 May, the enraptured headmaster, reporting to the Trust, believed that his building was "one of the noblest and most commodious in the kingdom". Yet it cannot have been all that luxurious, for as late as 1859 he was asking for a place where the boys could hang their coats; and he frequently reported the forms as very dilapidated; or required more. By 1863 even elementary schools were becoming aware of the advantage of classrooms as opposed to the open hall, and he wanted a curtain to divide the room. Pressure of growing numbers diminished the "commodious" feeling, and in 1864 he needed another room capable of holding 100 boys. This was added by 1865; and in 1871, when the hospital closed down, 90 boys moved into its dormitory.

Meanwhile those trustees in favour of a girls' school had been carrying on a war of attrition. In 1834 they carried a resolution that it must not be postponed beyond January 1836. In 1835 they were furious because the grammar school had another master. Could the girls not be taught in temporary premises? In fact a mistress was appointed in 1836, and she opened the school on 12 September in the front rooms of the hospital with 265 girls. She was directed to run the school with the utmost economy.

In 1840 the Harpur site was extended westward along what is now Midland Road (Well Street) by the acquisition of six small properties, thus clearing a space for both the girls' school and the infants' school now also envisaged, on two floors – girls above and infants below. The wing was built in that year with the materials stored from that first boys' school which had been taken down, and it was in the same style as the rest of the Harpur complex, presenting to the casual observer the appearance of being an integral part of the whole. Perhaps undue economy was used. There was intermittent trouble over the contract till 1842; the contractors by mistake made the building a foot higher than intended; and there was doubt about the security of the upper floor, which had to be strengthened with iron tension rods. The light was inadequate, and a Gothic window was added on the west. The heating was bad; it was said in 1868 that the children near the fire were scorched, while others could not feel the heat at all. The playground was only 25 yards wide by 40 yards long; and both girls and infants trespassed on that of the commercial school till an iron fence divided them.

When after 1860 numbers at the girls' school soared to over 400, and the Trust (preoccupied with extensions for the grammar school and a new building for the preparatory commercial school) could not undertake one for girls and infants, the infants were squeezed out of this shared building. This was more readily done as their numbers were then declining. Till the trustees could spare funds for further building, a room in Bromham Road known as Matthews' chapel was hired in 1860; and in the next year Holy Trinity Sunday school in Roise Street. The former was "most unsatisfactory . . . ill-ventilated, unwholesome, and at an extremity of the town". The Taunton commission of 1868 (see below) criticised the building, and it was decided to close the infants' school, and to give the master, Jagg, an almshouse in lieu of pension. In fact, for some time he carried on the infants' school privately in Matthews' chapel.[3]

STAFF 1815–73

Before the establishment of training colleges, indeed before teaching became a recognised profession, securing the right staff was a difficult matter. All that the Trust could do was to get a recommendation from an established school of recognised merit, or to send their appointee to such a school for a couple of weeks, training. Thus in 1815, Miss Smith, first teacher of girls, was sent to the National Society's Central School in Gray's Inn Lane; but for all that Miss Smith was not a success. Training colleges came slowly. In 1846 the government provided that pupil teachers who served five years at a recognised school were eligible for a grant to go to a training college; a certificate from such a college would then entitle them to a small grant in addition to their salary. Yet this did not mean that certificated teachers were soon available in the required numbers; at Bedford in 1860 it was said that certificated staff were simply "not to be obtained". On the other hand, the man or woman with a vocation to teach, whatever his or her training or lack of it, stands out at once; of these the Trust certainly had two in Mr. Riley at the boys' school and Mrs. Furze at the girls' school.

At first there was trial and error. Things began on a very modest scale. When the boys' school was opened in 1815, it was thought that Mr. Furze, master of the hospital (children's home), could very well combine responsibility for teaching with his other duties. Furze had formerly taught in the Central School in London and the trustees sent him back there for two weeks "to be instructed in improvements in the Madras system since he was there". (The Madras system was that of teaching by monitors.) The boys of the Newton charity school, which apparently was in difficulties, were admitted to the new school. Furze did well at first; and as this was in the Trust's golden age, the trustees in 1819 recorded their "perfect gratification" and presented him with a piece of plate worth 12 guineas. However they were not prepared to give him a rise. His zeal and ability were still noted in 1823. But the strain of coping with nearly 300 boys with no help other than that of monitors, promoted from among them, was wearing him out; and medical opinion reported that his health was impaired, and he must have an assistant. An assistant was appointed in 1824 at £30 p.a.

By 1831 things were not going well. Furze was getting increasingly deaf, and wanted to retire; and his assistant, who had at first been diligent, was discouraged Between them, with the help of 19 monitors, they managed 289 boys. The committee found – so they said – negligence, ignorance, and not even "useful exercises of memory"; and expressed their "disapprobation in very strong terms". One suspects that only a man with strong physique and with great drive and sense of purpose could rise above the deadening teaching methods of those days, and infuse large numbers with something of his own spirit. Failing health or inadequate vocation or capacity must have produced dreary stagnation.

Such a man now came in Mr. Riley. The trustees were lucky, for when they wrote for help to the National School, Westminster, Mr. Riley of that school, attracted perhaps by the very need in Bedford, signified his willingness to come himself for an adequate salary. What salary? £150 with residence. So, promising to use every exertion, Riley came to Bedford in 1831, and remained till 1869, when he was given a pension of £200, the salary which his post then carried.

Similarly at the girls' school there was at first a false start. The failure of the first part-time attempt to teach girls, 1815–31, may have been partly due to the teacher, Miss Smith. When the full-time school began in 1836, the first mistress, Miss Poole, held office only a few months. There were 265 girls and the only help was from two "gratuitous monitors". But almost at once Mrs. Furze took over, and things began to change. Maria Furze was the wife of the master of the hospital, and probably somewhat younger than her husband. Already she had the hospital girls well drilled. She continued also to act as mistress of the hospital till after her husband died in 1846, and to run the girls' school till 1860. Her salary in 1853 was £80. And Mrs. Furze, through whose hands some few thousand Bedford girls passed, was rewarded on retirement with a pension of £26 13s. 4d. p.a. and an almshouse.

For the most part these heroic figures of the Victorian age had to depend on assistants of their own training, and they were always on the look-out for talent among their pupils so that they might promote them to be monitors. (The assistant appointed to help Furze in his latter years was given notice when Riley came.) The monitors were meagrely paid, and the able ones all too soon secured posts elsewhere. Thus James Fisher, who was head monitor when Riley came, was encouraged by him, allowed to attend the French class at the commercial school, and was raised in 1836 to the magnificent wage of 8s. weekly; but in 1840 he obtained a post at Christ's Hospital, Hertford. He was followed by George Odell, who in 1843 left for the Greencoat School at Leicester.

The point of the monitorial system was that it enabled large numbers of children to receive some sort of teaching at small cost. The master taught and supervised the monitors, and these taught the other children. In 1815 monitors' rates were: head boy or usher, 6d. weekly; each teacher, 3d. weekly; each assistant teacher 2d. weekly. Such teaching was of a mechanical kind, and served for little more than reading, writing, the rudiments of arithmetic, and learning by heart. This "factory" aspect of education was not its only drawback. There was difficulty in getting sufficient monitors, as Riley explained in 1861. Boys left at an early age, so there were few to choose from. Those bigger boys who stayed at school did jobs before and after school hours; their parents were not indifferent to education, but needed the money thus gained. The only way to help both himself and them would have been to pay the monitors more. Again in 1862, Riley wished the trustees would come sometimes and see how boys of 10–13 years teach others for the trifling weekly rewards of 3d. to 1s., the entire cost of this being about £20 p.a., "while magnificent premiums amounting to hundreds per annum (i.e., capitation) are awarded to other departments".

Gradually the trustees became aware of these facts. After Fisher, Odell, and other assistants had lasted only a short time, Riley in 1853 obtained a really sound assistant in James Denyer at £30 p.a., whose "fidelity and efficiency" he constantly praised to the trustees. A second assistant was appointed in 1864 at £50 p.a. When Riley retired in the summer of 1869 there were 402 boys. The examiner's report of that year, though it praised the monitors, urged the need for more staff.

At the girls' school, at first the assistants were not paid at all. Miss Jones, in September 1836 when the school opened with 265 girls, was allowed to attend "as a gratuitous teacher"; and the next month she was joined in this lofty position by Miss Allen. In 1837 they were each allowed £20 p.a., but were never to expect an increase. Miss Allen left in 1840; but Miss Jones stayed the whole time with Mrs. Furze. By slow degrees she rose to the height of £55 in 1855. In 1860 she had some accident "in her duties" – the details are not given, but it would "probably render her a cripple for life". As compensation for this she received a lump sum of £50 (some trustees queried this as illegal), and she was given a pension of £15 13s. 4d. a year. This happened at about the time of Mrs. Furze's retirement; there were now three assistants: Miss Perfect at £35 (she had been a trainee of the school); and Mrs. Thompson and Miss Sarah Jones, each at £30; and a vacancy; for Miss Purser, another product of the school, resigned. The new headmistress, Miss C. J. Mitchell, under whom numbers shot up to over 400, belongs rather to the next period; she too was still depending heavily on monitors; and when in 1862 it was proposed to discontinue monitors' rewards, she protested that without them she would need two more staff.

The infants' school opened with 264 children under Mr. and Mrs. Jagg, who as usual were sent to be trained at the model school in London. Jagg seems to have done well, even if he was not outstanding like Riley and Mrs. Furze. A report of 1842 describes him as quiet, with a subdued manner, and praises the gentleness and decorum of the children. Incidentally, when there was an unsuccessful proposal to close the school in 1843 as an economy measure, a public meeting protested, and the proposal was dropped. Jagg seems to have had one or two monitors or assistants, who were paid small sums, such as Maria Wray (4s. weekly in 1843) and Ann Bailey (£15 p.a. in 1859). But Mrs. Jagg was perhaps overbearing. There was some trouble in 1843, not fully explained; and in 1848 she was even forbidden to enter the building in school hours; though in 1860 she seems to be participating. By this time the school was in some difficulties, partly perhaps owing to Jagg's health, already impaired in 1849; partly perhaps from the increased numbers of girls who shared the building. The inadequacy of the temporary premises (see above), hired in 1860 till more building could take place, did not help. Jagg, in spite of his ill health, must have had a good deal of quiet persistence, and he continued the school privately when the Trust closed it at the end of 1868.

CURRICULUM AND EXAMINATIONS, 1815–73

The standard aimed at in the boys' school during its first 15 years can be gathered from the committee's strictures in 1831 when Furze was old and deaf, and from Riley's report when he arrived as the new master. There were then 270 boys in 12 classes. The lowest classes (10–12) were taught the alphabet; classes 7–9 learnt words from cards; classes 4–6 read sentences in simple books; classes 2–3 read the New Testament and wrote on slates; class 1 read Old and New Testaments and wrote in copybooks. They also learnt the Lord's Prayer, the catechism, and arithmetical tables. It seems from a reference in 1824 that there was some singing. Prizes were given to the deserving.

In early years this system seems to have worked well, so far as its limited scope allowed. The trustees assumed that it continued to do so; and not until a committee visited in 1831 did they realise that the school was deteriorating fast, as, with such a system, it must do on the decline of its head. No registers were kept. The monitors were incompetent – i.e., not sufficiently taught and supervised. Some children two years in the school could not be sure of their alphabet or repeat the Lord's Prayer. When Riley came, he confirmed that there was "most lamentable ignorance throughout the school"; class 1 could not do compound addition; classes 2–3 could not count properly; most children in classes 5–12 could not make a letter; classes 7–9 were short of cards; the whole school was profoundly ignorant of arithmetical tables; and monitors did not know the boys' names. The whole was "an indistinguishable mass of confusion"; there was "rude and unmannerly conduct, want of cleanliness, and an unsatisfactory manner of assembling and dismissing", when even the head boy was inaccurate in saying the Lord's Prayer and the collect.

But Riley's strictures show how in his hands the Madras system could take on life. Thus when he objects to the upper classes' indistinct reading of the Bible without comprehension or stops, and in utter ignorance of sense, he clearly means to teach comprehension. He complains that the monitors have no notion of asking questions. He enforced strict discipline; indeed in 1832 he had to defend himself in this respect. He soon had over one-third of the school able to write in copybooks. Each class had a box for books, slates and pencils. And he persuaded trustees at least for a time to make weekly visits to help to enforce his standards. The trustees who did so commented on the children's neat, clean and orderly appearance. In 1848 the Duchess of Bedford came. With it all, his aim was to render boys "moral, useful and responsible members of society"; and from 1841 he secured that each deserving boy should have on leaving a prayerbook as well as a Bible. He seems soon to have expanded the curriculum, getting maps, borrowing books from the commercial school, and persuading the Trust in 1855 to subscribe to the National Society so as to get books at reduced prices. By 1868 he was teaching French; and by 1869 there was drawing.

Examinations by an outside examiner acted both as a spur and a test. When the government began to give grants to schools, such grants were dependent on inspection; and though the Trust received no such grant it invited inspection in 1843. The inspector declared the school "particularly well conducted, and the children better informed than any other National School with which I am acquainted". Later examinations were more usually by a local incumbent; thus in 1862 the Rev. C. J. Hillier of Cardington found the first or top class (aged 11) able to do compound division and some fractions, and to answer questions on scripture and on English history, while the second class knew a little geography. But he observed "288 is a large number of boys for two masters"; while in 1868 the Rev. J. W. Haddock said "370 is a very large number of boys in charge of three masters", but that the school was "highly creditable". In 1871 J. T. Hannam of Christ's Hospital set written papers; he thought more attention might be given to English literature – Shakespeare, Milton, Wordsworth; but he adds "I know the difficulty of dealing with masses". The lay observer cannot but think that successful teachers in these conditions were Titans.

The girls began with the handicap of preoccupation with needlework. In 1818 threads, cottons, needles, pins, calico, Holland and canvas were purchased for them. They were to sew and make samplers on Thursday and Saturday afternoons, and to read, spell and write on Tuesday afternoons; but when a committee came to examine them they seemed bewildered and unable to answer, except for two who had probably been taught at home or at Sunday school; and for the hospital girls, who could read, write, and say their catechism. But as soon as Mrs. Furze took charge of the new full-time school which opened in 1836, though sewing and knitting continued, regular attendance, clean appearance and progress in reading, writing and arithmetic are all found; and by 1841 the trustees are talking of the school's "high state of perfection". Here too the curriculum became diversified, but not so much as that of the boys. In 1853 French, English literature, music and drawing for an advanced class were urged at Trust meetings by Skene and Mantel, but they were out-voted; and Skene was again out-voted over French in 1856. Even after 1860, when Miss Mitchell came to build up the school still further, plain sewing was again required, and not fancywork. However, the Rev. R. Fitzpatrick, who examined the school several times, gave it the highest praise for Bible knowledge, English history, geography, grammar, arithmetic (including fractions); the girls were orderly, quiet, neat and clean; and the mistresses worked harmoniously together. He urged in 1862 "increased liberality" for the school, "considering how small a proportion of the funds of the charity is devoted to female education". In 1868, though he had been "exceedingly pleased before", he was now "if possible better pleased", especially with the written answers to printed papers on history, geography and grammar; and he felt sure the girls would become "good, intelligent and useful women".

Even the infants' school had examinations. In 1842 the Rev. H. H. Higgins (of the Liverpool Church of England School Society) found the staff qualified, the children clean, healthy and happy, the singing good, and scripture, history and arithmetic very good, though he made one or two specific suggestions for additional books.

It is worth remembering that at this time the "inspectors" were themselves untrained, and some were ignorant of young children's attainments. The son of a teacher of those days recalls a contemptuous sneer when a six-year old spelt tough as "tuff". They also criticised a teacher before the class.

EVENING EDUCATION

As the value of education gradually made itself felt, those who had insufficient opportunities in early life began to try to make them good by evening study later. Here the Trust's main contribution was by the loan of its premises (which were indeed constantly in demand for many activities), but it did also for a time pay teachers. The use of the boys' school premises for a night school was first suggested in 1850, but not actually begun till 1853, when after a month's trial it was allowed to continue. By the following year there were two night schools, one for boys taught by Denyer, and one in the girls' school for girls, taught by Mrs. Timaeus, each teacher being paid £10. These night schools were for young people aged 12–21 years, and took place on three evenings weekly for two hours. At the same time, militia officers taught privates; while, in the infants' school, older men met as members of the Working Men's Mutual Improvement Society; and in 1856 the Oral Classes Society was allowed to hold French classes in the commercial school. Economy in 1862 threatened the night school; but the Rev. W. Fitzgerald came forward to help with the cost, so the work was allowed to continue, provided the Trust's responsibility was limited to gas and firing.

NEW FACTORS, 1868–76

The Taunton commission of 1868 (ch. 2) to enquire into endowed grammar schools came to affect elementary education because these absorbed part of the endowment, and thus it enquired into the Trust's elementary schools. The figures that it reported for these schools were:

boys	370
girls	490
infants	250
	1,110

It noted that at the boys' school there was an average of 123 boys to a master, and that the monitors were very young; at the girls' school, where there were five trained mistresses and two untrained girls, the average was 70; at the infants' school (master and two mistresses) the average was 83, and the building was "destitute of all conveniences for teaching".

The commission's main recommendations were necessarily for secondary education, but since they had to consider the use of the endowment, their report affected the elementary schools. They conceded that these should continue; the Trust should "maintain in full efficiency the schools needed for Bedford". They thought that, with the elimination of all the welfare side except almshouses, the revenue would suffice for this as well as for the development of the grammar school as a boys' boarding school (ch. 4) and for the establishment of secondary schools for girls (ch. 6). They urged however the closing of the infants' school, and the removal of the girls' school from its then premises. And as they observed that "Bedford's population is but 15,000 and can hardly increase very much more", they saw no need to anticipate expansion on the elementary side. The elementary schools would remain static!

Under the endowed schools act which followed in 1869, a new scheme had to be prepared. To get approval, this must be based on the conclusions of the Taunton commission, and therefore devote the greater part of the Trust's income to secondary education. The commissioners even tried to limit elementary expenditure to £2,000 by their scheme of 1870, but the Trust in their eventual scheme, approved 1873, managed to secure 2/11 of income. Thus for the time being the Trust was able to continue and improve its provision for this purpose, but as the population of Bedford nearly doubled by 1891, while income merely rose from £14,000 to £15,000, this could not be for long.

Meanwhile there had been passed in 1870 an education act providing, where necessary, for locally elected school boards empowered to levy rates, build schools, and provide teachers. Children were to pay small fees unless their parents could not afford it. A government grant was payable, which was calculated from factors such as attendance, subjects and proficiency, but could not exceed the amount raised by school pence.

But in Bedford practically all children came to the Trust schools. The Newton charity boys had done so from the first. The Leith charity school gave up somewhat later. By 1867 some Roman Catholic children were being taught in Brereton Road, but the Anglican and nonconformist churches had limited their efforts to Sunday school teaching, except for the Moravian school for girls (ch. 6). So almost everything continued as before at Bedford.

Almost, but not quite. In 1873, when the new Trust scheme was approved, the 2/11 rule came into effect, as stated above; and under this scheme in 1874 the Trust was obliged to introduce fees into its elementary schools: 1d. weekly (in 1876 raised to 2d.) up to the age of 13; 3d. over 13 years. Even these fees were paid only by children entering the schools after this date, and so for several years the amount they produced was negligible. In 1876 the limit on government grant in relation to school pence was revised (for the year 1875–6 only £25 was received from this source, although £579 would have been "earned" but for the restriction), so there was some increase of help from this quarter. And in 1876 the school attendance act brought the first faint appearance on the scene of the local authority. In areas where there was no school board, there should be a school attendance committee. Thus arose the town council's school attendance committee, which continued till 1897, and which brought a certain number of prosecutions for absence; for instance, in 1880 a father was fined 5s. for keeping his son away from school to look after a stall at a fair. And finally the Trust declared their elementary schools open to government inspection.

PREMISES, 1873–1902

The Trust moved into the new era of general elementary education (compulsory from 1891 when fees were abolished) with two well-established but overcrowded schools for boys and girls respectively, and a third (infants) for the time being closed down.

The first need was for a new elementary school south of the river, which would cater for children in that growing area and draw away some coming into the town centre. A site was acquired in Ampthill Road, and here the new school (boys, girls, infants) was opened in 1876, with six classrooms. By 1880 it was needing accommodation for 200 more children; and in 1884 another new classroom.

It was probably the opening of this school which enabled the Trust and the town council to send a satisfactory joint reply to the Education Department's query in 1876. The department seems to have been uneasy at the non-emergence of a school board in Bedford, and questioned whether all appropriate action was being taken. The joint reply stated that school "accommodation was at present in excess of requirements", but it required a deputation to convince the government that the town council and the Trust should "be left for twelve months to pursue the course they deemed best".

There still was pressure on the girls' school in the northwest wing of the complex, and their vacation of this wing would release it for other purposes. There was land available to the rear, so here a girls' school was built in a modest architectural style, and hidden from general view by the main Harpur façade. Here the girls moved, 26 November 1879, "amidst a heavy fall of snow". A cookery school was built nearby in 1892, which was used also by senior girls from Ampthill Road.

By this time the infants were able to move. An infants' school was reopened in January 1874 by taking over (with staff) a small school in Hawes Street (now Tavistock Place) belonging to Mr. Turnley. The school continued in Hawes Street till the end of 1877; when it was transferred to Holy Trinity room in Roise Street. On the junior department of the former commercial (now Boys' Modern) school moving into the main block, the infants were able in 1880 to occupy their premises (built 1860 – ch. 4) adjoining the girls' school.

All this time the boys' school on the central site, with its high reputation, was under pressure of numbers. On one occasion in 1871 it is recorded that a master and one or two boys fainted.[4] Two classrooms were added in 1889.

Meanwhile the claims of north Bedford for a school were already acute. A site was secured in Clapham Road in 1883, and the contract for the building for a mixed school was finally sealed in 1893.

In 1895 the Trust elementary schools had on their registers 3,868 children, in buildings designed for 3,500 (central site 1,700; Ampthill Road 1,050; Clapham Road 750). At the meeting of the elementary committee on 12 December they recognised the urgent necessity and their inability to provide more. Children outside the borough boundary could be refused, but these were only 28. There was no money to build – there was still a debt on recent building. The committee considered various possibilities for renting premises, but there were difficulties; for instance Costin Street mission hall had no sanitary accommodation. In April 1897 the Trust gave notice to the town council that, in spite of "urgent necessity for increasing school accommodation", they were "not in a position to provide for more". In December 1898 the total excess at all schools was 788. The Education Department insisted that the rule of 10 sq. ft. per child must be kept; and in January 1899 the teachers were directed to admit no more children.

Something had been attempted by the churches. The Roman Catholics built a school in Priory Street in 1877, and for sometime the incumbent maintained it largely at his own expense, but when it closed in 1889 it had only about 100 children, of whom one-third were Roman Catholics. For a very short time there was a very small Primitive Methodist school. The Anglicans made three efforts. St. Paul's in 1877 built a school which was always in difficulties, and was handed over to the school board in 1900. In this school a class of 80 infants was taught by the mother of a Bedfordian, who recalls that only by repetition *en masse*, aided by unbending discipline, could any "instruction" be carried out.[5] Holy Trinity in 1876 opened a school which also was precarious and short-lived. The most successful effort was by St. Cuthbert's, opened in 1888, but even that closed in 1900. A Church Schools Association was promoted in 1896 by the mayor, F. A. Blaydes, with the object of buying a site in the Queen's Park area, but a house-to-house collection brought in only £149.

So at long last in 1897 a school board became inevitable in Bedford, where customary resistance to external direction (coupled here, it may be added, with lack of intelligent assessment of the situation or of effort sufficient to cope with it) had so long resisted such a measure. The mayor described it as "a bitter pill". The Trust promised the board every assistance. In 1900 the Trust offered the school board the Ampthill Road School, with its debt of £653, and the offer was accepted. The Clapham Road School was transferred in 1902 (£4,198). These two schools, and further expansion on Bedford's perimeter, would be the responsibility of the board till 1902; and thereafter (by the education act of 1902) of the town council. But the Trust schools on the central site, so integral a part of the complex, could not well be transferred, and remained the Trust's responsibility and the beneficiaries of 2/11 of its income.

STAFF, 1873–1902

As in the mid-19th century, so again in its latter years, two notable head-teachers stand out, so much so that both at the time and later their schools were known as Mr. Bates' and Miss Mitchell's schools.

G. M. T. Bates, B.A., (who came from Farnley) was headmaster of the boys' school on the central Harpur site, 1875–1911 (between Riley and Bates came F. Bannister). He was chosen from 94 applicants. One of his old boys now living at the age of 87 says "No elementary school had, or now has, a more capable head than old G.M.T." A redoubtable character, he was in appearance short and somewhat stout – "a little like Edward VII", compact of energy and enthusiasm, and a brilliant teacher. Something of his aura comes through even in official minutes – indeed at one stage he had a clash with the Trust over his salary, and came off with the honours at least even. He was (says F. D. Pryer who went to his school in 1892) very strict and very fair.[6] Characteristically, he brought on his death by cycling up a hill.

At the girls' school Miss Mitchell presided 1860–99. She knew well how to make a good impression, and W. E. Forster, who visited Bedford in 1869 when the education act of the following year was in preparation, said "One thing I can speak of with unqualified praise, and that is Miss Mitchell's school".[7] But another memory remained with one who was both pupil and later teacher under her. Her "reign was one of terror. She aped Queen Victoria in dress and deportment, but added an element of cruelty. It was her custom to inspect all classes every morning, accompanied by a trembling child carrying a shawl and duster – the first for comfort in the colder rooms, the second to remove any dust on the chair she condescended to use if she decided to hear a lesson". If she did, she usually slapped the children and left the teacher in tears. "She lived to an immense age and died a tyrant".[8] She was followed in 1899 by the humane and kindly Miss C. A, Etchells.

The other head-teachers, Miss Cooper at the infants' school, A. Corney and Miss Robinson at Ampthill Road, Miss Poynter at Clapham Road, all seem to have been efficient. Incidentally, economy was the cause of the Clapham Road school being a mixed school under mistresses; this meant a 30% saving on salaries.

There was a drive to raise the general level of teaching. Gradually monitors were eliminated from 1870 onwards, which of course meant more staff. Slowly the size of classes was reduced; in 1871 at the boys' school the ratio of staff to pupils was 1:89; in 1875 1:51. It was resolved in 1875 that in the boys' school only certificated teachers should be employed, or pupil teachers who were aiming at certificates. Eleven of the latter were fully trained in the first twelve years, and one went on to a university.[9] Intending pupil teachers, who qualified for exhibitions to the grammar or modern schools, were in 1885 allowed if they so wished to choose the alternative of having their training college entrance fee paid. Something was done to improve salaries, and even in 1897 to allow for modest regular increments; thus at the boys' school certificated teachers were to rise from £80 by £5 increments to £100; at the girls' school from £70 to £90; and at Clapham Road from £60 by increments of £2 10s. to £70. A local branch of the National Union of Teachers was established by 1898.

SUBJECTS AND CHILDREN, 1873–1902

These were simple days when, as in 1890, on a circus visiting the town, teachers were allowed to arrange for children to go; and when there was trouble in 1889 because the master did not allow Ampthill Road children to attend the Wesleyan Sunday school festival, but gave permission for attendance at an Anglican equivalent (the perplexed trustees wished all churches could choose the same day, but affirmed that each child must be allowed to attend the festival of its denomination). It was a time when the school image was being built up by prize-days, when prizes were distributed by the Trust chairman, Whitbread, who in 1878 told the children how their prowess had won increased government grants.[10] To each recipient this kind old gentleman uttered a simple adage or homily, e.g. "Better be good than clever", or "Waste not, want not".[11]

There were entertainments where the children displayed their games, recitations, drill and music to trustees and parents. For Empire Day, generally celebrated after 1902, the girls at Miss Etchells' school wore white dresses, and wreaths, bracelets and necklaces of daisies which they had picked in the park on the previous day. It was also a time when better conditions for cleanliness were still being attained; children were sometimes sent home for being dirty – thus in 1879 "no child could sit near them on account of the unpleasant smell – the mother came and was most insolent".[12] Health, too, was more precarious; there was diphtheria at Ampthill Road school 1877–8, and was thought to come from Pilcroft Street (a mean little street of Cauldwell Street and now swept away); or there were cases of ringworm (1881), or an epidemic of scarlet fever, as at Miss Mitchell's school in 1886; and a heavy fall of snow would mean absence from school because there was not available the protective clothing of today. It was a time of severe discipline; an old boy of Bates' school can remember that when he was given two cuts on each hand "my hands were so swollen, I could not close them"; and for "getting fresh" with girls from Miss Mitchell's school the whole class was kept in half an hour extra for a week.[13] The Trust committee enquired into corporal punishment after a disputed case in 1880, but thought it was "under proper rules and control".

Yet standards of attainment were rising. Some of the praise given in this period by inspectors might be doubted, were it not that it can be set against criticism on other occasions. Thus the first teacher of infants at Ampthill Road was not successful; in 1886 there was a warning that grant might be reduced; and she resigned. When Bates came to the boys' school in 1875 it seems that things had gone down slightly in the six years since Riley left; the inspector went so far as to say that in the lower classes "general attainments scarcely reach the level of a good elementary school"; and even in 1878, though the boys were "very satisfactory", the girls' work was of higher quality. By 1884 the boys were "good"; in 1892 their "high reputation" was maintained. Of Miss Mitchell's girls it was said as long ago as 1869 that they were taught to think as well as recollect; their intelligent knowledge was mentioned in 1875; in 1888 the inspector said that it was "the best girls' school I have ever had the pleasure of examining"; while in 1892 the inspector "cannot speak too highly". At Ampthill Road all was well long before 1900, when the inspector wrote in the logbook "I wish to put on record my high appreciation". The Cross commission, giving percentage passes at government examinations in 1884–5, shows Bedford elementary schools averaging a 95% pass, equalled only by three other places in the country.[14]

The curriculum was slightly extended. French and cookery were taught to the older girls, and pianette and harmonium were bought for the school. Mr. Bates was allowed to spend £8 on the "scientific apparatus of the late Mr. Glover", and from time to time had small grants for his library – in 1888 he bought a new set of Scott's novels. Religious teaching was based on the Bible, and was undenominational, as a report of 1894 shows. In the country generally there was at this time a movement towards what were known as higher grade elementary schools. The Bryce commission's report of 1894 describes Bates' school as "in fact if not in name higher grade"; several boys of 15 were then attending, and one of 16; and subjects mentioned include English literature and mathematics. Mr. Bates' only fault, says an old boy, Mr. F. D. Pryer, "was that he could get impatient if you could not readily master the higher mathematics which he taught" – but then his own favourite subject was drawing.

Looking back from the context of 1972, Mr. Pryer's memory is that there was still a concentration on "the three Rs"; "I did not really like school; it was rather grim". Zeal, discipline, and use of corporal punishment to exact the highest performance of which the student was capable were in accordance with the ideas of the time – a similar account of his own experience in a London elementary school is given by the late C. S. Forester. "Life is real, life is earnest" was a watchword of the day.

Physical education was not omitted. Sergeant-Major Dawson taught drill. In

1893 the corporation were asked to allow the schools to use the baths for one or two hours weekly. A field in Goldington Road was rented for football in 1884; and in 1893 there were grants for "materials" for cricket, both for Bates' school and the Ampthill Road school.

One feature of this period is that, though there were only a few exhibitions from the elementary to the secondary schools, yet these were not highly prized. Masters wished to retain their clever boys, and parents were not anxious for the boys to be transferred. At first in 1875 there were two exhibitions for boys, one to the grammar, one to the modern school; in 1881 for instance, George Gibbs went from Ampthill Road to the modern school. But it was reported in 1882 that in seven years only five exhibitions had been taken up.[15] Later, two similar exhibitions were available for girls.

The Trust elementary schools were often able to claim distinguished old boys; thus at Ampthill Road speech day in 1900 it was said that old boys included "two B.A.s, one B.Sc., a doctor, a chemist, and a Cambridge wrangler".[16] Not surprisingly there was in existence by 1907 a Bedford Elementary Old Boys' Association.

On the girls' later careers, some light is thrown by admission registers. Of about 180 girls admitted in 1894 to the girls' school in Horne Lane, 51 left the town, 33 went to another school or became pupil teachers or took Kindergarten training, 20 to some form of work or to learn dressmaking, 19 to domestic service, 10 went for reasons of health, and 48 were required to help at home.

EVENING TEACHING, 1873–1902

Evening teaching continued in some of the Trust schools. Grants were now available from the government department of science and art; and these were paid to the teachers, who, the Bryce commission reports, were mainly the same as the day teachers, i.e. Harpur Trust staff. Under the technical instruction act, 1889, county councils were the appropriate authority, and by a curious arrangement were able to get funds from local taxation (customs and excise, known as "whisky money"),[17] which in Bedfordshire at the time of the Bryce report amounted to £4,500.

1902–65

From the passing of the education act of 1902, the elementary schools remaining to the Harpur Trust – those for boys, girls and infants in Horne Lane on the central site – are more properly studied as part of the wider pattern of elementary education in Bedford generally. With the 1870 act the government had assumed direction of elementary education; and with the 1902 act its instrument in Bedford became the education committee of the town council. From 1903 there ceased to be an elementary education committee of the Harpur Trust, but there were managers for the three Trust elementary schools. The Trust owned the premises and carried out repairs. It also in 1904 increased the number of exhibitions to 12 at the Boys' Modern School, 6 at the Girls' Modern School, and two each at the Grammar School and the High School; and these exhibitions now begin to be fully taken up.

With the education act of 1918 there came another change. National policy was beginning to see education more as a whole, and to provide for dovetailing the hitherto nearly separate strands of "elementary" and "secondary". Thus on the one hand, direct grants were available to secondary schools which allotted a required proportion of free places (chs. 4, 6), and the number of free places at what were now the four main Trust schools shot up in 1920 to:

Bedford Modern School	96
Girls' Modern School	82
Grammar School	40
High School	27

The Harpur Trust also where necessary made grants for maintenance and books. On the other hand, for those who did not obtain these free places, the act directed the setting up of central schools to which transfer could be made at 11 plus, and which aimed at a higher standard than the old "elementary" schools. In Bedford, both because of their tradition and of their site in the heart of the town, the Harpur boys' and girls' schools in Horne Lane were the obvious choice for a central school, which they became (after a reconditioning of their premises) in 1921, when the infants' school closed down. Laboratories were built in 1929. From 1930 staff were appointed by the local education authority.

The position continued thus until the next education act in 1944. This brought still closer approximation by setting up secondary modern schools, and thus the Harpur central school became secondary modern. But by now standards of school accommodation had risen so much that it was impossible to continue much longer on the limited Horne Lane site. The LEA erected a new building on the edge of the town in Chester Road, and to this Harpur secondary modern school transferred in 1965, taking the name of Westfield School (thus leaving the old premises available for the use of Bedford Modern School – ch. 7). The last link with Harpur was broken except for an eagle badge.

There remained the question of how best to apply the 2/11 of revenue which under the 1873 scheme was devoted to "elementary" purposes. Latterly an accumulation was built up, which in 1954 reached £14,000. Anxiety grew in the town lest this be diverted; yet it was difficult to find uses for which the local education authority could not provide. The then M.P. for Bedford, Christopher Soames, helped in negotiations with the ministry of education, and reported on 29 April 1954 that the principle remained that the original scheme's intention was that elementary school children in Bedford should have better advantages than elsewhere. An amending scheme was approved by the minister in 1956. Under this grants are made for many purposes to the school children or young people of Bedford; thus in 1961, 54 were helped: 24 at universities and training colleges; 3 at Trust schools; 2 at other schools; 11 with professional education; 10 with tools; and 4 with sports' clothes; and in 1966 a grant of £1,181 was made towards Westfield School's organ. Block grants are also made – for instance to scouts groups. There are two endowed berths (one for boys, one for girls) on training ships for working cruises. The Trust is now planning in Wales a field centre in charge of a warden; this will be available for parties from all the schools.

Applicants for help from the 2/11 elementary section of Trust income must have two qualifications: parents (or, if independent, the applicant) must reside in Bedford; and the applicant must have attended for not less than two years a non fee-paying school, though this need not necessarily be in Bedfordshire.

6 *The Four Main Schools 1873–1920*

A NEW OUTLOOK

The period of roughly 50 years from the emergence of a national policy for education to the end of the 1914–18 war, approximately 1870–1920, was a high-water period for the public schools, not absolutely, but relatively in the national esteem.[1] The older public schools had for the first time been brought before a royal commission. Those founded in the 19th century had acquired standing. As the result of another commission the old endowed schools, like Bedford, were being encouraged to develop on similar lines. There was a national awareness on the part of them all. The Public Schools Yearbook appeared for the first time in 1889, listing 30 schools – the Grammar School at Bedford among them.[2]

In 1869 twelve headmasters met to discuss their common problems. The idea of meeting was conceived by John Mitchinson of Canterbury; eventually Edward Thring of Uppingham took the lead. Some 60-odd headmasters had been invited, among them Fanshawe of Bedford, but he was not well, nor was his an out-going personality. Those who went wished to co-ordinate their attitude in face of possible further government intervention – it was a kind of league of self-defence. Out of this grew the Headmasters' Conference.[3] Fanshawe's ebullient successor, Phillpotts, attended. Bedford Modern School, so called from 1877, has been represented since 1929, when H. W. Liddle was headmaster.

In the ethos than current, boarding was seen as a major factor. This was largely coincidental, because the dynamic headmasters of the 19th century were headmasters of boarding schools. Boarding, as has been seen, originated as a practical convenience for boys not near a school, and developed because it provided a financial incentive for headmasters; thus a notable headmaster would almost certainly be a headmaster of a boarding school. Moreover, in a mainly boarding community, the headmaster's influence and inspiration could have maximum effect. The headmaster who of all others caught the public imagination was Thomas Arnold of Rugby;[4] in his lifetime he was not always successful or well-judging; but his promptness in taking a public line on national questions, his early death, and his commemoration almost at once in A. P. Stanley's *Life* (1845) and T. Hughes' *Tom Brown's School Days* (1856) made him known all over England, so that even the radical Bedford draper, George Hurst, whose real interests were in the Trust's other schools, wanted an Arnold for the Grammar School in 1855. Till 1873 boarders had been tolerated at Bedford as long as there were not so many as to put pressure on requirements for space and staff. In 1882 boarders were to be allowed at the Grammar School up to one-quarter of the school number, and by 1903 there were ten houses taking 230 boys. At the Modern School up to 100 boarders were allowed in 1884 – an old boy remembers that boarders in the VI wore top hats. When Bedford High School opened in 1882 there were three boarding-houses, and in 1919 boarders were allowed up to one-fifth. Even the Girls' Modern School had boarders from 1895. But however influential the boarding element, even at the Grammar School the majority remained day-pupils.

The main characteristic of this period in the country's important schools was its belief in leadership. National policy provided for a dual system: the elementary schools now at last becoming universal, in which the great mass of children would receive limited education, which was all that they would require; and the endowed schools, plus other schools added by local authorities after the 1902 act, for the middle and professional classes, with a few children of exceptional ability from the "lower" classes gaining free places. This concept of leadership must be seen against the background of the British Empire, which then seemed founded as a rock. The South African war showed that it could be challenged, and so devotion was needed to uphold and defend it; devotion too was required to administer its far-flung domains. "For God, King and Empire" was a rallying cry till at least the end of the 1914–18 war, in which 383 boys from Bedford School (it took this name in 1917) and 133 from Bedford Modern School lost their lives, while three and one respectively gained the V.C. Boys who were at school in Bedford in the early years of the century were even in the 1930s gaining such posts as Postmaster-General in Nigeria, or Director of Education in Kenya, and also overseas posts outside the Empire, such as Director of Railway Transport in Bolivia.

For the young people who were to be thus educated, clearly much must be done. Premises must be on a more generous scale. Teaching must cover a wider range of subjects, including science. Playing space must be adequate for the achievement of physical prowess. Responsibility must be developed, and consciousness of school identity fostered. Parents' co-operation must be enlisted. In fact, parents no longer clamoured for their "rights", and they accepted the introduction of fees. They might occasionally memorialise the Trust, as they did in 1877, but in a more constructive spirit; they had a better understanding of the limits of Trust resources, and would accept a reasoned answer calling for their patience and co-operation. The schools became not merely something from which one took, but to which one also gave.

The importance of good modern schools and their relative scarcity began to be recognised. The Samuelson commission, appointed to investigate technical education abroad, reported in 1884: "the best preparation for technical study is a good modern secondary school of the types of the Manchester Grammar School, Bedford Modern School and the Allan Glenns Institute at Glasgow university.

Our middle classes are at a great disadvantage compared with those of the continent for want of a sufficient number of such schools".

THE BOYS' SCHOOLS

There was a new confidence. Hitherto the schools which were to become Bedford School and Bedford Modern School had had to compete with the three elementary schools for their share of the Trust's educational resources (i.e., that part of the revenue which was left after the fixed welfare charge had been met). Now the two boys' schools, and the sister schools for girls which were to be established to accompany them, had the prior claim, and were entitled to 8/11 of Trust income.

All this has to be seen against the background from which the boys' schools were emerging: a building on a cramped central site; the teaching of more than one class in a room or hall; that teaching a severe and sometimes almost mechanical drilling enforced by frequent corporal punishment; little physical exercise; and little attention paid to the development of character. If today much of what the schools then strove for, or the methods used, seems either obvious or in its turn to be questioned, that is a measure of the advance they achieved over the conditions of the mid-19th century. For they did not achieve it all at once; in 1873 they were, so to speak, beginning to emerge from a chrysalis; they were feeling their way towards a new conception, and striving for it as it began to take shape. Their success – and success it was in the contemporary setting – is mirrored in the subsequent emergence of a critical outlook as still another conception began to develop, and in the love-hate image which public schools have in the public mind today.

Headmasters in those authoritarian days were all-important, and were more powerful than before because under the new scheme they appointed their own staff. They soon began to reflect a wider range of contacts. J. S. Phillpotts (1874–1903) of the Grammar School, "Chief", a classicist, all-round sportsman and layman, was the last Wykehamist from New College. He, however, had taught for several years at Rugby, where the Modern School headmaster of the day, R. B. Poole (1877–1900) was educated. Poole was a cleric of the school of "muscular Christianity", a modernist in education, whose aim, like Saunderson's at Oundle, was "to develop every faculty a boy has, with special care to bring out those qualities which are likely to make a man of him".[5] Poole had taught at Clifton; and at Clifton the two next headmasters of the Grammar School were educated: J. E. King (1903–10) and R. Carter (1910–28). Carter, a head in the paternal, authoritarian tradition but essentially a kindly man, inspired confidence alike in boys and parents, and he also did much to encourage music. At the Modern School, Poole was followed by C. W. Kaye (1901–16), who had taught at Loughborough Grammar School. An ex-headmaster wrote recently "Kaye taught us to walk tall". His imposing presence in his unfailing topper and morning suit is still remembered by some Old Modernians, to whom he seemed remote from ordinary mortals.

Staff salaries became more realistic, and by the time a national (Burnham) scale was introduced they were above that scale. The old system under which a pension, if granted, was a matter of grace from the Trust and uncertain in amount, had meant that staff dared not retire as their powers declined. A contributory scheme for pensions at 60 was adopted in 1903.

A wider curriculum gained ground slowly. As regards science, there was not only the question of laboratories but the practical problem of staffing, because of the few qualified people available, since the universities themselves did not cater adequately for science. For years the classical side at the Grammar School maintained a strong position. In 1875 at the examination for university exhibitions, 2,000 marks could be awarded for classical subjects, but for non-classical subjects such as mathematics, languages and science 200 marks each. Science was still to some extent considered an extra; in 1876 a laboratory fee of a guinea a head per term was payable. However, the Board of Education began to discountenance this policy, and fees became inclusive in 1908.

At the Modern School the development of VI form work in general was somewhat handicapped till 1880 by the limit of 17 years as leaving age, and from 1880 to 1928 of 18 years, unless permission were obtained. In fact permission seems never to have been refused, and applications to stay on continually increased.

The schools developed a consciousness of identity. One way of promoting this was the school badge. The Bedford eagle was first appropriated by the Grammar School, and when it was worn also by the Modern School Phillpotts in 1876 protested to Finlinson. As a result the latter school adopted a red ground to differentiate it from the Grammar School's blue.[6] School magazines appeared: the *Ousel* at the Grammar School from 1876 (there was a collection of essays in 1845–6 called *Harper's Magazine*); the *Eagle* at the Modern School from 1881. Founder's Day became an event.[7] At the Modern School it began in 1878, and was celebrated with a concert and a dinner at the Assembly Rooms; by 1891 it had become a three-day affair. School songs were composed: at the Grammar School speech day in 1880 – held at the time in the Corn Exchange – the founder's hymn (*Domus pater Harperiae*) was sung; and in 1899 came the well-known "Oh, north and south and east and west . . . You will find the boys of the eagle crest". A Modern School song written by Poole himself has now dropped out of use; it included the verse:

> Away with all selfish ones, idlers and loafers,
> We need no such fellows among us at all;
> Let them lie at their ease on their hammocks or sofas
> While their muscles grow soft and their biceps grow small.

The present "Song of the Black and Red" dates from 1919.

Responsibility given to senior boys (monitors or options – *optio* was a Roman adjutant) was intended both to develop the boys' character and to promote the new outlook. Phillpotts' rules for monitors say that they are chosen on grounds of character, influence and discretion; that punishment is to be inflicted by the head boy or his delegate and only after a meeting of monitors for deliberation, to enforce the tradition of a careful hearing; and that there must always be liberty to appeal to the headmaster.[8] The Modern School VI book, instituted by Poole and continued by Kaye, still survives. Each boy promised "to maintain a good, honourable and manly tone in the school". In this book successive head-boys recorded their suggestions: "avoid trying to get up cases"; compulsory games would be "a very great benefit" (1909); "do all you can to make the fellows turn up at school matches" (1912); "do not be swollen-headed" (1916); caning "must be used with great discretion" (1919); and in 1915 "My ambition – to see the school a school of the first water. It *can* be done if the chaps at the top stick to it".

At the Modern School there was one unfortunate occasion when Dr. Poole found the head of the school playing "small" cricket in the library with the fire-shovel and a tennis ball, and closed the library for the rest of term – not perhaps the best form of punishment.[9]

Fagging existed to some extent in the boarding-houses at the Grammar School and consisted mainly of cleaning shoes and Corps buttons for seniors.

Suitable premises in which the new-type school could develop were achieved in this period only by the Grammar School. Even this was not thought possible for some years. Late Victorian Bedford was still small (population in 1891 under 30,000), and the school had occupied its position for more than 300 years. At first there were expedients, such as using the Castle Rooms and the (old) Corn Exchange on St. Paul's Square, till minor extensions were made in 1880 and 1882. Science teaching made its demands, first met in 1875 by converting the upper floor of the original school building to a lecture hall for science, with a small adjoining room as a laboratory. In this provision Modern School boys were allowed to share. The purchase by the Trust of the St. Paul's Square brewery (once associated with Woodward, later with Belsham, and then with Sir William Long, but now owned by Jarvis) gave a little scope. In 1876 part of the house was adapted for engineering and carpentry workshops, while the remaining buildings were pulled down in 1884 to make room for 11 classrooms (architect Basil Champneys). This was opened by Lord Cowper and became known as the Cowper building.

Clearly the ultimate solution was a move to a new site on the edge of the town. The first move towards this was the purchase in 1883 of $8\frac{1}{2}$ acres, the present school field. This was gradually extended by a further 10 acres up to 1891, including the old St. Peter's rectory, giving access to St. Peter's Street. Further enlarged as opportunity offered, it has been adequate for the eventual demands of a large up-to-date school, with boarding-houses on its perimeter.

The process took many years.[10] First an iron building, known as the tabernacle and secured by the headmaster's initiative, provided temporary classrooms till the new building could be erected; it was later converted to laboratories and gymnasium. Meanwhile a deputation visited other schools to get ideas, and decided against the old system of the encased hall. The headmaster strenuously urged taking a long view for a century ahead, and allowing for a hall that would seat over a thousand. The opening of the new school (architect – after some dispute – E. C. Robins) took place in October 1891. A senior Bedford resident still remembers as a very small boy being taken to see the firework display, when the crowd was so great that he would have been badly trampled if not lifted up on his father's shoulders. There followed workshops in 1895, used also by the Evening Institution; a preparatory department (Inky) in 1899 on the site of St. Peter's rectory; and chapel (architect G. F. Bodley) in 1908. The old school buildings were sold to the corporation; they served for about 70 years as the town hall, and are now the mayoral suite and civic theatre. The Cowper building however was for a time retained for another purpose.

The Modern School expanded and rebuilt on the Harpur Street site, gradually taking over further accommodation. A fine hall with organ was opened under Poole in 1881 (in what is now the old gymnasium). The first gymnasium (1891) was on the field. Laboratories (1880) were devised out of the old kitchen and dormitory of the former children's home (ch. 8), while a range of new buildings, including 16 classrooms and a large workshop, was added on the east of the quad in 1908 under Kaye.

Fees were now paid, except for boys already in the schools, but were very low. At first yearly fees at the Grammar School were £7 up to 13 years and £9 thereafter; at the Modern School £1 10s. to 14 years and £3 thereafter. They soon began slowly to rise. In 1920 upper school yearly fees were as follows: Bedford School, £22; Modern School, £17; High School, £7; Girls' Modern School, £6.

Parental support began to be available, because of the schools' extensive needs and the obvious high cost of meeting them, and parents collected money to supplement the Trust's work. The first of these efforts was to secure for the Grammar School a gymnasium in part of the old brewery premises which were then being adapted. An exhibition of art and science was opened in 1879 by the mayor; it illustrated "archaeology, bibliography, oriental objects, photography, natural history and microscopy, applied mechanics, musical instruments", and "crowds flocked day after day" to it.[11] Another opportunity came over the new Grammar School building: here in 1882 Phillpotts acted quickly to secure the site, which might have been lost while the Trust was awaiting the Lord Chancellor's consent (on behalf of the Charities Commission) to the purchase; and when it came to the building, £7,000 was raised by appeal, the Duke of Bedford and Samuel Whitbread giving £1,000 each. Similarly Kaye raised £6,000 for the Modern School additions of 1908; here a grant of £3,000 was forthcoming from the county council, now responsible for secondary education (ch. 3); and here again the Duke gave £1,000 and Samuel Whitbread £500, and there were many smaller donations. In 1912 a two-day bazaar raised £600 for sports purposes at the Modern School.

A smaller matter was the creation of prizes. In 1884 the parents of Bedford School collected £200 to be invested for this purpose.[12] Since then many prizes have been added at all the schools by old boys or girls or parents.

Sport gradually became organised.[13] Till the 1880s boys played in the restricted playgrounds with marbles or conkers, or at prisoner's base, or a primitive hockey with a brewer's bung. On the old shared field, imperfectly levelled, some played football and cricket. There was also a little rowing: a four from the Grammar School rowed in Bedford regatta in 1872; and the Modern School Boat Club was formed in 1878. On half-holidays boys wandered out into the country; some collected birds' eggs or wild flowers or picked blackberries; some shot with catapults or even guns – one boy in 1873 was killed in a gun accident.

Now sport began to be seen, not only as needed to develop a boy's physical potential, but to encourage team spirit, either for the house or for the school. Houses were introduced at the Grammar School by Phillpotts in 1876.[14] They were named, as they still are, after areas of the town, and the *Ousel* of 1876 reports a football match on 2 October between St. Peter's, Pontine and Trinity, and St. Paul's, Ashburnham and Bromham. Later St. Paul's and Pontine were merged, and St. Cuthbert's added. The *Ousel* comments that collective life involves some sacrifice on the part of the individual, but the latter gains in energy, power and pride; let each house see which can do the most. House races and house steeplechases followed. At the Modern School Poole introduced houses; they bore the names of North, South, East and West; and in 1887 a distinctive badge was introduced, North being a silver star on black, West an anchor on green. Soon non-swimmers (drowners) had to wear a white button on their caps until they could swim 75 yards. At the Grammar School the Corps was re-formed in 1887 – it provided a guard of honour at the move to the new building; at the Modern School a Corps was revived in 1900. At the Grammar School the annual gym display (assault-at-arms) was a feature.

Matches against other schools or colleges began. For instance, the Grammar School in 1876 played cricket against the County School and against Magdalene College Cambridge. The acquisition by each school of its own field made better organisation possible. The Modern School's first field was in Ford End Road, near the gas-works; in 1882 the (old) Clapham Road field was acquired, and gradually levelled and turfed. In the early 1900s, Modern School teams were playing the County School, Leys School and Perse School at Cambridge, Merchant Taylors', Mill Hill and Oakham. Oddly enough, however, the two schools did not play each other, though they competed on the river. By the 1880s crews were being sent regularly to Henley regatta.

Other activities developed, in some of which also the house system could be made to serve. At the Grammar School there were "house recitations", entertainments given by each house in turn, with prizes for the best items.[15] Years later an old boy said he found the experience useful in keeping up the spirits of his regiment on the Indian frontier. The School Musical Society rose to 240 members under Carter, and a house glee competition developed. At the Modern School, Poole established a Reading and Debating Society, and there were sometimes plays or concerts. In 1886, with the help of an old boy, C. E. C. Prichard, a museum was established, the first permanent one of its kind in Bedford. It owed much to its honorary curator, the Rev. P. G. Langdon, and in a later period to F. W. Kuhlicke.

With this consciousness of identity at the schools came a growing pride and awareness of the part of old boys. In 1880 there was the first annual dinner for Old Bedfordians, presided over by Sir Thomas Erskine May.[16] The Old Modernians' Club was formed in 1892, and over a hundred old boys sat down to dinner in the school hall. Overseas branches developed: there were even 35 Old Modernians who could meet in Buenos Aires in 1899.

Already there was a close feeling of contact between the schools and their old boys overseas. Fred Burnaby's *Ride to Khiva* (1876) fired the imagination of boys at the Grammar School. George Farrar went from the Modern School to South Africa about 1879 to become notable in mining and in public work. The *Eagle* in the 1880s has as recurring items not merely the Oxford letter and the Cambridge letter, but news from India, South Africa, Australia and Canada; and a little later comes a report of troubled conditions in China. The South African war came home closely to both schools. The *Ousel* of 1900 gives over 60 Old Bedfordians serving; and the *Eagle*, which at first printed 21 names, found that in fact there were many more. Henry Cross, a Grammar School master, was with the Kharthum expedition at Omdurman in 1898 and died of fever shortly afterwards.[17] In these circumstances more importance came to attach to the Cadet Corps at both schools, first begun in the 1860s when (after the Crimean war) military preparedness began to seem more necessary. The 1914–18 war was to enhance the Corps' standing yet more.

One less favourable factor should perhaps be noted. In the early years of this century numbers fell somewhat, possibly partly because the former County School, now Elstow School, was doing better as a private school under C. F. Farrar, but this closed in 1916.

THE GIRLS' SCHOOLS

In Bedford the first effective girls' school was that kept in St. Peter's Street by the Moravians.[18] Here the school accounts for 1824–37, with names like Hillyard, Leech, Maclear, Ommaney, Pearse, Trollope and Wing, show clearly that this is where sisters of several boys at the grammar school were educated at this time. (There had been a Moravian boys' school, but that declined because the Harpur Trust provided for boys.) Later there sprang up a number of private schools. In the 1877 directory, no fewer than nine schools for young ladies are listed; one in Western Street was probably a modest affair for tradesmen's daughters; but three were on St. Peter's green and five in the new residential area, such as the Crescent and Adelaide Square; and a very successful one, Howard College run by Mrs. Compton Burnett, was yet to come.

Elsewhere a movement for better education for girls had begun some years previously. As long ago as the 1850s Miss Buss was teaching at the North London Collegiate school and Miss Beale at Cheltenham. However, though at Bedford it was government pressure which led to the setting-up of the girls' schools, yet these were among the earlier ones of the new movement, which spread only slowly.

The government's attitude was itself hesitant: the Taunton commission (ch. 3) had said "We do not go into particulars as to the share which girls should have in the proposed system. It should be an integral but an inferior share", and this was reflected in the 1873 scheme. Under this, 8/11 of income was allotted to secondary education. This sum was divided between the Grammar and High Schools on the one hand (4/11) and the Boys' and Girls' Modern Schools on the other (4/11). But as between boys and girls in either group, the division of funds was according to the average number of scholars during the previous five years, "reckoning for this purpose three boys as earning the same amount as five girls".

Governors were appointed in 1874 to begin to plan. For the first time women were introduced, five being co-opted on to the committee; some, like Miss Mary Ewart, were educational pioneers, others were local ladies like Lady Ampthill and Lady St. John. Funds had to accumulate before building could begin.

Though two Trust secondary schools for girls were required by the 1873 scheme, it was in 1878 proposed to begin only with a Girls' Modern School, till a petition from the town pleaded for both. It was then decided to erect adjoining buildings with a shared hall, which had a sliding partition. Since the 1873 scheme had reduced the number of almshouses, the obvious course was to pull down the older ones on Harpur Green (see ch. 8) and use this site. No plan pleases everyone, and the town council in 1878 viewed with deep concern the prospect of a building on this "salubrious and picturesque" green, with its limes and chestnuts. However, in the next decade the town council made up for it by planning for parks and for the river embankment.

In May 1882, with evergreen arches across Bromham Road and be-ribboned Venetian masts lining it, the building (by Basil Champneys) was opened by Lady Isabella Whitbread, the High School having 43 girls, the Modern School about the same. Numbers increased so much that in 1892 other arrangements had to be made. The High School was left in possession of the original building; and even then the hall had to be enlarged in 1897, and later a junior school and art room were added. Meanwhile the Girls' Modern School moved to St. Paul's Square into the Cowper building left vacant by the Grammar School.

Old girls at the Girls' Modern School remember the dark cold classrooms, and at both the welcome interruption when the caretaker entered to make up the fire or to light the gas. At the Girls' Modern School the windows were so high that one could not see out of them except when standing on a desk to open them. At both schools, however, old girls still recall a notable occasion early in the 1914–18 war when they saw and waved to a Highland regiment marching past. In St. Paul's Square the carillon made the teacher's voice inaudible at 3-hourly intervals. Here the annual school concert, at which for many years certificates were presented by the Duchess of Bedford, had to be held in the Town Hall or the Corn Exchange. Numbers here too continued to grow, and extensions were added in 1904 and 1909, while East Lodge (later Dame Alice House) in Cardington Road was used, at first by juniors. The house was not actually bought till later.

The whole background to girls' education was different from that of boys. In the first place, the concept of young ladyhood survived: education must not make a girl un-feminine. At the end of term the form mistress kissed each of her girls. When the first headmistress of the High School died within a few months of its opening, the girls sat in darkened rooms, while extracts from Tennyson's *In Memoriam* were read to them. Gloves must always be worn, and girls went to school in buttoned boots, there exchanged for slippers – the architect at first made no adequate provision for cloakrooms in which to do this. While in school, girls wore pinafores. When gym was introduced, a pleated dress was used, but a long skirt must be worn on top outside the gymnasium. (The long dresses of those days had large calico pockets inside the skirt, and one girl brought to the Girls' Modern School in her pocket a bottle containing tadpoles, with unfortunate results when the cork came out.) Boarders wore cream suits on Sundays. At concerts the whole school appeared in white.

Rules were stricter at the High School than at the Girls' Modern School. Until 1920 two girls might not walk to school together unless each mother had previously sent written permission to the headmistress. As late as 1914, girls might not acknowledge polite cap-raising by young male acquaintances, even across the safe expanse of Bromham Road. Modern School girls were somewhat freer; one girl remembers bowling her hoop along High Street on the way to school – she was also the second girl at her school to have a bicycle. Older girls were sometimes escorted to the parting of the ways (Boot's corner) by cavaliers who carried their books.

But against the lingering concept of young ladyhood worked a newer and stronger force: dedication to that learning so recently available to women to any wide extent, and to teaching by which it might be passed on to a younger generation. This first generation of women teachers was dedicated in a special sense and to a greater degree than male counterparts. While men had a range of careers from which to choose, teaching was almost the only opening for women, and so these were some of the finest spirits of their generation. They cared for their pupils to an extent which later generations do not require. Moreover, at that time Bedford had no public library, only an inadequate subscription library, and school was to many girls a revelation. To discover ability in girls who had had few opportunities, to foster it and eventually hand them on to the universities, was the delight of these teachers. And they had few others.

They led restricted lives socially. On Friday evenings the Modern School headmistress entertained her staff, reading an educational book to them while they crocheted shawls. They welcomed the coming of bicycles in the 1890s which enabled them to get out into the country at weekends. Even they were under supervision. As late as 1919 a young mistress at the High School, who went a few yards up the street to post a letter without putting on gloves, was reported to the headmistress and reprimanded. As restrictions were relaxed, they might be asked to tea at their pupils' homes; and one girl, who then had scarcely heard of opera, remembers being invited by a mistress for a weekend in her London home and taken to Covent Garden.

In early years the financial reward of these teachers was meagre. Even their future was ill provided for. When a superannuation scheme was first planned, even the headmistress of the High School thought it was "not a necessity" – £50 would be enough for a pension.

The headmistresses were significant. The High School had strong connections with Cheltenham Ladies' College. This was not indeed through the first headmistress, Ada Benson (Mrs. McDowall), who had already been the first headmistress of Norwich High School, and was the sister of Archbishop Benson (headmaster of Wellington); she died in her first year. The connection came through the next two headmistresses, Marian Belcher (1883–98) and Susan Collie (1898–1920), both of whom had taught at Cheltenham. Soon after Miss Belcher became headmistress, that redoubtable pioneer of Cheltenham's early days, Dorothea Beale, came to Bedford to visit her former assistant and to address the staff. Miss Belcher is remembered for her kind friendliness, her thoughtful teaching, and her encouragement of music. Her weekly mark-reading was never to be forgotten. "She believed the best of everybody."[19] Miss Collie had for years been Miss Belcher's second mistress. She was scrupulously just and true, her insight into character was pre-eminent, and she had a gift for remembering everyone.[20] Old girls remember her as a stately figure in her long rustling skirts.

At the Girls' Modern School the first headmistress was Mary Porter (1882–94). One of her addresses to the school was remembered years afterwards. "A piece of rough wood in itself is not beautiful, but if it is good close-grained wood it will take a high polish. Then you see the beauty of the wood, the colour and the variety and beauty of the marking. These qualities were there before but were concealed."[21] After Miss Porter came Edith E. Dolby (1894–1925), a young mathematics graduate from Cambridge, who had taught at Manchester High School. Miss Dolby in particular, with her headship of 31 years, was the main creator of her school. An old girl writes "She was fair and kindly and understanding, had great patience and a sense of humour, and was always full of encouragement. I have never forgotten how much we owed to her wise guidance".[22]

Soon girls began to go to the university, more especially from the High School (for limitations on Modern School VI, see above). In 1912 there were seven old girls at Oxford, five at Cambridge, and seven at London; and in 1915 an old girl was house-surgeon at the Liverpool Royal Infirmary – this was the more remarkable as science teaching at both schools was minimal. Sometimes an able girl had to transfer for her last year or two from the Modern School to the High School. But in 1905 there was an old girl at Newnham and in 1907 two at Royal Holloway College.

Much that was characteristic of the boys' schools at this time came only later at the girls' schools and in a modified form. Thus there was at first no provision for games. Seniors played a kind of hockey in the playground on Saturday afternoons. About 1892 on each school playground a tennis court was marked out on the asphalt, and matches began to be played against other schools. There was drill, at first taught by a man; from 1887 by Miss Stansfeld, later Principal of the new Physical Training College, opened 1903. Cricket and netball began to be played. Then fields were acquired. The High School field off Bromham Road was bought in 1899 and a pavilion (given by Mr. T. Rose in memory of his daughter) opened in 1913. The Girls' Modern School field in Chaucer Road was bought in 1910 and enlarged in 1921. But there was a subscription to the field, and many girls did not attend, either for financial reasons or because their parents did not think it necessary for girls. Guides were introduced at both schools in 1918.

At both schools the badges have been subject to change. The High School began with a red and green ribbon. It was not till Miss Tonkin's day (1925–46) that the Girls' Modern School adopted the emblem of the cornflower and the motto "ardent au devoir quotidien". The High School magazine, the *Aquila*, began in 1911; the *Uisage* at the Girls' Modern School somewhat later. Division into houses did not come at the High School till about 1920: East, West and Central, with corresponding colours; and one old girl remembers the initial meeting at which the prefects explained the system, and being bored by the suggestion of getting excited about the "honour" of such an artificial creation as the house. At the Girls' Modern School houses were introduced in 1930, and called after Saints Bridget, Etheldreda, Hilda and Ursula. A head girl was not appointed at the Girls' Modern School till 1917,[23] and on the first occasion of her having to propose a vote of thanks to a visiting speaker she was too petrified to do so (Miss Dolby, wise and kind as usual, perceived what had happened and unobtrusively covered up). For a time at both schools prefects were elected; later those at the High School were appointed.

One feature of building up the school ethos – an association of old girls – was if possible stronger at the High School than at the boys' schools. Founded about 1892, the Guild claimed almost universal membership. At its biennial celebrations, the school hall, decorated with delphiniums and furnished with carpets and armchairs for the Friday evening conversazione, took on the appearance of the palm court of a Grand Hotel; old girls attended in evening dress, and prefects, honoured to be invited, looked forward to the day when they would join this august assembly as of right. A full weekend of events followed, including a garden party at the field, where strawberries and cream were consumed while a band played music from Gilbert and Sullivan; a Sunday service; and on the Monday morning old girls were at liberty to attend and disrupt all classes. At the Girls' Modern School, the Old Girls' Association formed in 1911 functioned on a more modest scale.

A WIDER SOCIAL INTAKE

One factor of the 1873 scheme affected all four schools, though not to the same extent: the boys' schools were open to country boys, and the girls' schools when built similarly took country girls. Ashton Grammar School at Dunstable was the only other grammar school in the county, and boys and girls came to Bedford even from Luton. There were some country boys at the Grammar School, but more at the Modern School. The railways in 1894 brought to the Modern School 43 boys from the south, 34 from the southwest, and 9 from the east. The late C. D. Linnell recalled walking to Pavenham six miles when he missed the train home. Others came by bicycle. In 1900 one boy in seven at the Modern School came from the country. The prestige of the Harpur schools was such that, even though there had been set up in 1869 a so-called County School in Kempston parish on the Ampthill Road, it attracted few local boys and soon became a private school. Railways and bicycles brought girls to the girls' schools too.

There were also the holders of free places. From 1875 the Trust offered free places at the boys' schools, but in the early period these were seldom taken up. In 1885 two were offered at the Girls' Modern School and one at the High School. The 1902 education act gave Bedfordshire county council the power to supply or aid what was called higher education; within a few years schools were built at

Luton, but north, mid and east Bedfordshire relied on the Harpur Trust schools. The Board of Education itself speeded up the process by national direct grant if the proportion of places was sufficiently high, and in 1917–18 the Trust schools became direct grant, with 25% free places at the two Modern Schools and 10% at the other two.

Thus to sons and daughters of service families and of Bedford professional classes were added boys and girls drawn from other backgrounds. In consequence there were social pressures, not overt but felt. Here the Trust schools reflected the general attitude of the day, when class distinctions were more marked. Individual cases and memories vary, but it is clear that, the older the old boy or old girl, the more definite his or her memory on the subject. The Grammar and High Schools believed themselves superior to the Modern Schools. In the earlier period there tended to be within each school socially homogeneous groups. Boarders were the elite; this was so even at the Girls' Modern School, where they were fewest; some of these girls were conscious of their connection with the British Raj in an Empire on which the sun never set, and behaved accordingly. Next came the town fee-paying pupils, of whom many came from Anglo-Indian families who had come to Bedford for education. It was said that the richer ones went to Cheltenham, the poorer came to Bedford, and that Bedford "society" was a closed circle of retired military and naval officers, civil servants, planters and engineers, together with local doctors, lawyers and schoolmasters.[24] (Perhaps this genteel poverty explains why Bedford till 1935 was content with an inadequate and deteriorating subscription library, while Luton had a public library in 1883.) Then there were those who held free places: these, while they did not snub overtures, tended not to respond to them. Last of all were the country boys and girls. In the VI, the ranks closed up, and a country girl might find that a colonel's daughter was not necessarily stand-offish and had an equal interest in books.

Even the staff might be unsympathetic. An Old Modernian recalls that about 1913 the son of the blacksmith from a neighbouring village was ridiculed by a master before the class because of his hobnailed boots and bucolic accent – he left soon after. Old Bedfordians remember that such conduct was not unknown at their school. And there were other pitfalls. On one occasion a form at the Grammar School was set to write an essay on the summer holidays; a country boy for financial reasons had had to spend the whole time working on his father's land; to describe his holiday truthfully would be to court derision; so he wrote an imaginary account of the Isle of Wight.

At this distance of time, it can be seen that, while the Trust schools reflected the class distinctions of the day, they also helped to erode them. The contacts were in fact good, and the cross-fertilisation an intangible asset. Those who were then free-placers and country boys now swell the number of eminent Old Bedfordians and Old Modernians.

The 1914–18 war took its toll. For a time school buildings and fields were occupied (a Highland regiment camped on the High School field). The workshops were organised for war work. By October 1915 102 boys from the Grammar School had been killed and 150 wounded. The final figures from the two boys' schools were 516 killed; with still more awarded decorations and many mentioned in despatches. In 1918 King George V and Queen Mary visited the four schools. In the peace celebrations of 1919 the Harpur Trust boys and girls joined the massed schools of Bedford in the park, singing "Land of Hope and Glory". War memorials were planned: at the Grammar School (now Bedford) a reredos in the chapel; at the Modern School a Memorial Hall at the school entrance and a Memorial Library. A new era was at hand.

7 *The Four Main Schools 1920–1970*

1920–40

The generation growing up in the 1920s found a changing world. The League of Nations seemed to offer the prospect that in future international change could come by peaceful means. The British Empire still stood – in fact a school essay could still suggest that the best outcome for the human race would be the Empire's peaceful extension to cover the globe, bringing to all nations peace, order and liberty; but part of it was now known as the Commonwealth; and in the rest there were signs of change, such as the progressive Indianisation of the Indian civil service. Even Bedford was altering; it was no longer mainly residential, for the development of industry during three decades had mounting effects.

The general educational outlook was being revised. Under the 1918 act the Board of Education tried to improve the "elementary "schools by transferring children at 11+ to senior or modern schools; and from 1921 the Trust's own voluntary school in Horne Lane became such a school. In time the LEA built others in Bedford (Silver Jubilee) and in the county (such as Harrold and Stewartby). At the time this seemed a notable advance, for it was not long since elementary schools had emerged from the monitorial system, in which huge classes were drilled mechanically by monitors who knew little more than the class. In retrospect the advance seems pitifully small and painfully slow.

But though the gap between public schools and other schools, between those of the Harpur Trust and the rest of the county, was narrowing very slightly, the former were unchallenged. Indeed this might be called a period of fruition, in which so much matured that had been planned and striven for in the last 50 years. The goal had not been entirely reached, especially as regards premises. But in the main the Harpur Trust schools could legitimately think of themselves as fulfilling a high function in training future senior service personnel, administrators, and professional classes in a country of world-wide influence, and could feel that their methods were successful. The headmaster of Bedford School in his annual report listed along with examination successes the honours or important appointments awarded to old boys in the current year: in 1934–5 there were 30, including a G.C.B. for a general and a knighthood for a medical professor.

Each of the four schools during this period had a head who remained for more than 20 years. At Bedford School was Humfrey Grose-Hodge (1928–51), a Cambridge man who had been in the I.C.S. and had taught at Charterhouse. He was perhaps a "Chief" on the old lines. An authoritarian, he also promoted high academic standards. He himself in 1936 gave some land near St. Peter's entrance to the school. Kate Westaway, D.Litt., (1924–49) at the High School, appointed at the age of 31, was an old girl. She too encouraged high academic standards and drew out the best in staff and girls, inspiring at least 12 of her staff to become headmistresses elsewhere. While carrying on old traditions, she looked forward, widening the curriculum, particularly in science, and experimenting with new VI form courses – she built up a strong nursing tradition. She knew every girl, yet found time to serve on national committees.

At the Modern School the headmaster was H. W. Liddle (1922–46), who had been wounded and a prisoner-of-war. He was always ready to experiment, as with the scout movement, or taking boys abroad. The school historian says that he opened the school to the influences of a new age. His wide interests included the W.E.A. and the promotion (at long last) of a public library in Bedford. At the Girls' Modern School was Beatrice Tonkin (1925–46), of whom it was said that "no one sought her sympathy or advice in vain". Elegant in appearance, she had a personal and unconventional approach. She knew each parent and child, and to her each was an individual. She tried to open the minds of her girls to the problems and opportunities of the day by her Society of the Open Mind, and she was active in the League of Nations' Union.

In honouring these heads for their long service, we may remember that the short-term head may render a service of his or her own. At the Modern School Arnold Powell (1917–22), it has been said, let in light and air. At the High School Emmeline Tanner (1920–4), afterwards D.B.E. and head of Roedean, was a vital personality and full of fresh ideas. She will never be forgotten by her girls. An incident is characteristic. There were a dozen or so country girls who brought packed lunches, and through some reorganisation they were placed at lunch-time in a room where boarders dumped their satchels. (Boarders were too much of ladies to carry their satchels – this was done by a little man with a handcart.) Miss Tanner transferred the country girls elsewhere and occasionally joined them, implying that she herself liked a packed lunch occasionally and then was glad of company.

Premises, the unceasing requirement of schools, were still a preoccupation, even with Bedford School, which in 1920 was the only one on a self-contained site. Here the purchase of an adjoining building (the Moravian school, later Howard building) in 1921 made possible better provision for country boys; their facilities were transferred to the Craig building in 1936. As part of the war memorial, the library was re-housed. The old iron building, so long gymnasium and laboratory, was pulled down, and a science block rose in 1933, followed by a gymnasium in 1934. The hall was panelled in oak.

The next school to move to the outskirts of the town was the Girls' Modern School, for long cramped in St. Paul's Square. The purchase in 1927 of a new field in Cardington Road eventually made practicable a school on the same site. The building (architect Oswald Milne, OB) featured in textbooks as an example of good new building, and was enhanced by the established trees.[1] It had an oak-panelled hall, a gymnasium with changing rooms and showers, laboratories, art room and library; and included a curved corridor over the historic King's Ditch. The mound in the grounds over four air-raid shelters later contributed to out-of-door dramatic work. The move was made in 1938, and in 1946 the name of the school was changed to The Dame Alice Harpur School, to avoid confusion with secondary modern schools. But the building was planned only for 350 girls, and as numbers grew the school spread into houses in Cardington Road.

At the High School there was considerable development. It was possible to expand on the existing site with the addition of houses in Adelaide Square. A science block, with laboratories ahead of those in most girls' schools at the time, was opened in 1927. There was a new gymnasium in 1931, the old one being converted to a handsome library. In 1935 came the Susan Collie wing, on the site of the old passage-room and the land acquired in Adelaide Square.

At the Modern School it was a case of using the old premises of the Harpur complex. A new hall which could hold all the school was contrived in 1929, and the old one became the gymnasium, while the museum was moved and enlarged. In 1930 came new workshops. A house for country boys, now County House, was acquired in the Crescent.

For these various purposes, much of the money was raised by appeals and fund-raising efforts by parents and by the schools themselves. Incidentally, parent co-operation with the schools has become more organised. At the Modern School a Parents' Association was formed in Liddle's day, and about the same time Mrs. Perry founded a Mothers' Guild at Bedford School. Since then the High School and Dame Alice have acquired similar associations.

Sports too acquired better facilities in addition to the gymnasiums mentioned above. There was the new boathouse in 1922, and new swimming-pools for Bedford School in 1930 and for the Modern School in 1935 (the latter covered and heated).

There was more academic achievement at Bedford School and at the High School, for the two Modern Schools had smaller VI forms. The leaving age of 18, which had irked Kaye in his day – "an anachronism, contrary to the whole trend of modern educational views" – was removed in 1928, but probably financial reasons deterred some parents from allowing boys to stay on. While at Bedford School the headmaster in 1930 could report that out of his 862 boys, 26 had obtained higher certificates and 117 school certificates, the corresponding figures for 582 boys at the Modern School were 12 higher certificates and 39 school certificates. For 599 girls at the High School, the figures were 7 and 59; and for the Girls' Modern School 2 and 18.

To look a few years ahead, the climax to this period of growth was in 1952, when Princess Margaret visited Bedford to celebrate the 400th anniversary of the 1552 letters patent, granting Bedford corporation leave to obtain an endowment for the original school (ch. 1).

1940–72

The storm clouds over Europe broke in 1939, and in 1940 this country was threatened with invasion. Rye Grammar School, Victoria College from Jersey, Woodford High School, King's Warren School, Plumstead, and Owen's School were evacuated to Bedford. The new extension to the Modern School field was given over to growing crops, and allotments were worked by boys not in the Corps. Again many old boys were in the forces. Among the letters from overseas received by H. W. Liddle are some referring to his 1944 broadcast: "In our Naafi somewhere in Palestine it came as a very pleasant surprise to hear the broadcast from Bedford and your voice again"; (from Kashmir) "the reception was excellent"; (from Ceylon) "I was walking through the jungle, keeping the heavy rain of the monsoon period off with my cape, when I heard the strains of the old school song"; (from Tanganyika) "the reception was particularly clear, considering that I am living on the slopes of Mt. Kilimanjaro". This time the girls' schools were represented in the services: the High School had 81 in the W.R.N.S., 58 in the A.T.S., 56 in the W.A.A.F., and 37 in the Women's Land Army, besides 74 nurses. Girls at school worked on the land one afternoon weekly. The High School staff manned a canteen at the Corn Exchange on Sunday evenings. Losses by death were less severe than in the previous war; the Modern School lost 124; but it was calculated that out of the entire dead for the Commonwealth and Empire, one in every thousand was an Old Bedfordian.

The war acted as a forcing-house on tendencies already growing. No longer did it seem right to rule an Empire even paternally; rather, Britain's role was seen as having helped African and Asian countries to nationhood, and those who went overseas must think mainly in terms of service. At home, Bedford became cosmopolitan: first from the Poles and others who remained after the war; then came Italians, Caribbeans, Indians and Pakistanis. Where formerly Anglo-Indian colonels had strolled down a quiet High Street, now amid a roar of traffic Pakistani workers embussed for Stewartby brickworks.

There was a new approach to education. The 1944 act laid down that secondary education was to be available for all: each child was to have what was suited to his or her ability and aptitude. To facilitate this, schools receiving direct grants might be required to receive free-placers to the extent of 50%. At the time, Bedford School and the High School were receiving 10%, the Modern Schools 25%. Thus there would be a great change. Withdrawal of direct grant would mean that fees must rise to make good the deficiency, and there was already difficulty as the result of war damage to the Holborn estate (ch. 2).

Bedford School and the High School became independent. The 10% of free places in these schools remained, being taken up by the LEA. The fees rose. The following table shows upper school yearly tuition fees:

	1940	1950	1960	1970
Bedford School	£32	£68	£144	£297
High School	25	52	126	249

The two modern schools remained direct grant. Over 50% of their places were taken up by the LEA as free places; in fact in 1968 when the Public Schools Commission visited Bedford the percentage was 65% and 74%. Their fees remained comparatively low:

	1940	1950	1960	1970	
Modern School	£15	£30	£54	£153	distorted by
Girls' Modern/ Dame Alice	10	24	51	144	cut in capitation grant 1968

The overseas' connection of the schools was still maintained. In 1968 there were at the four schools 28 children from Europe, 45 from Asia, 43 from Africa, and 8 from America. These were mainly children of Britons overseas, though at Bedford School and the High School there were respectively 12 and 6 of other nationalities.

North, east and mid-Bedfordshire could not in any case have long found room in the Harpur Trust schools with the great expansion of secondary educational requirements that followed the 1944 act. Moreover, the effect of this act was enhanced by the increase in the county's population. Bedfordshire has shared in the post-war development of southeast England. Between 1931 and 1961, Bedford's population increased by 50% (from 40,554 to 63,334), and the county population by 75% (from 220,525 to 380,837). Thus in time there was a sufficient continuing age-group to allow the LEA to build a selective school in east Bedfordshire. The first classes were taught at Stratton in 1950, though the completion of the building and formal opening came later. The same point was reached a little later for north Bedfordshire, and Pilgrim at Bedford began to function in 1962. For mid-Bedfordshire Redborne, near Ampthill, also provided education of this kind from 1954. Many secondary modern schools were built also.

In this period, the new headmasters at the Trust schools were: at Bedford School, C. M. E. Seaman (1951–5), who left to take over the headship of his old school, Christ's Hospital; and W. M. Brown, the first Old Bedfordian to become headmaster. At the Modern School came J. E. Taylor (1946–65), a master in the mould of Arnold, and descended from headmasters. He enforced discipline, improved academic standards, and raised the school's standing in Bedford. He was followed by B. H. Kemball-Cook.

To the High School came Gwendolen Watkins (1949–65), an Oxford scholar, who had previously taught at the school. She adapted the school to the post-war age, modifying rules without relaxing standards, and encouraged older girls to discuss problems. After her came Miss Ella K. Wallen. To Dame Alice came Irene Forster (1946–55), a physicist, who extended interest in music among the girls. Under her came an expansion of VI form work made possible by more enlightened national policy. Hilda Lawson-Brown (1955–70), herself a classicist, further expanded VI form work, especially in science, and raised its standards. She was followed by Miss Suzanne M. Morse.

The present heads of the four schools show a widening range of contact both by education and experience. While three were at Oxford or Cambridge, the fourth has a Bristol degree. The schools with which they have been associated range from Repton, Shrewsbury and Wellington to Blackburn, Camden, Colston, Gloucester, Leamington and Stockton-on-Tees. One of the heads has seen war service.

In academic matters in this period two features are notable. One is the widening of the curriculum: the old emphasis on classics, so long a feature at Bedford School and others like it, disappeared. Instead VI formers were studying a wide range of arts and science subjects, and increasingly choosing combinations from both these broad groups. There has also been a steady advance in senior work at the two modern schools.

	1972 passes at A level			*at O level*		
	Latin	Greek	Science	Latin	Greek	Science
Bedford School	3	3	82	56	2	296
Modern School	3	1	96	11	3	211

At the Modern School the percentage of passes at A level has risen between 1967 and 1972 from 70% to 79%. In terms, not of girls but of subject passes, these at Dame Alice (863 pupils) were 151 and 842, a percentage pass rate of 88%. Here the large VI form, 166 in 1972, divides into eight or nine groups.

In music, drama and art, the wide interests of all the schools and the high standard of their productions defy adequate notice here. In this direction the increasing co-operation between the schools offers particular scope. At Bedford School the annual school play alternates between modern and classic subjects – in 1971 it was Gogol's *The Government Inspector*, while house plays follow in the Easter term. All afford opportunities for scene painting. The Modern School in 1971 performed *Peer Gynt*, for which music was composed by the boys, and over a hundred costumes designed by the art master. In both these productions girls took part, while boys assisted with the High School's production of *The Miracle Worker*. Orchestral work has developed greatly. Bedford School Choral Society recently performed Mozart's *Requiem*, and the Lower School put on an outstanding production of *H.M.S. Pinafore*. At the Modern School Vivaldi's work featured in two concerts, and the school orchestra and junior school choir were successful (not for the first time) in the Bedfordshire Music Festival. In Dame Alice's performance of *Die Fledermaus* boys from the Modern School assisted. The High School recently gave Pergolesi's *Stabat Mater*.

Details of the four schools for the year 1971–2 are as follows:

	Bedford School	High School	Modern School	Dame Alice
total pupils	946	654	1,041	863
boarders	337	134	103	50
LEA scholars	96	67	547	524
A level pupils	224	93	210	152
pupil teacher ratio	11.3	13.7	16.3	16.3
day fees	£255–£384	£213–£285	£138–£186	£135–£165
boarding fees	£345	£270	£306	£282

The total number of pupils was 3,495; and the contribution made by the endowment towards the education of each pupil averages £27.

Below is given a comparison with two other educational trusts, though for an earlier year. When the Taunton commission reported on endowed grammar schools in 1868, only two had an income higher than Bedford. The order of precedence of 1868 is not that of 1973, since some endowments have appreciated more than others. However, it may be of interest to see how those nearest to Bedford then fare now.

The second in 1868 was Dulwich, which then had an income of £16,829 as against Bedford's £13,121. Its income in 1969–70 was £131,474. This foundation's beneficiaries include the picture gallery and two aided schools. The share of the endowment received by Dulwich College, Alleyn's School, and James Allen's Girls' School was £103,454, and their fees and numbers as at September 1970 were as follows:

	pupils	day fees
Dulwich College (independent)	1,392	£300
Alleyn's School (direct grant)	794	£207
James Allen's Girls' School (independent)	528	£216

The next nearest to Bedford in 1868 was King Edward's School, Birmingham, with £12,218. In 1971–2 the income for this trust was £323,000, considerably more than that of Bedford. It supports a day school for boys and one for girls (1971–2: total 1,200 places; fees £141); and also five voluntary aided schools.

Premises have developed further at Bedford during the period. At Bedford School the main extension was the building in 1966 of central dining halls for the houses, a development found at similar schools elsewhere. At the High School dining rooms were added, and also the Westaway wing with geography rooms and a cooking room; while a fund of £32,000 was raised which provided a swimming pool. Dame Alice's extension included dining hall, increase of laboratory space, and purpose-built specialist rooms for geography, history, mathematics, and also for needlework, art and cookery; besides a swimming pool towards which £11,000 was raised. The High School remains on its old site, though transfer has been considered.

The chief change in prospect is for the Modern School. Till recently its needs were still met, so far as possible, on the original site of the Harpur complex. A splendid science building was opened at the rear in 1958, more than half the cost being met by the Industrial Fund for the Advancement of Science Teaching. The departure of the (voluntary) Harpur Central School to Westfield (ch. 5) made it possible to take over the premises vacated. More space was also found by the removal between 1959 and 1962 of the museum to the Embankment, where it is now in the care of the town council, though the collection is still owned by the Trust, who pay half the curator's honorarium. But behind the unruffled front of Blore's façade is a labyrinth. There are metal workshops in what was once the elementary infants' school; woodwork in the former cookery school; art in the original elementary girls' school; and music in another of the old buildings. Infinite ingenuity must be required to run the whole. At last an entirely new school is being built in Manton Lane on a wooded hill overlooking the field. The school (architects: Greenwood & Abercrombie) is costing upwards of £1,280,000. The appeal for money for additional facilities had raised over £100,000 by the end of 1972. It has been designed to meet the requirement of the new agreement (ch. 9) for co-operation with the Bedfordshire system of reorganisation. Everything will be in its place: hall, library, laboratories, workshops, art and craft rooms, special rooms for history, economics, geography, languages, music and so on; and there will be a dining area. The new premises are due to open in 1974.

In ethos, at Bedford as in comparable schools elsewhere, a more subtle development has taken place. Perhaps three stages may be distinguished in older schools generally: these are not clear-cut, owing to age ranges and individual approaches. What follows is an attempt to give trends in broad outline, not to give exact details for each school.

Very roughly, before 1870 mechanical methods of teaching depended heavily on flogging. "All the great headmasters were renowned floggers" [2] – Moss of Shrewsbury is said to hold the record with 88 lashes, though at Eton in 1832 Keate flogged 80 in one day and was cheered. Physical training was minimal, and for character it was enough to inculcate Christian doctrine.

Towards the end of the century, the aim was to train mind, body and character. Students should think deeply and without prejudice, and value freedom. Facilities for games developed to a high standard, and prowess commanded boys' respect, with games' idols sometimes a consequence. The approach to character emphasised leadership, team spirit and discipline; lines of authority ran from the man at the top, the headmaster, down through staff and options or monitors, and there might be a temptation to look on authority as a reward. The wearing of uniform, even out of school hours, was enforced. The Corps was compulsory.

However, the school prepares for the outside world, and both change. Matthew Arnold said that education's "prime aim is to enable a man to know himself and the world". Today authority does not command automatic obedience: should there not be more room for service? The old system did not succeed equally with all: should there not be more scope for choice? The new will perhaps be fully achieved when a new generation who have experienced these changes from below comes to take charge.

In the new approach all schools are feeling their way on similar lines.[3] Authority is a social necessity and an opportunity for service. An enormous co-operative effort is required. Young people do not like to be told; they learn more informally than formally; hence training must move from being direct to indirect, and a framework has to be constructed in which they can learn.

Nowadays masters can queue in the cafeteria or are waited on by spontaneous-volunteers. They can address boys by their Christian names. Options and monitors, though not elected, are chosen after careful consideration; at Bedford School names are put forward by house committees and at the Modern School by the staff, but this is combined with opportunity for the boys to vote. They are still responsible for discipline at break and in the lunch hour, for arrangements at entertainments and expeditions, for lost property and bicycles. They no longer hold hair-cut inspections, nor make cycle raids to check that country boys are wearing uniforms out of school hours (an old boy from Ampthill can remember being found outside his house as a team of monitors swept over the brow of the hill). They do not cane boys, nor sentence juniors to an hour's exercise (after the last war a Modern School punishment was to pick up a bucket of stones on the school field). However, in a boarding house, monitors have rather more authority, since they can feel responsible for a basic group.

The term "fag" is still in use at Bedford School, but its meaning has changed. Fagging, once approved by Dr. Arnold of Rugby, as a means of securing "regular government among the boys themselves and avoiding the evils of anarchy", could nevertheless sometimes involve exploitation of younger boys by older ones. Some old boys who were boarders at Bedford School remember being made to do chores. Now there are few fags, and they volunteer to do helpful tasks (brew a cup of coffee or clean shoes) for older boys; they often receive special reward for this: and it exempts them from other duties. This can bring a more personal contact between the new boy and the more responsible members of the community. All juniors in boarding houses perform the more routine jobs for the house, such as washing up or tidying common rooms, as indeed do many day boys in their own homes.

A school with a large boarding element is in a stronger position to enforce its ways than one with a large number of free-placers. At a debate, Bedford School boys tend to speak alike more than do those from the Modern School, in spite of the modern customary preference for diversity as opposed to Oxbridge. Perhaps the Modern School is successful in getting all boys to speak out with confidence. On the other hand, if we compare Bedford School with self-contained boarding schools on country sites, it ranks as middle-of-the-road, for it has always had one foot firmly planted in the local scene.

Individuality is allowed more play. School caps are seldom worn, and leisure clothes are used out of school. The Combined Cadet Corps is no longer compulsory, yet has enough volunteers to be viable: it has three sections: Navy, Army and Air Force. At Bedford School a boy can choose a pursuit, such as printing, art, library work, beekeeping, home economy; undertake a project in electronics, boatbuildings, metalwork; or follow a course with police, fire service, industry, computers. At the Modern School all boys over 14 have to undertake one of a range of service activities: Cadet Force, Venture Scouts, Duke of Edinburgh Award, Social Service, Fire Cadets, Local History Research, School Working Party. In sport too there is a variety of choice, including fives, tennis, sailing, hiking, fencing and judo.

The concept of service perhaps began at Bedford School with the Holborn Boys' Club in 1920 (the Hobos, as it was known in school), followed after the 1939–45 war by the Holborn Girls' Club at the High School; both closed in 1970. In such clubs there might be an element of condescension: now young people are involved in the community outside the school. A central organisation, Youth Action, has been set up to coordinate this for the Trust schools and other schools; boys and girls serve on the committee, and the organiser is a Community Service Volunteer. Pairs do practical jobs for elderly or disabled: taking out, window-cleaning, gardening, fetching provisions and changing library books. Blitz teams of three to five tackle bigger jobs, such as decorating. Some are attached to centres for handicapped children. Girls help feed geriatric and other hospital patients, and provide at the High School an annual tea for old people following an outing; here also the annual harvest sale raises a large sum for charity.

Religious teaching has changed, since unthinking conformity has gone and formality is suspect. The young want a new contact with the substance of life. At Bedford School a Chapel Council, representing each house, suggests new ideas. At the Modern School experiments are being made in the form of morning assembly; musical performance is a regular feature; and readings are sometimes secular as well as from the Bible. Discussion covers a wide range. Yet some tradition remains: at Bedford School chapel voluntary and compulsory services alternate; and the Modern School has a communion service twice a term at St. Paul's church. Here there is also a small spontaneous lunch-time group. At the High School prayers are regularly taken by staff and girls, and girls take part in the boarders' service at Holy Trinity. At Dame Alice too girls are encouraged to help plan and participate; and in the V and VI social, moral and theological problems are discussed. All schools study other faiths.

Some of the increased feeling for service carries on after school. Young people have done voluntary service overseas in countries ranging from Borneo to Kenya. Even the retiring headmistress of 1965 from the High School taught for a year in Papua/New Guinea. In fact, to illustrate the change in attitude from the days of Fred Burnaby and George Farrar a century ago we could take as examples of today: an old girl of the High School, a colonel's daughter, who has spent her life as a doctor in the Indian sub-continent since 1939, at first in a teaching hospital in the Punjab, where she experienced the troubles of partition in 1947, and later in what is now Bangladesh, where she was working during its struggle for independence; and from Dame Alice a teacher in Hong Kong and a veterinary surgeon in Kenya.

The career destination has changed. It is not easy to indicate this precisely, because so many on leaving are entering university courses and their final destination is not yet certain. The figures for 1971 were:

Bedford School	47	Modern School	53
High School	14	Dame Alice	22

At Bedford School that year only two leavers were aiming at the army, which in the earlier period was a frequent choice. The most popular fields were medicine, engineering, commerce, accountancy, science. At the Modern School careers for leavers cover a wide spectrum of industry, commerce and public service. For girls, other destinations include nursing, art and drama, and it is no longer unusual for them to embark on careers in computing, commerce, business management, pharmacy, and town-planning, as well as medicine and law.

The disparity between the Trust's financial support of the education of boys and girls respectively has been resolved. The occasion was marked by verses from the headmaster of the Modern School.

Fair Shares for the Fair Sex

How balance each respective need?
  Do girls require more books – or less?
Do boys cost more than girls to feed?
  Do girls cost more than boys to dress?

Does it take more to float a boat
  Or start electric cookers cooking?
How long have women had the vote?
  Steady! Mrs. Pankhurst's looking?

The best laid schemes of mice and men
Do not appeal to women's wit.
Ope education's door? Ah, then
You'll wish you hadn't opened it.

In 1969 the formula 3 boys = 5 girls was discarded, and parity will be reached in 1973–4.

How far has the ethos of the girls' schools been modified? One change was natural. Though it is to be hoped there will always be dedicated teachers, that crusading spirit of a century ago, and the complete dedication that sometimes went with it, are not appropriate when the education of a girl for a career is normal. Further, the coming of married women and of men teachers has changed the atmosphere of the staffroom.

There neither has been nor should be changes in the effort to help each girl to realise her own potential academically and in every other way in which the school can assist her, both for her own benefit and satisfaction, and as a means to the service of any sort of community in which she may find herself, in the encouragement of good manners, self-control, consideration for others, a neat and workmanlike appearance during school hours, and good grooming at all times; and, especially for the senior girls, the experience of exercising responsibility for and some degree of authority over other people. But there have been some changes in method.

Methods like those of the boys' schools, in so far as they were at one time adopted, came later and were never so strongly entrenched. Some, like the house system, have been discarded. At the High School the institution of prefects has gone also; the head-girl is elected by the VI; there is a school committee of headmistress, staff and girls; and all girls in the VI are expected to feel responsibility. At Dame Alice too all VI form girls are expected to shoulder responsibility, and many run clubs for juniors. Here the prefects are elected by their own year, but the head-girl is chosen from among second year prefects by the staff.

Physical exercise is more varied, including (for the VI) fencing, judo, badminton, squash, modern dance, and "keep fit". The High School's annual hockey match with Cheltenham, maintained for years, is now dropped. At the Guild's buffet wine and cheese supper there is modern informality, with every kind of costume in evidence.

All four schools have been inspected by H.M. inspectors of the department of education several times during this century, the last occasion being that of the Modern School in 1968.

Meanwhile the educational milieu in which the Trust schools are set has changed. In the country as a whole there has been a movement towards a comprehensive system of education. The public schools commission was appointed under Sir

John Newsom to recommend methods of integrating the public schools within such a national system, and reported in 1968 on independent boarding schools. It summarised its proposals thus: "the proportion in any integrated school of pupils who are assisted and have previously attended maintained schools for at least three years must be at least half the total number of boarding pupils in the school"; further that "as the development of schools in the maintained sector is governed by the policy of comprehensiveness, independent schools which are integrated must conform as far as possible".

The same commission, now under the chairmanship of Professor D. Donnison, reported in 1970 on independent day schools and direct grant grammar schools, but without knowing whether the previous proposals would be implemented. It noted that the Harpur Trust had "offered to admit local authority pupils to the direct grant schools from 60% of the ability range at 13+ in order to co-operate with the local authority's scheme". It concluded "schools which want to play their part within the national framework that serves children throughout the country, and to secure the continuing flow of public funds which enables them to do that, must enter a comprehensive system of education in which no fees would be charged". There was, however, difference of opinion as to whether the direct grant system should be preserved. But these two reports have not been implemented.

In Bedfordshire, however, as in some other parts of the country, steps were taken to reorganise the county's educational system on comprehensive lines. To resolve the situation which seemed in danger of arising – a confrontation between a selective and a comprehensive system – a working party was set up by the Harpur Trust and the LEA. In 1971 a basis of co-operation was reached. This agreement is given in chapter 9: The Trust Today.

8 *Welfare 1764–1973*

OUTLINE AND REASSESSMENT

Harpur had directed that, after the needs of the school had been met, his bequest should be used to endow poor girls, "nourish and inform" poor children, and the residue be distributed in alms. These provisions were to be expected from a public-spirited man of his day, when few would have thought of teaching girls. By the 18th century enlightened benefactors even in Bedfordshire villages, like Elizabeth Emery of Meppershall, laid down that girls should be taught at least to "read and work"; and also in more important endowed schools: James Allen did it for Dulwich in 1741. Since, however, girls' dowries had been explicitly mentioned by Harpur, the framers of the 1764 act hesitated to convert this to teaching girls, and provided that there should be each year 40 marriage portions of £20 each. "Nourishing and informing poor children" was interpreted in two ways. By the 18th century, the apprenticeship system, already in existence in Harpur's day, was at its height; £600 was therefore allotted annually to apprentice 40 poor children who should also receive a benefaction of from £10 to £20 on completing their apprenticeship. For poor children in real need a home or "hospital" was to be built; its running cost was not to exceed £200 p.a. The residue of the income was to be distributed annually among the old or unfortunate; this was known as hall money; it was meant to be provisional; but alms distributed in mid-winter soon came to be looked on as certain, and curtailment or suspension to seem hardship.

These rules were designed to see that the superfluous income of the Harpur estate did in fact reach those for whom it was intended, and to close loopholes by which it might be wasted or misapplied. They could – for instance, by adding almshouses for the old, as was actually done in 1793, have been slightly more up to date; but they kept as closely as practicable to the letter rather than the spirit of Harpur's wishes. They had the usual drawback of acts: rigidity. This drawback was (as regards the future) intensified by the act of 1793, when the sum for apprenticeship was raised to £700, for the hospital to £300, for hall money to £500; while the trustees were at last empowered to build twenty almshouses. The 1826 act still further increased the allowance for apprentices (to £1,500), while the almshouses were now 66, for after a disastrous fire in Bedford in 1802 the Trust had generously, if rashly, built houses for the homeless, and these were subsequently declared almshouses. This act also provided for donations for equipping boys and girls not apprenticed, and for rewarding them for up to five years of service.

The main welfare provisions lasted for more than a century: 1764–1873; some being increased in 1793 and 1826; and the almshouses, added in 1793, still continue though reduced in number. For much of this time they were fiercely disputed or passionately defended. A printed memorial of 1790 complained that they attracted poor strangers to the town, who after five years' settlement could participate, and that poor rates had risen from 2s. 6d. to nearly 7s. in the £.[1] It is true that in the 18th century Bedford's population was growing and its rates rising; but this was a general feature of the times. In spite of the laws of settlement, which provided for the compulsory return of wandering poor to their original parish, many did manage to evade discovery, and this was easier in a town than in a village, while in a town there might be more hope of work. But it is doubtful how much of Bedford's increase was due to the hope of benefiting from Harpur's welfare provisions, which would be after five years' settlement and then only if successful in drawing a lot. The only detailed population estimates before the 1801 census have been compiled for 1671.[2] Between 1671 and 1801 Bedford's population grew by 86%, whereas Luton and Leighton grew by only 50%; but Dunstable and Ampthill increased by 100% and Biggleswade by 130%. Thus Bedford was not outstanding.

Still less valid is the charge (on the face of it illogical) that one effect of the Trust was to raise Bedford's rates.[3] Rates were rising everywhere in the 18th century, from increase of population and pressure on opportunities for employment. A rise from 2s. 6d. to "nearly 7s." in the pound is not as much as trebling the rate; in some parts of the county rates more than quadrupled. The help for apprentices alone which the Trust provided meant less outlay for the overseers, whose responsibility it was to apprentice needy children.

Some years after the welfare payments under the 1764 act had become operative, their political implications were called in question. In 1690 there had been a house of commons ruling that "the right of election of burgesses to serve in parliament for the borough of Bedford is in the burgesses, freemen and inhabitants, being householders of Bedford, not receiving alms". A petition after the disputed election of 1774 claimed that the candidates returned, Sir William Wake and Robert Sparrow, had bought their seats, one of the points raised being that beneficiaries of the Harpur Trust should not vote, and Sparrow was unseated in favour of Samuel Whitbread the elder.[4]

Visitors to Bedford praised the Trust. John Byng in 1789 admired the looks and cleanliness of two boys from the children's home, out with their (presumably widowed) mother; "two fine boys dressed in light blue, the livery of the great Harpur charity here"; their mother "thanked God for her luck in getting them upon so good a foundation".[5] That intelligent radical, Sir Richard Phillips, in 1828 had nothing but praise for the Trust and all its works: its "salutary effects are visible in the manners and morals of the people", and servants entitled to Trust benefactions "are anxiously sought for".[6]

There were three reasons why the growth in its first 60 years of what may be called the welfare side of the Trust's work was to make increasing problems for it later.

One was that it took place while revenue was rising sharply; but when the rise ceased or greatly slowed down, the provisions which allocated definite sums remained in the act then operative.

Again, it was impossible in 1764 or 1793 to foresee the tremendous growth in educational demand that was to come in the 19th century. Already from 1779 to 1783, because of the capital outlay for school repairs, teacher's houses, and the purchase of the hospital, there was for a time insufficient to pay marriage portions. Had Bedford grammar school grown under Hook, as Rugby did under James, more building would have been desirable; Hook's lack of enterprise left this need to develop later. Given 19th century accelerating demand for education, growth was bound to come at Bedford at the grammar school as soon as there was an enterprising headmaster. By 1815 it had been realised that more education was needed than the grammar and writing schools together provided; and in their plans for a range of buildings (completed 1838) the trustees no doubt thought they had provided for Bedford's educational needs for a long time to come.

When to increasing educational demand is added a population which quadrupled between 1801 and 1871, it is clear that the attempts from 1764 to 1826 to allocate to appropriate welfare objects revenue, which it was anticipated would be surplus to educational requirements, were to prove in future almost suicidal.

On the other hand, during the period 1764–1826 (previously the welfare payments had been negligible), so much had these become part of Bedford life that it was politically extremely difficult for locally elected trustees to curtail them. After major financial difficulties in the stormy 1840s, culminating in the new scheme of 1853, they did in fact begin to dismantle the welfare system, by discontinuing hall money, benefactions on completing apprenticeship, and donations on going out to service. This was not enough to enable them to meet adequately the greatly enlarged educational needs of Bedford. The revenue could not, in fact, cover both education and even limited welfare; and it was government policy under the endowed schools act of 1869 which resulted in the scheme of 1873. This reduced the welfare commitments to a small number of almshouses, and so completed the process of getting the trustees "off the hook".

Yet opinion today is better able to appreciate the position of the trustees than was the Taunton commission, which thundered against the "unrestrained application of local and indiscriminate lavishness". It was no such thing. In the first place, the mid-Victorian trustees did not rate welfare above education; they were the victims of the misjudgement (or more correctly, inability to foresee the future) of their predecessors in 1826, who had supposed the revenue would greatly increase and had not supposed that population and the quality of educational need

17a T. Riley, headmaster of boys' elementary school, 1831–69

17b G. M. T. Bates, headmaster of boys' elementary school, 1875–1911

17c Class at boys' elementary school, c. 1910

17d Miss C. A. Etchells, headmistress of girls' elementary school from 1899

18a Ampthill Road elementary school, 1876

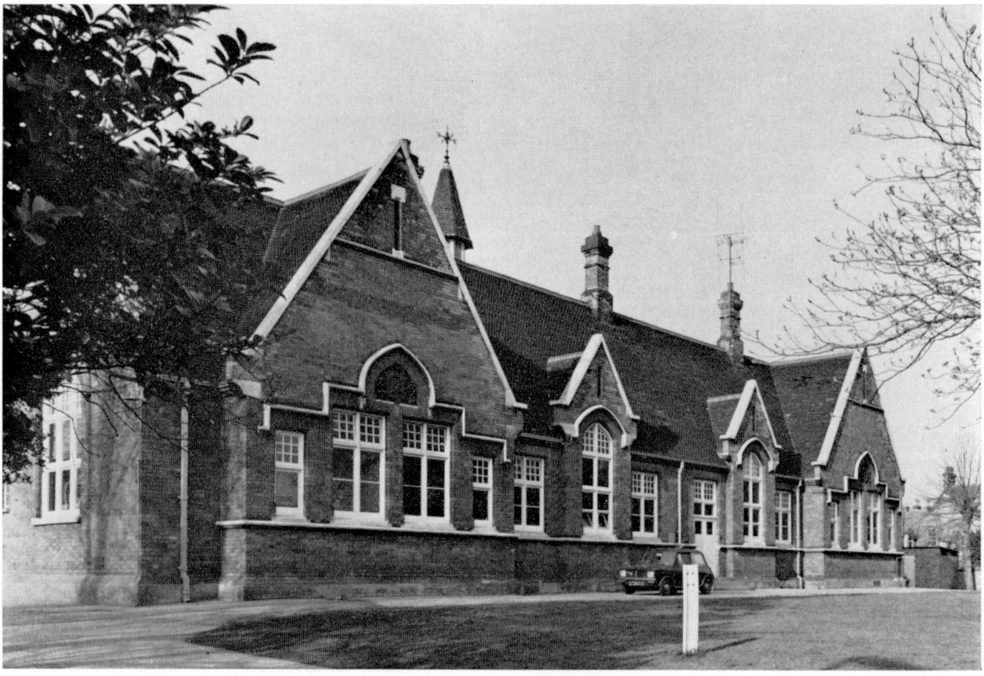

18b Clapham Road elementary school, 1894

19a Staff of Girls' Modern School, 1897

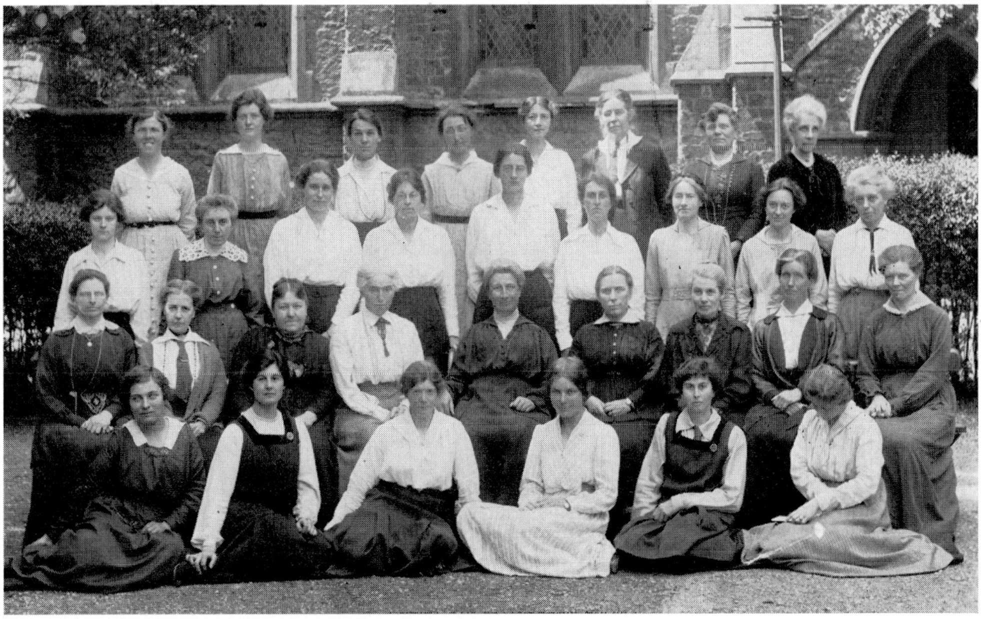

19b Staff of Bedford High School, 1920

20a R. Carter, headmaster of Bedford School, 1910–28

20b H. W. Liddle, headmaster of Bedford Modern School, 1922–46

20c Susan Collie, headmistress of Bedford High School, 1898–1920

20d Edith E. Dolby, headmistress of Girls' Modern School, 1894–1925

21a H. Grose-Hodge, headmaster of Bedford School, 1928–51

21b J. E. Taylor, headmaster of Bedford Modern School, 1946–65

21c Kate Westaway, headmistress of Bedford High School, 1924–49

21d Beatrice Tonkin, headmistress of Girls' Modern School, 1925–46

22a Bedford School, 1891

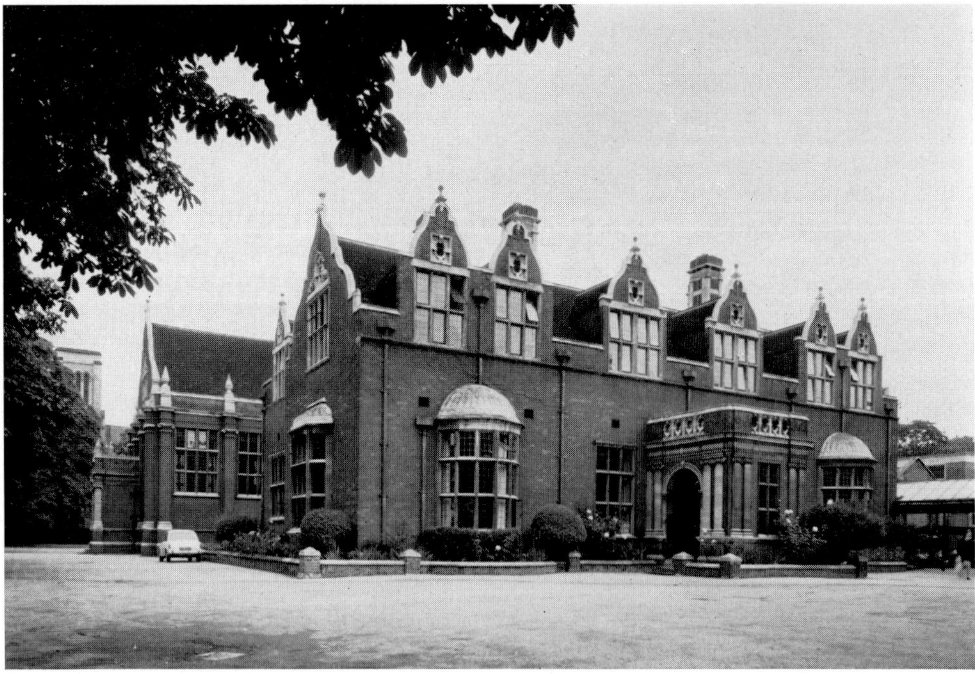

22b Bedford High School, 1882 (then also housing Girls' Modern School)

23a Bedford Modern School (model of new building), 1974

23b Dame Alice School, 1938

24a Bedford School chapel, 1908

24b Bedford Modern School swimming baths, 1935

25a Bedford High School library, 1931 (originally gymnasium)

25b Dame Alice School: a laboratory

26a Almshouses in Dame Alice Street as first built, 1804

26b Almshouses in Dame Alice Street, refronted 1882–95

27a New almshouses (Harpur House), 1970

27b The prospective Harpur Centre (model)

28a An eight on the river (boathouse, 1922)

28b Governors present 30 July 1970

would much expand; and had therefore thought they must allocate a surplus. Once each act was passed, the successive trustees were legally bound to carry it out until a new scheme could be agreed upon. Further, the social conscience has developed much since Victorian days. We look back to Harpur, and see that he had some feeling for the welfare of the community as a whole. We ourselves make some effort in the welfare state to provide for the sick, the old, and the unemployed, and for children in need. And so we can understand that the Victorian trustees, in a fumbling manner not altogether suited to the needs of their time, did believe that they had on Harpur's account a responsibility towards the less well-off inhabitants of Bedford.

Thus it is worth enquiring how the Trust's welfare provisions worked. They dealt with the young (apprenticeship, benefactions, donations, marriage portions and a children's home); the unfortunate (hall money); and the old (almshouses).

THE YOUNG: APPRENTICESHIP AND SERVICE

The Trust's provisions for the young were designed to start them in life by training, equipment, encouragement of steadiness, and help in setting up housekeeping; and (for those in need of it) by residential care.

A boy's training in 1764, when the Trust began, was in general by apprenticeship. Normally this would be the parents' responsibility; and frequently a parent would train a child in his own calling; but children left destitute were apprenticed by parish overseers. There must, however, have been many parents, not poor enough to obtain help from the overseers, who would find it difficult to pay an apprenticeship premium. There was further the question whether the father who trained his own child was not also entitled to help; this was hotly debated for years, and finally disallowed under the 1853 scheme. It was not possible to grant help in apprenticeship to all applicants, and lots were drawn quarterly. Boys from 1793 had the larger number and the larger sums; the 1764 act specified "40 poor children" who would each have an apprenticeship fee of £15; the 1793 act provided for 30 boys at £20 and 10 girls at £10; the 1826 act for 40 boys at £30 and 20 girls at £15; and the 1853 scheme only for 40 boys at £30. The total number of apprentices remained constant from 1764, when the population was below 2,000, to 1826; from 1826 to 1853 it was 60; but reverted to the original 40 in 1853 and so remained till 1873 when the population was nearly 17,000. The age for apprenticeship was specified in 1764 as 12–15 years, but the minimum was raised by 1853 to 14 years. A benefaction of from £10 to £20 was payable on completing service. The greater emphasis on boys is partly explained by the fact that the girls could later apply for marriage portions. Apprenticeship could be indoor or outdoor; it was not till 1843 that the Trust insisted that an indoor apprentice must have his own bed.

There is seldom evidence of applicants being newcomers to Bedford, but the case of Ben Spence was discussed in 1799. He had occupied a house for more than ten years, and it was remarked that the parish officers had not done their duty in either removing him or demanding a certificate; but he had an established good character and was not likely to be chargeable; and his claim to apply for help with the apprenticeship of his son Thomas was allowed. In 1845 Joseph Treganza, son of the keeper of the prison, was at first not allowed, as his father resided in Bedford only by virtue of his office; but subsequently the trustees gave way.

The trades to which boys were apprenticed in the Trust's first 50 years number about 150, reflecting the wide range of skills then required. The most popular were cobbling and carpentry. They covered building (stonemason, bricklayer, thatcher, later plumber and glazier, sawyer, painter, bellhanger); clothing (weaver, dyer, tailor, glover, framework knitter, staymaker, breeches maker, hosier, hatter, haberdasher, peruke maker, fringe-maker, straw manufacturer, lace buyer); food (brewer, butcher, grocer, fishmonger, gingerbread-maker, pastrycook, biscuit baker, victualler); leather trades (tanner, currier, leather-dresser, saddler); furnishing (chair maker, turner, gilder, matmaker, upholsterer, rush-chair bottomer); auxiliary agricultural trades (miller, millwright, wheelwright, collarmaker, woolstapler, blacksmith, corn factor, ploughwright); and miscellaneous (whitesmith, basketmaker, hempdresser, ropemaker, cooper, pipemaker, fellmonger and parchmentmaker, watch or clockmaker, bottle-maker, tallow chandler, chemist, apothecary, plate-burnisher, perfumer, lime burner, silversmith, lapidary). Girls' trades included lacemakers, mantua-makers, milliners, sempstresses, laundresses and clear-starchers.

The boy or girl benefited by training, but the actual fee did not necessarily benefit Bedford. In the 1760s the percentage of apprentices in Bedford itself was 73, in the county 18%, elsewhere 9%. By the 1840s the proportion of young Bedfordians apprenticed outside the town was much increased: in Bedford 33%; in the county 24%; adjoining counties, 37%; London and elsewhere 6%. Thus in 1805 the future industrialist John Howard was apprenticed to an Olney ironmonger, and in 1847 W. Berrill was apprenticed to a printer in London; S. Negus, however, in 1848, was apprenticed to a Bedford carpenter.

There were many uncertainties to be encountered. In the early years there were often "turnovers" to another master, if the initial arrangement proved unsatisfactory; to obviate this there was later a trial period to see whether apprentice and master suited; thus Frederick Hockliffe went "on liking" to a Bedford printer in 1847. There are cases, as in 1779, of an apprentice being reported "very ill and in a decline". On the other hand, the master might be unsatisfactory. In 1788 William Lawson begged to be released from his master, William Howe of Bedford, tailor, who either neglected or beat him. Apparently as a result of this, a committee was appointed in 1789 to examine masters and mistresses. Attempts were made in 1826 to safeguard the system by paying only half the fee at binding, and the remainder halfway through the term; and from 1845 the payment was made on three occasions, at binding and at the end of the third and sixth years. Yet there were always human failures, especially at a distance. A Hornsey master sent a forged certificate in 1816; while in 1833 there was a case of gross fraud by an Arlesey blacksmith, George Harris, whose apprentice had absented himself for five years. In 1835 a Potton shoemaker, James Carr, treated his apprentice (possibly delicate?) so brutally that he died, and the coroner's verdict censured the master; Carr had the impudence to apply for the second instalment of his fee, but was refused and told that he would never be allowed another Trust apprentice. Thereafter prospective masters had to produce a certificate from the minister, churchwardens and overseers of their parish. One master, John Smethures of Wellingborough, tailor, emigrated to America in 1842, and his apprentice was re-bound. However, apprentices themselves were sometimes in fault, as was James Smith at Newport Pagnell in 1822. Apprenticeship to publicans was discouraged; in 1833 it was resolved that such cases must be strictly investigated. Straw-bonnet sewing was disallowed entirely in 1846, as it was said it could be easily learned in two years. One unusual apprenticeship was in 1857, that of a blind boy to a teacher of music at Henshaw Blind Asylum, Manchester.

By the middle of the century, the utility of the apprenticeship system had much declined. Openings for vocational training were fewer, because the English economy no longer depended on a wide range of small skills; while the days of modern technological training were not yet come. In 1838 the Trust called for a report on the twelve years 1832–46; this showed the main trades as:

tailors	111
shoemakers	78
carpenters	53
plumbers	28
blacksmiths	23
bakers	22

Trades numbering less than 20 apprentices were 17 hairdressers, 15 wheelwrights, 9 saddlers, 5 watchmakers, 5 chemists, 4 curriers, 2 pianoforte makers, 2 coachbuilders, surgeon, auctioneer, ropemaker, pipemaker, whipmaker. The ten-year period 1845–55 yields 35 trades. With a hundred boys apprenticed, 1846–48, only 22 callings are to be found, the chief being cobbling and tailoring, though there are 6 plumbers and 5 cabinet-makers; and a number of boys are apprenticed at Howard's works.

The need was for increased education, a need which the Trust was trying to meet in its various schools. This the trustees themselves recognised in 1842, when they deplored the great evil of leaving school at an early age; for parents improperly withdrew their children from the schools, depriving them of sound and useful learning, of service to them in after life. The Trust was in fact trying to cater for both old and new needs. In 1853 the number of apprenticeships reverted to the original figure of 40, and benefactions on satisfactory completion of service were dropped. The population multiplied about nine times between 1764 and 1871, so that apprenticeships had become relatively much fewer. By 1871 there were over a thousand boys in the schools. But it was left for the 1873 scheme to bring the Trust apprenticeships to an end.

The boy or girl who missed apprenticeship, either from not drawing a lot or because family circumstances required the child to earn at once, could from 1826 to 1853 hope for a grant of £2 to fit him or her out with clothes on going into service. Steady service in the same place had a further reward at the end of each successive year, up to £5 after five years. But this was available only for 10 boys and 30 girls. These grants were called donations.

THE YOUNG: MARRIAGE PORTIONS

For girls there was the additional provision of marriage portions, for which again lots were drawn. A few were given in the early 18th century (ch. 1). From 1764 the portion was £20, and there were 40 of them. The age range for applicants was at first 16–50 years; from 1826 to 1853 18–50 years; and in 1853 applicants must be 21 years of age. There were various provisions relating to their fathers; in 1764 the girls must be either daughters of freemen or of inhabitants who had occupied premises in Bedford for five years and were not certificated from an outside parish. In 1793 fathers must either have been born in Bedford or have occupied premises for ten years. The 1826 act required a ten-year residence. In 1798 there was a question as to whether Ann Course was entitled to a portion; her father Thomas had once resided in Bedford more than ten years, but ran away about three years previously; and her mother was in the House of Industry. After debate, Ann's claim was allowed. Should there not be sufficient applicants from Bedford girls, girls who had been maid-servants in Bedford for five years could apply.

It was early found that it was necessary to take account also of the character of intended husbands. From 1794 character certificates were required, and the application might be held up if these were delayed, as happened in 1798. Elizabeth Smith was refused in 1810, "it not appearing that Thomas Croft is a person of that good fame and reputation required by the act", but she persevered, and ultimately Thomas was thought to pass muster. The same thing happened to Sally Bonfield in 1836. Her fiancé, Charles Clark, was "not of steady industrious habits"; but perhaps he reformed, for after a delay of three months, the minister and churchwardens were able to give him a certificate, and the couple were allowed to marry in a month's time, with the promise of receiving the portion at Christmas. A similar case occurred in 1842. In 1844 a printed form was adopted for such certificates of character. A case of bigamy occurred in 1841; Richard

Kelly, who married Mary Ann Crawley, was found to have a wife living, and the trustees prosecuted him.

The Napoleonic wars, which meant that there were from time to time soldiers in the town, brought a special danger. The girl who drew a marriage portion might too easily attract a soldier husband. Particular cases are not cited in the minutes, but in 1807 it was said that "very great abuses (had) arisen in consequence of girls claiming marriage portions being married to soldiers of marching regiments and having in a short time returned to the town deserted by their husbands and their fortunes spent". In future a girl making such a marriage would not be paid her portion till a year had elapsed. Even after the war, suspicion of soldiers lingered; in 1826 payment to a soldier husband was still to be deferred for a year unless the trustees judged otherwise; and as late as 1842, Elizabeth Cosford was directed to get the permission of her husband's commanding officer.

The marriage portions were an anachronism, and as such were the first to suffer in times of financial difficulty. They were stopped from 1779 to 1783, and then were resumed by notes at 24 months' date. The establishment of the girls' school in 1836 was the real answer to the needs of girls. The number of portions was reduced in 1853 to 28. Because of population increase they were fewer relatively to the population, and inflation had diminished their value. They were abolished altogether in 1873.

THE YOUNG: RESIDENTIAL CARE

For a limited number of poor children, residential care was provided by the Trust in a children's home, which went by the medieval name of hospital (the medical hospital in Bedford was known as the infirmary). The 1764 act did not specify the number of children, but laid down that the running cost should not exceed £200 p.a. This sum was raised to £300 by the 1793 act, which provided for 26 children to be inmates. Rising costs showed the unwisdom of fixing an arbitrary ceiling, and this was omitted in later acts. The trustees had become aware of the fact, well known today, that residential care is expensive. As however in 1826 it was still expected that revenue would continue to rise indefinitely, the number of children permitted was increased: there were to be not less than 26 nor more than 50. This higher figure was never reached, for increasing general expenditure, with a comparative decline in income, made it impracticable. In 1861 the number was reduced to 26. The children's home, frowned on by the Taunton report, was closed in 1871, even before the adoption of the 1873 scheme. As regards the number of children affected, it was a comparatively minor feature of the Trust's welfare system; yet the information available has some interest in comparison with official children's homes in this century. This information covers premises, Trust administration, staffing, dietary and clothing, education and leisure, medical care, and finally closure.

The first premises were a converted house in Angel (now Harpur) Street, – it is visible on Dawson's panorama (Pl. 7). It was bought for £1,000 in 1771, although the act had laid down a cost of £500. It seems however to have been a suitable choice, partly because it had large grounds – it was at one time the property of John Hawes, a leading burgess; and partly because it was near the school and turned out to be the first step in securing the whole west side of the street on which later the Harpur complex was to arise. It opened in 1773 with 30 children, 19 boys and 11 girls, several of whom were fatherless. The children were not to leave the premises (except when going to church), and the street gate was to have iron spikes and be kept locked. In their brief playtime they played in the grounds, which were also used for drying laundry and growing vegetables.

One room, equipped with a 10 ft. deal table and four forms, was kept as a committee room for the trustees. There were two rooms for the master and mistress. It seems that the children slept in the garrets, where were bedsteads with sacking bottoms and flock beds, and the windows had iron bars. Each child had two blankets and a coverlet (these last were apparently green), and the sheets were made from a roll of linen and kept in two large deal chests. The kitchen was equipped with grate, dresser, and 16-gallon copper; also three saucepans (gallon, quart and pint) and a large iron frying-pan. The tableware consisted of wooden trenchers, of which there were six dozen, tinware, and horn cups.

When the Harpur complex was built – it was completed in 1838 – the children's home moved into purpose-built premises, disguised, like the other buildings of the complex, behind Blore's façade; and no committee room was required, as there were purpose-built boardroom and office in the complex to the south. Girls and boys had separate day rooms. A laundry was provided, and later a sick-bay built above it; and a bath was procured in 1857. The boys' and girls' playgrounds were divided by a pale fence.

The trustees' methods of administration varied, for they had many other responsibilities and preoccupations. Rules were drawn up in 1773 covering timetable, dietary, tuition and leisure, visiting-hours (Saturdays, 2–3 p.m.), and even such matters as the issue of clean linen on Saturday evenings, and clean sheets once a month. The usual punishment was to be losing the next meal; for lying, the child should be set on a stool with a paper inscribed "Infamous Lyar" (one wonders whether this was done); for more serious offences it should be as the trustees directed, with dismissal if necessary. In 1828 visiting day was altered to the first Thursday in the month. The rules of 1866 provide for family worship morning and evening.

At times the master and mistress seem to be left to their own devices, apart from an attempt to share out fairly among local tradesmen the contracts for shoes, clothes and provisions. Throughout the 1780s there was a committee of management of three trustees, changed quarterly. In 1793 the committee was enlarged to seven and was to hold office for a year; and one of the trustees undertook to attend the market personally and order the meat required. There seems to have been no regular inspection at this stage; and when a special committee visited unexpectedly in March 1815, they were horrified with what they found. There was no fire in the dining room; the tablecloths were dirty, and so were the vegetables (carrots); there was no order among the children, the boys' hands being unwashed, some clothes ragged, and caps thrown on the floor. There was no beer to drink; some children got water from the pump in tin cups. In the bedrooms the sheets were dirty and the boys had no nightcaps. The whole house needed painting and whitewashing. The mistress was by no means so clean or so neatly dressed as would have been becoming. An entire change was required; and there should be henceforth a regular visiting committee. It seems only fair to add that the master, Thomas Sheppard, was of advanced age and blind, of which the trustees should have been aware; and that though his wife was censured as negligent and inattentive, she clearly had a heavy load of responsibility. The couple were dismissed; and the new master and mistress, John and Maria Furze, were of very different quality.

After this mishap, the trustees were more watchful. The visiting committee of 1817 recommended that each boy should have two clean shirts a week instead of one; ventilation should be improved; bedspreads re-dyed; a plate-rack should be added over the sink; and in the playground the fence between the boys' and girls' sections should have the pales closed up to prevent conversation!

From 1853 the visiting committee's minutes have survived; the trustees went quarterly, and seem to have been so assiduous that in November 1866 some spirited boys, perhaps rather resenting inspection, treated the committee with disrespect, and were ordered bread and water for dinner.

The master and mistress of the home were of the first importance, and the trustees' first choice was unfortunate; John Field, appointed with his wife in June 1773 at £20 p.a. with board, was dismissed in December for "a very great misdemeanour". Then came Richard Freeborn; he was only moderately successful and was dismissed in 1782. He was replaced by Robert Clements (1782–96) and Edward Jeffrey (1796–1805); both these resigned. Then came the Thomas Sheppard (1805–15) whose age and blindness contributed to the debacle of 1815. A new chapter opened with the appointment of John Furze (1815–46) and his wife Maria. The salary was raised to £40 p.a. for the children's home, while at the same time the master and mistress were to teach in the "National" school (ch. 5) about to be opened, where their salary would be £60. When in 1833 the clerk to the Trust was ageing and in poor health, Furze was also called in to assist him in arranging contracts, keeping accounts, and regulating the applicants who came to wait on trustees' meetings. At the same time Mrs. Furze became the redoubtable headmistress of the new girls' school. When her husband died in

1846, she carried on single-handed at the home for a further year; but even her energy could not continue the dual responsibility alone; and in 1847 she resigned from the children's home to concentrate on the girls' school.

The next master was George Winwood (1847–65), who combined the post with teaching duties at the commercial school, and who died in office. Then came Peter Passmore (1866–71), in whose time the home was closed down, but he was retained as a teacher.

There was a varying number of domestic staff, of whom details are occasionally found; but much of the housework was done by the girls.

Meals, as provided by the rules of 1773, were to be:

9 a.m. breakfast (porridge, broth or gruel)

12.30 dinner (beef or mutton three days a week, cold meat or cheese on the remaining days)

6 or 7 p.m. supper of bread and cheese

The normal drink was small beer. Bread was to be a day old.

In wartime the cost of food rose, and in 1799 the master was allowed an extra £3 a month "during the present high price of provisions". The diet was revised in 1815 on the advice of the medical attendant; but further details are not given till 1843. At this date breakfast still consisted of porridge; for dinner every day there were meat, vegetables and pudding, with water to drink; except on Saturday, when there were bread, cheese and beer; and this last was also the daily menu for supper. On Sunday the children had tea. (The master and mistress had long had a tea allowance: two guineas a year from 1782.)

The clothes were a soft mid-blue in colour; a pattern is stuck in the minute-book. The girls wore gown, petticoat, round-eared cap and tippet; seven-year-old Sarah Lightwood modelled the outfit for the trustees to approve. They had also black aprons and worsted mittens, and later black bonnets. The boys had leather breeches. Some changes were made over the years. In 1825 the girls had cloaks; and in 1843 straw bonnets, apparently in addition to their black stuff ones; while in 1854 the visiting committee recommended a woollen scarf for going to church in cold weather. In 1853 the boys' outfit was changed to cloth jacket, waistcoat, corduroy trousers, and greatcoat or cape; and in 1867 they had tweed trousers for Sundays. When leaving for apprenticeship or service, each child was given an outfit; and from 1819 each girl had a deal box to put it in.

With regard to education and leisure, it is sometimes difficult to distinguish theory from practice. The rising-hour was 6 a.m. in summer, 7 a.m. in winter; and bedtime varied from 7.30 to 8.30 p.m. Apart from meal times, normally an hour, but "dinner and play" were to occupy $1\frac{1}{2}$ hours in summer, the children were expected in the early years to be occupied the whole time, either in "such work as they are fit for" (spinning, carding wool, or lacemaking); or from 11 am–12 noon and 3–4 pm in learning to read. The girls were to learn cookery, housework and laundry. For a time, special teachers were appointed for lacemaking, but this seems not to have worked satisfactorily; however, lace was made; for in 1776 150 yards were bought by a Bedford lace-buyer, Thomas Rush; but 47 yards were of poor quality.

On Sundays the children were to go to morning and evening service; and after service the master was to hear each child who could do so read a chapter from the Bible. Although it was not till 1826 that the act specified that the children should worship according to the Church of England, it is clear that they went to St. Paul's church; for details of their pew are often mentioned. It was to be so arranged as to give the master and mistress command of the children (1782); and was in the centre of the front gallery (1798); and a grant was made towards it in 1831. For a time from 1828 the children also attended here on weekdays to practise singing, which necessitated a payment of 7s. 6d. a quarter to the organ-blower; but the next year this singing practice was transferred to the preparatory school; it was still directed by the organist, who was paid ten guineas p.a. for his teaching, later £15; but in 1843 economy dispensed with his services. In 1863 the children's place in the gallery was required by the church choir, and the children were transferred elsewhere.

The rules as to children's employment were more strictly kept as regards girls than boys. A report of 1793 says that girls were taught needlework by Mrs. Clements. In 1815 we hear that girls were kept too much to lacemaking; they should learn plain work, reading, writing, and household duties. Next year their samplers are mentioned. In 1843 six girls helped at the home till 10 a.m., while on three days a fortnight three girls took it in turns to help with the laundry. This was in Mrs. Furze's day, and no doubt she kept them hard at it. On another occasion (1854) they were found diligently scouring. In 1866 they were required to make their own dresses, but the rules of this year specify that the master and mistress are to teach them reading, writing, arithmetic, Bible history and geography. It was reported in 1869 on their examination by John Brown that they answered reasonably well, considering that they had only two hours' instruction daily.

But the boys in 1793 were found by the visiting committee wholly unemployed, and the wheels formerly provided for spinning jersey – still there – did not appear worn. The boys seem very soon to have attended school, apparently the commercial school, from references in 1839 and 1866.

Exercise and recreation are mentioned later. In 1848 the visiting committee recommended that the children should walk out at least three times a week, weather permitting. In the summer of 1866 the children had a picnic and sports in Mr. Harrison's field. On regatta-day of that year many were allowed out on a visit, and the mistress purchased a few buns for those who remained at the home. A local incumbent gave a magic lantern show, and in 1867 a magic lantern was bought for the home. Later that year the children went for a trip to the Crystal Palace. On the day of the October fair, the master again took the children for a picnic, but the mayor allowed them to see General Tom Thumb. And the 1866 rules allow an expenditure of 10s. p.a. on toys.

From the first a medical attendant (apothecary and surgeon) was appointed at £20 p.a., who was to attend once a week at least, and oftener if required. The first was Alderman Gidney Phillips, and the first trouble he had was an outbreak of smallpox in April 1777 – in October of that year the maids were each given a guinea for their very extraordinary trouble and fatigue at this time. When a later apothecary, Charles Short, was mayor in 1836, he gave his services free; but in 1840 had to remind the Trust that his fee was again payable. The fee had now risen to £60, for it included the occupants of the many almshouses.

Other illnesses mentioned are scrofula (1841), wasting disease, fever and ringworm (1843). Thomas Paviour died in 1854 after a short illness. A boy had an ulcerated throat (1859), and Annie Carter died from consumption in 1862; while typhoid occurred in 1866. This last was limited to one girl, who was delirious, and as the sick bay was a room over the washhouse, her convalescence was not helped by the noise of pumps and mangle, nor by her mother bringing her "eatables" (sweets?). Incidentally there had recently been in Bedford a battle over piped water and main drainage, and Bedford's waterworks were erected in this year.[7]

Little comes through of the personalities of individual children, save for the occasional scapegrace. The first of these was a girl Downman; in 1774 her mother was told to take her away, and if she refused the master was to carry her and deliver her to her parents. John Sisson was expelled for thieving and lying in 1796. In 1817 no less than four boys and six girls were expelled for "flagitious conduct"; one of them was William Hockliffe; perhaps their unruliness was the result of bad habits formed during Sheppard's old age and blindness. Joseph Catlin was insubordinate and insolent in 1858. The tone of the house seems to have deteriorated in the last few years before the then master, George Winwood, died; the want of discipline was said to be injurious to the girls' morals and character; but this improved when the Passmores came in 1866. However, Henry Sweatman absconded in 1869.

When the children's home was wound up in 1871, there were 18 children. Seven were aged 14 in the coming summer; they were apprenticed or put to service. For three orphans foster-homes were found, and the remainder were put with relatives or friends; all these had a maintenance allowance of 6s. weekly and were given a new outfit. There was some discussion about the boy Henry Rabbit; his father, who kept the Saracen's Head, was not badly off, and the boy "ought not to have been admitted". His was probably a marginal case, accepted in order to fill a vacancy at a time when there happened to be a dearth of applicants, and afterwards regretted. However, Henry Rabbit was treated the same as the rest. When in 1874 he got a post as clerk on the Midland Railway, his father applied for an outfit for him, but that was going too far!

It is difficult to assess the contribution made to Bedford by the children's home, without making, so far as practicable, a study of case-histories. But it is probable that, even with mid-Victorian strictness, there was a more homelike atmosphere there than at the poor law institution (the House of Industry), to which some of these children might otherwise have gone.

THE UNFORTUNATE (HALL MONEY)

Harpur had provided that the reminader of his benefaction was to be distributed in alms to the poor. In pre-Trust days the corporation did in fact distribute small sums on St. Thomas' day, 29 December. In 1751 378 people participated in a distribution of £37 15s. 0d.

St. Paul's parish	227
St. Mary's	57
St. John's	24
St. Peter's	37
St. Cuthbert's	33

They received sums varying from 1s. to 4s. During the 1750s the amount distributed rose slowly to £72; then in 1762 sharply to £200. Henceforth until the 1793 act of parliament, this was the usual sum, though the 1764 act only spoke of the residue, and stipulated that the recipients were to be poor decayed householders who had lived in Bedford for five years. The sums received varied from 4s. to 12s., and they were distributed in the hall of the children's home; hence hall money. The clerk was ordered in 1770 to make out the list in co-operation with the overseers; and in 1774 he was directed to go from house to house. In February 1784 there was a distribution of bread and meat to the most distressed poor. Sometimes the allocation of funds was made well in advance at the November meeting; but sometimes when funds were low it was delayed; and from 1788 it was rarely made before February. The 1793 act specified that recipients must have lived in Bedford for ten years; and it fixed a ceiling of £200 until the almshouses had been built; after which it could rise to £500, as it in fact did in 1810 and 1815. The act of 1826, rash in this as in other respects, fixed the sum at £500. The trustees probably had in mind that population was growing; in 1801 Bedford's population was 3,948; in 1821 5,466. In fact after 1826 the level of £500 was not reached till 1832, after which it became constant during all the difficulties of the next 20 years, till hall money was discontinued under the 1853 scheme.

Early in the 19th century the growing population made compiling the list difficult. A list was kept from year to year, but that of 1815 was mislaid, and "by some unaccountable accident" a hundred people were omitted in 1816. Attempts in 1817 and 1818 to draw up more precise guidelines for compiling the list resulted in a printed form of certificate which must be signed by a trustee; but this was not foolproof, for the trustees could not know everyone; and in 1829 it was resolved to print in red on each form that a trustee must only sign for an applicant known to him personally. In 1833 an attempt was made to revise the list to exclude bad characters, but the task presented "insuperable difficulties". However, the trustees persevered, and in 1835 proposed to disqualify inmates of almshouses, keepers of beer-shops, and those having apprentices from the Trust; while they fixed an astonishingly low age rate: 40 for a single man, 30 for a single woman, and 25 for a married couple. They wished that the distribution could encourage industry and good conduct, but could not see how to bring this about; sometimes the money was used to pay debts. They found that some trustees still signed certificates irresponsibly. One precaution might be to circulate to each trustee the provisional list in print, so that unsuitable applicants might be better detected. They had tried very hard, but from the difficulty of getting the facts right they feared the list might still contain some unqualified persons; and so it proved; for in April John Cook was suspended for fraud. With growing financial stringency it became more and more difficult to find the money; and in March 1851 the trustees resolved that the distribution should be made "when possible"; and in 1852 it was held up till May. It was during this time of difficulty (1852) that there occurred the only recorded specific case of attempted misuse of hall money (to reimburse trustees for legal costs disallowed: see ch. 3).

When hall money came to an end under the 1853 scheme, distribution was phased out over a period of years. A questionnaire was got out in 1852, on which the applicant had to answer 17 questions, including age; how many years' residence in Bedford; whether housekeeper or lodger; rent; occupation; total family wages; children under 14 years. There were 96 applicants, of whom 37 had been born in Bedford, and 42 rented premises there; while others had acquired settlement by apprenticeship, service or marriage. The largest age-group was the 50s, there being only 16 in the 60s, two in the 70s, and one widow of 81, who said that she received 2s. 6d. and a loaf from the parish; while a widow of 66 received 1s. 6d. "from the Union". The expectation of life was of course shorter then than now. The majority of the applicants had incomes of less than 10s. weekly; 38 had weekly incomes from 10s. to 12s.; nine had more. Of these 96 applications, over 50 were disallowed, including that of George Perkins, an unemployed labourer aged 52 with two children, on whose form the clerk or a trustee has written "gets gloriously drunk".

It is probable that there was some abuse in the distribution of hall money, especially in the twenty years 1832–52 when the maximum of £500 was reached. But this £500 included over £200 in regular allowances to occupants of the Christie and Hawes almshouses, so that less than £300 was left for distribution.

Moreover, in this period the population doubled; in 1831 it was 6,959; in 1851 it was 11,693. Detailed distribution accounts have not survived, and it is difficult to ascertain how much each recipient had. On the credit side may be postulated at least some cases where an unfortunate family would feel less damage to their self-respect through help from the Trust than from the poor law overseers out of the rates. In fact the trustees were amateurs, trying to discharge a task which today is not found easy by professionals in the Ministry of Social Security.

THE OLD: ALMSHOUSES

Almshouses were introduced by the act of 1793. At the time, Bedford was not well supplied in this respect: there were some founded by Thomas Hawes in 1619 and eight by Thomas Christie in 1697. The 1793 act provided for 20 houses (for 10 men and 10 women) who should receive a weekly allowance of 5s. for married couples or 3s. for a single person; and these beneficiaries must go to worship on Sundays. If there were a surplus, the trustees could build cottages at low rents for the industrious poor; this advanced provision, long before the day of municipal housing, may have been inspired by the humanitarian Samuel Whitbread, so closely connected with this act. As will be seen, it was acted on by erecting 46 houses after a fire of 1802. By 1816 the original conception had been forgotten; the trustees declared the 46 new houses to be almshouses; and this was confirmed by the act of 1826. This act of 1826 also increased the allowances in the 20 older (or "best") almshouses to 15s. and 10s., plus a clothes allowance (£5 or £3); and in the 46 newer almshouses it provided an allowance of 10s. 6d. and 7s. (clothes £3 and £2). The occupants were not to pay rates, and a medical attendant could be provided. Street replanning reduced the number of the newer almshouses to 45; and these were continued, with the existing allowances, by the scheme of 1853, with the proviso that residents should be born in Bedford or have lived there 30 years. The almshouses were the only part of the welfare side to survive under the 1873 scheme. This omitted the 20 older almshouses (the site being used for the girls' school); and continued the 45 in what is now Dame Alice Street, or others "equally commodious", on the same conditions as before; 1/11 of Trust income being set aside for the purpose. In 1965–6 the eastern section of the Dame Alice Street almshouses, 25 in number, was modernised with the aid of an improvement grant from the town council. In 1970 the western section was sold, and 24 "equally commodious" modern flats were provided in entirely new premises in Cardington Road.

The initial almshouses took some little time to get under way. In fact, a blind couple, Thomas and Elizabeth Thompson, selected in 1797 before building began, never in fact seem to have got an almshouse at all. The trustees thought there was no urgency; the project could be carried out at such intervals of time as would avoid debt. The almshouses were not to be for the lowest class, but to have a kitchen and two other rooms, and a low range of detached offices; and the rooms were to be 8 ft. high. Part of Hill close in Bromham Road was bought for £160 in 1796, west of the site where the new gaol was to rise in 1801. The leading architect, John Wing, got out a plan, which was framed and hung in the board-room. There seems to have been uncertainty about the plans, for Salmon was at first appointed surveyor, then asked to "draw up the particular", and finally in 1801 Salmon's plan was adopted and to be immediately executed. Perhaps his was a modification of Wing's. The first 20 occupants were named in 1803. The pleasant site of these almshouses, although near the gaol, was on the edge of the town; it came to be known as Harpur Green, and to be looked on as a public open space where residents could wander or young people play – sometimes causing trouble. There were lime trees; some were cut down in 1816, but others planted in 1820. When the site was allocated for the girls' school which opened in 1882, there was an outcry. These 20 on Harpur Green were the "best" alms-houses.

Before these first almshouses were completed came the disastrous fire of 1802, which made homeless many families in the nearby district of St. Loyes. Startled out of their hitherto leisurely proceedings, the trustees decided to raise £600 on notes of hand to complete the first almshouses, and to build ten more to alleviate the poor's distress, a number raised later in the year to 26. Between the gaol and St. Peter's green was a farm belonging to the Duke of Bedford and occupied by William Sharp. Part of Dovehouse close, $\frac{1}{2}$ acre, was released at once by the Duke to the Trust, and completely built on by July 1804. The rest was secured in 1805, the price for the entire area being £500, with the proviso that Sharp should be allowed to occupy the house for at least five years. In 1815, as there was a considerable surplus of revenue, the trustees thought it would be expedient to build 20 more almshouses in line with those built after the fire; and these again were planned by Wing. There was thus a continuous row running from St. Peter's green to the gaol (the 46, which were declared almshouses in April 1816), and beyond the gaol the "best" almshouses on Harpur Green. Money by now was running short, and the contractors for the last ten houses had to be paid by notes of hand. At the eastern end of the 46 almshouses was a house which served as the clerk's residence till the Harpur complex (ch. 3) was built, after which it was taken over by Mr. Riley (ch. 5). At the western end was another staff house. The street thus created was called Harpur Street (now Dame Alice).

The trustees, as has been said, thought of the almshouses as not destined for the lowest class (who would go to the House of Industry), and they did not expect the occupants to be in receipt of a parish allowance. Yet some were in fact needy, and the trustees found it necessary to give extra help. Thus in 1808 Widow Coleman was allowed £2 p.a. for clothes, and this is the beginning of the clothing allowance which became statutory in 1826. They also in 1809 doubled the weekly allowance laid down by the 1793 act, because it was clearly inadequate with rising prices in wartime.

In 1822 the trustees began to be worried about medical care for the inmates; hence the provision in the 1826 act to cover this, and it continued till the 1860s. Charles Short, the then apothecary, waived his fee when mayor in 1836. Isaac Hurst, who died in 1856, was said to have ably filled the office.

The trustees provided pews in St. Paul's church, and also paid a 3-guinea Easter offering to cover almshouses, children's home and schools.

Vacancies were allocated at Trust meetings. In 1836 names of those having a trustee as proposer and seconder were put in a bag and drawn. In 1845 it was laid down that applicants must be at least 60 years of age. When the number of almshouses was reduced in 1871, names were drawn from the oldest and most necessitous of those over 70. The trustees found the almshouses useful for providing for some of their own ageing staff, such as masters of the children's home (Robert Clements and Edward Jeffrey), and the headmistress, Mrs. Furze.

But they insisted on certain rules. A widow in 1819 had to leave after her husband's death, though she was given three months' grace. Leave of absence had to be obtained when going on a visit. They were especially suspicious of a possible abuse through the inmates taking lodgers. An enquiry was made in 1820, when it was found that ten inmates had others living with them. Some of the extras were lodgers paying weekly sums from 8d. to 2s. 6d.; one was John Woodham's own journeyman, so Woodham was still pursuing his trade; another was a lacemaker. The remainder seem to be dependents, such as a child, and a married daughter. The decree went forth against them. But it was found to be not as simple as that. Nearly the whole of the inmates petitioned for people to live with them, though not as lodgers; and in fact when all the cases were sifted, the trustees found themselves obliged to concede the request in nearly every case. For instance, Thomas Goodman and his wife, who were in an infirm state, really needed the help of Sarah Crofts.

There was another drive against lodgers in 1835. Widow Norris was not allowed to have her daughter with her, and Widow Zachary's daughter was told to leave at once. The only result was to show again that it was often "absolutely requisite" for an old inmate to have someone with him or her, and no improper advantage was taken. It was concluded that complaints of lodgers of improper character had either by now been remedied, or never existed to the extent believed. But in 1837 Widow Zachary, though frequently admonished, was again found to have with her her daughter and four grandchildren, while in two or three houses there were schools of 10–15 children (possibly lace schools).

Disturbances at the almshouses were rare. Thomas Pirton was expelled in 1823. In 1857 there was some trouble, after which Merry, the inmate concerned, expressed deep regret, and the mayor had to reprimand William Kay.

The almshouses did not escape the economy drives of the middle of the century: in 1843 inmates must mend their own broken windows; and in 1862 must even be responsible for repairs.

Meanwhile in 1819 the Trust had developed the area on either side of the road leading northward to the 46 almshouses. This land was let on building leases, and the street called Harpur Place. In 1841 it was extended northward, the extension making it necessary to break the continuous line of almshouses from St. Peter's green to the gaol: three were pulled down, temporary arrangements being made for occupants, but two were rebuilt round the corner in the new street, making a total of 45. This long street, comprising the one-time Angel Street, the section known as Harpur Place, and the new extension, became Harpur Street as it is today; while that which crossed it, and which had hitherto been known as Harpur Street, was renamed Dame Alice Street. Under the 1873 scheme, when the 20 older or "best" almshouses on Harpur Green were pulled down to make room for the girls' school, the 45 almshouses in Dame Alice Street were overhauled and given a mock-Tudor front by stages between 1882 and 1895.

The inmates of these 45 re-fronted almshouses had, in place of the former medical attendant, the services of a nurse. Sister Fanny Eagles (foundress of the diocesan orphanage in Bromham Road), who died in 1907, did this for some years. When state retirement pensions were introduced, the weekly allowance was reduced and eventually discontinued. Rules of 1925 reaffirmed the old prohibition against underletting, and also forbade pets without permission.

As housing standards improved in the present century, the trustees became uneasy that their accommodation was falling behind; and in the spring of 1939 they were considering putting up new buildings on the edge of the town. The war held up all such plans. After the war, the need was urged, for instance by Dr. Towers. One proposal was to obtain funds by developing the site, and a local enquiry was proposed in 1961. Sir Albert Richardson defended the almshouses. A way was found to achieve both aims, i.e. to preserve the character of at least part of Dame Alice Street and yet to modernise. The eastern section was modernised at a cost of £47,000. The western section was sold for £75,000, and replaced by modern premises in Cardington Road. For the modernisation of the eastern section the town council gave an improvement grant. To the casual observer, this section looks exactly as it was before, save that one door bears the word "Warden". Inside however are 25 flatlets with modern kitchen and bathroom, and looking out to the rear on a long strip of garden.

The new building in Cardington Road is called Harpur House. It has a garden maintained by the residents and is a short distance from the river. The flats are self-contained; two on the ground floor are especially equipped for the disabled (wheelchair cases), having cupboards with revolving interiors and devices to help in using the bath. Two flats are for married couples and 20 for single persons;

and two bedrooms for visitors can be hired for a small charge; there is also a communal room.

Both premises are centrally heated; and in both, residents have their own furniture and cater for themselves. In both premises there is a resident warden, who visits each flat daily, and who can be summoned in an emergency by an alarm bell or a flashing light. No rent is paid.

Application is made to the Trust, but notified to the Town Hall; and although the requirement of 30 years' residence in Bedford is still a condition, there is a waiting-list of about 80.

9 *The Trust Today*

THE TRUSTEES

The Trust consists of 30 members, under the chairmanship of Sir John Howard, D.Sc., F.I.C.E.; the vice-chairman being the mayor of Bedford. There are five ex-officio members, the lord lieutenant, the mayor, and the three members of parliament. The nominated members are 13: two from New College; one nominated by the lord chancellor; one each by the universities of Cambridge and London; four by the school staffs; four by the parents. There are twelve representative members: six each from the town and county councils.

THE ENDOWMENT AND THE HARPUR COMPLEX

The revenue from the London estate 1971–2 was £196,356, and from the Bedford estate £965. The present gross area of the former is 6.08 acres, and the net area (less the roads) 3.77 acres.

The present policy is both to conserve and to look forward: that is to say, as regards the London estate, the policy is to allow no further diminution of the freehold, to promote the most beneficial use of the estate, and so far as practicable to conserve and where necessary and possible to restore the best buildings of the past. In the last decade major works of rehabilitation have been carried out on four premises in Bedford Row.

As regards the Bedford estate, a bold initiative has been taken. The trustees were faced with the problem of what to do with the central site, so long occupied by the Harpur complex, when the Modern School moves to the outskirts of Bedford in 1974. Blore's façade has been an essential part of the character of central Bedford, as is the original school (now owned and preserved by the town council). Yet the value of this central site is an asset which the Trust cannot afford to forgo. After elaborate consultation, the Trust accepted the advice of their architect, Sir Frederick Gibberd, and a brave decision was taken. This is to preserve the façade at considerable cost (and façade it is, and not integrally related to the buildings in its rear – see ch. 3), and to develop behind it a shopping centre with pedestrian precincts. The west side of Harpur Street will preserve the appearance it has had for more than a century, but behind it will be a modern development covering the rest of the site, and entered from Midland Road or Horne Lane. It is hoped that this development will substantially increase the Trust's income and therefore its capacity to carry out its functions.

THE SCHOOLS AND THE AGREEMENT OF 1971 WITH THE COUNTY COUNCIL

All past history, especially that of the Trust, warns that there are no permanent educational solutions, and that each generation must feel its way forward. This has been done in Bedfordshire by an agreement with the county council, for approximately 1,300 school places, planned to last for 15 years "subject to local and national circumstances remaining unchanged". This provides for co-operation, and each party – the LEA and the Trust – takes a step to meet the other.

The Trust schools will take a wider ability range than hitherto. The two independent schools require pupils to be able to follow a GCE course at least to O level; and the two direct grant schools to CSE level. On the other hand, the LEA will have in its own upper schools sufficient pupils to benefit from VI form teaching to enable such work to be organised.

The method of selection will be as follows. The catchment area will be the whole county, instead of (as hitherto) north and mid-Bedfordshire. Parents will say if they wish a child at 13+ to be considered for a Trust school. All pupils must, however, be in the top half of the ability range (only the two direct grant schools will take pupils from the whole of the top half of this range), and capable of following a public examination course in a reasonable number of academic subjects; thus there will not necessarily be the same percentage at each school. If the number applying is greater than the number of places available, the places will be allocated in accordance with pre-determined criteria on a random basis, using a computer.

This will be done by the heads of middle schools dividing their applicants into five numerically equal groups in descending order of ability. The computer will be programmed to take an equal number of children from each of the five groups on an agreed area basis, thus ensuring a reasonable spread of ability (yet reserving for the upper schools sufficient for a viable academic VI). The criteria will be: parental request, sex, suitability for particular school, ability group, and area.

This will be the scheme as it takes effect when reorganisation into comprehensive schools is complete in Bedfordshire. In the short term, in areas not yet reorganised, transfers take place at 11+ under the old procedure of academic selection; but as an area becomes comprehensive, transfers will take place at 13+ under the new procedure. During the transition period a child may be considered at one age but not at both. The first transfers of free-placers at 13 will be made in 1974, and the transition period should end by 1976.

THE FORMER ELEMENTARY SIDE

The rules governing this part of the income (2/11) are those approved by the ministry of education in 1956. Here again a forward-looking move has been made. In recent years the grant has been used for a number of comparatively small purposes and individual applications; thus in 1971–2 grants were made, not only to Youth Action, but to a mini-bus for Goldington Road PTA, and £4,813 was given for further education expenses. Some larger project however seemed required. This has been found in the Blue Peris Outdoor Activities Centre now being established in Snowdonia, expenditure on which amounted in 1971–2 to £4,234.

WELFARE

There are 49 almshouses: 25 modernised flatlets in Dame Alice Street, and 24 modern purpose-built ones in Harpur House in Cardington Road, each set of premises having a resident warden. In 1971–2 they cost £9,297 to run. All flats are occupied by Bedfordians with over 30 years' residence in the town, and there is a waiting-list of over 80. Places are allocated in conjunction with the town council.

CONCLUSION

It is over 400 years since Sir William Harpur's deed of gift to Bedford corporation in 1566, and over 200 years since its administration was transferred from the town council to the Harpur Trust in 1764. This Trust developed to a remarkable degree an elective basis. It has had its times of difficulty, and sometimes trustees have been more zealous than wise. From time to time it has not clearly seen future lines of development, but he would be rash today who would predict the educational development of the next generation. Till 1873 the Trust tried to serve Bedford; since then trustees have thought in wider terms. Till 1873 they had a partnership with New College; in the present century they have worked with the LEA, the county council. Till 1873 parents' attitude was sometimes one of querulous complaint; since then they have supported the Trust and helped to raise funds. All in all, it may be fairly said that the Trust all through its history has been an institution of which Bedford may be justly proud, that in the last century its schools have been of national importance, and that it has made Bedford known all over the world. Today the Trust is one of the first governing bodies to succeed in making an agreement for co-operation with a local authority which has reorganised its schools on comprehensive lines. It is forwarding a modern educational development, the outdoor activities centre. It also makes excellent provision for the old. And it has taken a bold initiative to develop its resources.

Perhaps it is not without significance that Bedford is in the heart of England. Over a thousand years ago it was on the edge of the Danelaw, where Dane and Saxon met. Harpur's endowment was used by elective trustees to create, not one large boarding-school, but a wide system of schools, and to help the unfortunate when statutory provision was less adequate than it is today. Now Bedford is cosmopolitan; there are already some immigrant children in the Trust schools, and when others have overcome their language handicap, there may be for these schools a further experimental role ahead.

SOURCES

MSS. The Harpur Trust

The Trust has a splendid series of MS minute books and of printed accounts, and most of the information in the volume is drawn from these. As the date of the item quoted automatically gives the reference, individual references will not in the main be given for these sources.

The exceptions to the above are as follows:

HT pkt.: a small packet containing a few miscellaneous items apparently preserved by chance (all early correspondence and papers having disappeared).

BS.: a few items which by some unknown method found their way to Bedford School and were there mounted in a volume.

Application forms and lists relating to the welfare side; a limited number of these survive.

Committee minutes: these survive only from the 1870s, and the system changes:

Estate: 1876–1938 (numbered 25–32)
Special: 1886–1925 (41–42)
Elementary: 1875–1960 (36–37 and unnumbered)
Grammar: 1875–1923 (33–35)
Modern: 1876–1916 (38–39)
Girls: 1874–1919 (43, 45)
Schools: 1930–48 (46–48)

MSS. New College

The most important of the MSS. relating to Bedford and preserved at New College are letters written to the Warden. They are arranged in chronological order, and the bundles are numbered 1123–4, 3329–3, 3337, 3340–3. A printed catalogue is about to be issued. The *Victoria County History*, ii, 152–77, prints some of the earlier letters in more detail than the citations in this text.

Printed

For the great mass of printed material relating to the Trust, see L. R. Conisbee's *Bedfordshire Bibliography*, pp. 147–9; 1st *Supplt.*, pp. 48–9; 2nd *Supplt.*, pp. 75–6.

C. F. Farrar, *Harpur's Bedford Charity*, summarises Trust history to 1873. Farrar was a trustee.

The *Victoria County History* (see above) gives some detail of the early history of the grammar school, but is unsatisfactory on the writing (later Modern) school.

School histories exist for three of the schools (not as yet for Dame Alice):

Bedford School. J. Sargeaunt and E. Hockliffe, 1925. This is good for the period of Fanshawe and Phillpotts, but the early part is marred by insufficient historical understanding and by ignorance of the Trust.

Modern School. L. R. Conisbee, 1944. To this the reader is referred for more detail. See also F. W. Kuhlicke's series in *The Eagle*; xxvi–xxx; the reminiscences of C. D. Linnell in the same, xxvii; Linnell's memoir of Poole (pamphlet); and Conisbee on Kaye (*B. Mag.* xiii, 305–9).

High School. K. Westaway (ed.), 1932. This contains reminiscences by staff and old girls, and was re-issued in extended form in 1957. See also K. Westaway, *Old Girls in New Times, 1939–45*.

Dame Alice. Articles in *Uisage*, x.

NOTES

CHAPTER I

1. *B.H.R.S.* xliii, 127.
2. For the Harper family in east Bedfordshire, see *B.H.R.S.* xiii, 24, 80, 195, 197–8, 220, 223, 225, 266. For Harpers at Biddenham and Bedford, see *B.H.R.S.* xxxvii, 14, 42, and xlv, 91. For William Harper senior at Bedford, see Corpn. MSS., court of pleas, 22 Oct. 1509 and 15 July 1510. (I am indebted to Mr. F. W. Kuhlicke for this reference.) For further information on the Harpers at Biddenham and their connections the Greens, see CRO, TW 259–309. A Franciscan Friar, John Green, in 1521 gave the Bedford Franciscans a book he had bought in Oxford with alms (*B. Mag.*, xiii, 326).
3. For Harpur, see *D.N.B.* (which however gives a wrong year for his shrievalty); and a life by J. G. Nichols in *London & Middlesex Archaeological Society Trans.*, 1st ser., iv, 1875, 70–93. See however especially C. M. Clode, 'Sir William Harpur', in *Early History of the Merchant Taylors' Company*, ii, 240–61, in particular for contemporary quotations on Harpur. The Merchant Taylors' minutes date from 1562 and show him as attending regularly. There are also references in London corporation minutes.
4. For the Merchant Taylors' Company, see C. M. Clode, *Memorials of the Guild of Merchant Taylors*, and his *Early History*, 2 vols.
5. Alice's history is obscure. Earlier writers depended on the 1568 visitation of London printed by the Harleian Society, but this edition does not distinguish later additions. It gives her maiden name as Tomlinson and her first husband as Richard Harrison of Shropshire. But Mr. F. W. Kuhlicke in *The Coat of Arms* (Heraldry Society), vii, 137–44 (1962) quotes further evidence from the Gloucestershire visitation of 1623 (*Harleian Society* xxi), and shows her to be the daughter of Robert Thorne of Bristol. She first married Thomas Jackman and subsequently John Chauntrell, who must have died by 1547. Incidentally this visitation shows that Harpur's second wife and eventual widow, Margaret, subsequently married Edward Thorne, Alice's nephew.
6. *V.C.H.* ii, 158, but see also Clode, *Early History*, ii, 262–70, for full details.
7. Machyn, cited by Clode, *op.cit.*, ii, 246, 248, 251–2.
8. Merchant Taylors' records.
9. Clode, *op. cit.*, ii, 253.
10. For background information on the corporation throughout the period of this volume, see the writer's *History of Beds.*, 194–200, 259–65, 322–8. The corporation minutes preserved at the Town Hall date from 1647, and the volume 1647–64 is printed as *B.H.R.S.* xxvi.
11. Among the corporation MSS. is preserved a Chancery brief of 1650 which gives a history of lettings, and a plan.
12. There is still a Three Cups Inn at 22 Sandland Street, off Bedford Row, but the original inn was slightly to the south in a now vanished street which was at one time called Featherstone Buildings (see *B.H.R.S.* xxvi).
13. In 1965 three St. Clement Dane's boundary stones were found at 42–43 Bedford Row. On these premises are also stones marked Kitt Catt and Little Whig (see *O.E.D.*), but their presence here is a mystery.
14. *B.H.R.S.* xxvi, 61–2, 78. Mr. F. Kelsall of the Historic Buildings Division of the Greater London Council, to whom I am indebted for advice on this section, gives the Chancery reference as PRO/C. 7/55/33 and 40.
15. PRO/C. 78/1269 No. 2. This decree, which had somehow eluded the Public Record Office indexing system, and of which no copy survived at Bedford, nor deed of exchange, nor reference in the corporation minutes, was discovered by the ingenuity and persistence of Mr. Frank Kelsall of GLC's Historic Buildings Div. He traced it back from a recital in a deed of 1718. Thus a baffling problem in the history of Harpur's endowment is at last made clear. A summary of the decree is given in Appendix 4.
16. *B.H.R.S.* xxvi, 64, 66, 87–8, 94, 125.
17. PRO/C. 5/442/19–21, C. 5/447/25 and 38, C. 10/160/104.
18. PRO/C. 8/302/60 and C. 8/337/139.
19. *D.N.B.*; see also N. G. Brett-James, *The growth of Stuart London*. However, the story of Barbon instructing his executors not to pay his debts is not, Mr. Kelsall tells me, borne out by his will.
20. Roger North; A. Jessopp, *Lives of the Norths*, iii, 53.
21. Narcissus Luttrell, *Brief Relation*, i, 309.
22. PRO/C. 5/72/88 and C. 10/336/74 give Barbon's lease as 9 Dec. 1684 and his assignment from Thompson as 16 Feb. 1687.
23. Corpn. minutes. Farrar, *op. cit.*, 10, prints Cobb's bill in full.
24. Stow's *Survey of London*, iii, 254.
25. PRO/C. 5/72/88.
26. Godber, *Hist. Beds.*, 323.
27. *V.C.H.* ii, 162–6; CRO, OR 1718.
28. New Coll. 1731.
29. Hardwicke's judgement, cited Farrar, *Bedford Charity*, 20.
30. New Coll. 1726, 1731.

31. Cf. Farrar, 20. For details of the Woodward family, see CRO, WL.
32. For the background to the act of 1764, see the Russell papers in CRO.

CHAPTER 2

1. *B.H.R.S.* xlix, 135–47.
2. Original minutes in Public Library, 32 Theobald's Road.
3. D. J. Olsen, *Townplanning in London.*
4. See *A note on the firm of Budd, Brodie and Hart*, 1933.
5. *Report of the Public School Commissioners* (1864), i, 291 ff.
6. Olsen, *op. cit.*, 182.
7. *B.H.R.S.* xiii, 220.

CHAPTER 3

1. CRO, W 1/827.
2. New Coll. 3341.
3. H. G. Tibbutt, *History of Howard Congregational Church*, 15, 17, 50, 55, n. 3; *B. Mag.* v, 74–6. Belsham's essays include one on education. This dismisses the outward graces advocated by Chesterfield, or the freedom desired by Rousseau, but is also against over-severity, as failing of the desired effect. "Much may be effected by parental attention"; "the first principles of knowledge and virtue may be inculcated in a thousand different ways"; "all recreations, tending either to health or rational amusement, should be not only allowed but encouraged".
4. For the whole background to this act, see the Whitbread MSS. in CRO, in particular W 1/827–46 and 2401.
5. Sir Richard Phillips, *Personal tour*, 1828.
6. Mainly at Belsham's instigation: see CRO, BD 1191.
7. J. Sargeaunt & E. Hockliffe, *Bedford School*, 67, relate an anecdote purporting to be of Dr. Brereton (whom they knew only from hearsay) abusing a trustee over a coal contract. No one who has read Brereton's letters – the letters of an able and wise man and a gentleman – could imagine him indulging in petulant abuse, and this before the boys. The alleged authority is suspect, since the Mellor boys were not at school till the 1850s. That the no-contract rule, when finally passed, was enforced, seems to be borne out by an occasion in Dec. 1847 when the clerk reissued notices asking for tenders, because inadvertently a firm connected with a trustee had tendered. For another piece of anti-Trust folk lore, see n. 26 below.
8. Told to the Clerk by Sam Smith, horsedealer, Garfield St.
9. Thus *V.C.H.* ii, 173. Blundells School cannot confirm this, but believe it may be so.
10. CRO, Russell papers. See also *Eagle*, xix, 508–10, for an article on Blore by F. W. Kuhlicke.
11. See the history of the school by T. W. Hutton, 81–4.
12. Hutton, *op. cit.*, 46, 49. For the general picture as to local reactions to the existence of an important school, see Bamford, *Public Schools*, ch. 8.
13. Corpn. MSS.
14. *Loc. cit.*
15. New Coll. 1124.
16. New Coll, 873.
17. For the whole background from the point of view of the "respectable", see New Coll. 873 and 1123–4; and for both sides see the contemporary press in CRO.
18. Printed Poor Law reports.
19. New Coll. 1124.
20. *Loc. cit.*
21. Trust minutes, committee report 5 October 1848.
22. *Bedford Times* 27 March 1852.
23. *Ibid.*, 1 May 1852.
24. T. W. Bamford, *Public Schools*, p. 167.
25. New Coll. 1123.
26. In after years a piece of anti-Trust folklore, comparable to the story of Dr. Brereton and the coal contracts – see n. 7 – grew up about this appointment. It was alleged that the chairman was George Hurst, who is supposed to have said "Gentlemen, we 'ave 'ere the letters of some very learned persons. Please look at 'em. I 'ope you will be able to read them – I can't . . . What we want is that they (our boys) should write a good 'and." Hurst's later mayoralties were 1873, 1874, 1878 and 1886, and this seems to indicate a late 19th century date for the story. Probably some wag invented it in the 1890s, and it came to be accepted as true – so much so that G. E. Langley in extreme old age included it in his reminiscences written down in 1922, and it was printed in the *Eagle* in 1942 (p. 51) without being checked against the relevant Trust minutes.
27. Bamford, *op. cit.*, 168.
28. C. D. Linnell in the *Eagle*, xxvii, 39.

CHAPTER 4

1. New Coll. 3341.
2. Corpn. MSS., chamberlains' accounts.
3. Letter from the usher, Abbot, HT pkt.
4. New Coll. 3342.

5. New Coll. 3342.
6. N. Carlisle, *Endowed grammar schools*, i, 547, 557; ii, 210.
7. BS, p. 11.
8. BS, p. 13.
9. *V.C.H.* ii, 173; but no evidence survives at Tiverton.
10. New Coll. 1123.
11. E.g. 19 June 1821 (New Coll. 3343).
12. Some figures for local salaries in Brereton's earlier days have been kindly supplied by the County Record Office. At the infirmary (medical hospital) in 1826 the house surgeon had £63 p.a. and the cook £12 12s. p.a. (the same as the matron or head nurse). The master of the asylum had £80 p.a. The governor of the gaol, appointed in 1814, had £190 p.a. The Duke of Bedford's chief agent, administering one-tenth of the county, appointed 1822, had £250 p.a. Comparable figures for other incomes are hard to come by. Probably Thomas Barnard, owner of a private bank, had an income similar to that of Brereton at its height. John Howard the industrialist was prospering, though the Britannia works were not yet built. Well-to-do families would be those of Nash, brewers, and Green, coal merchants. Alexander Sharman the solicitor probably did well. In the church there was variation. In the medical profession rewards were low. It should perhaps be noted that the living of Thurleigh was in 1832 offered to the school for an exhibitioner, and as there was no one immediately eligible, Dr. Brereton held it till 1837. By the standards of the day, this was not objectionable, but radical trustees were angry (4 Aug. and 6 Oct. 1836). It took Brereton 37 years to reach his peak, and the peak was short-lived. However, he was far better off than all his staff except Le Mesurier. In 19th century public schools "the usual situation was for the head to receive ten times the salary of the assistant" (Bamford, *Rise of Public Schools*, 129–30). At Rugby Dr. Arnold's income reached exceptional heights: Bamford in his *Life*, p. 178, estimates it as between £3,600 and £4,000; he also points out that assistants at Eton, Rugby and Harrow were more highly paid than at other public schools. Today the ratio between heads of the Harpur Trust schools and the salaries of junior staff might be from $3\frac{1}{2}$ to 4 times.
13. Pearse, in *Ousel* 19 Dec. 1882. His memory for numbers however does not accord with the admissions register.
14. Carlisle, *op. cit.*, i, 1–26.
15. *Loc. cit.*
16. Register at Bedford School.
17. *B.H.R.S.* xl, 145, 147.
18. Bamford, *Arnold*, p. 178.
19. New Coll. 1123.
20. A. Cooper (1821–1914), Reminiscences of the school 1831–9, in *O.B. Register*, 1912, 83–5.
21. Bamford, *Public Schools*, 2–3. Abrupt departures were trying for a headmaster. Brereton sometimes noted in his register "father's caprice", or "mother's whim", and in one case "unhandsomely removed".
22. Lists at Bedford School.
23. Cf. n. 12 above.
24. New Coll. 1123.
25. The name of English school signified that Latin was not taught, but was no longer applicable when Latin was introduced in 1837. "Commercial" stressed the enlargement of the curriculum from the original reading, writing and arithmetic.
26. New Coll. 3342.
27. *Ousel*, 23 March 1891.
28. Matthiason, *Bedford and its environs*.
29. New Coll. 3342.
30. New Coll. 1124.
31. J. Sargeaunt & E. Hockliffe, *Bedford School*, 95–6, give more details.
32. Bamford, *Public Schools*, ch. 5.
33. F. McKinnon, *On Circuit 1924–37*, 117. *"Si modo tu orabis archididaskalon nostrum, ut, parte de solido die dempta, laboribus vacemus, gratias maximas feres"* – 1928.
34. Bamford, *op. cit.*, 87–8.
35. New Coll. 1123.
36. New Coll. 3343.
37. Mark Rutherford, *Early Life*.
38. Sargeaunt & Hockliffe, 85–7.
39. *Ousel* 28 Nov. 1883.
40. Mark Rutherford, *Autobiography*.
41. *Ousel* 28 Nov. 1883.
42. See n. 20.
43. *B. Mag.* ix, 179, 245; *Eagle*, summer 1972, pp. 28–30; Sargeaunt & Hockliffe, 95–6.
44. Sargeaunt & Hockliffe, 78–104.
45. *Op. cit.*, 122. ("Two" on p. 98 is apparently a misprint.) The Trust minutes 11 March 1875 speak of removing the partition into the centre to make the classrooms equal, but on 10 June of a lecture hall for science, with laboratory adjoining.
46. L. R. Conisbee, *Modern School*, 29.

CHAPTER 5

1. Godber, *Hist. Beds.*, 429–32.
2. Tibbutt, *Howard Congregational Church*, 22.
3. Godber, *op. cit.*, 504.
4. *Beds. Times & Independent*, 11 April 1871. I am indebted for this and other press references in this chapter to Mr. David Bushby, whose history of elementary education in Bedford will, it is hoped, shortly be published, and who kindly lent me his text.
5. Mr. L. R. Conisbee kindly told me what he had gleaned of education in Bedford in the 1890s from the reminiscences of his mother, Rose Trasler, who taught 1888–96.
6. Letter from F. D. Pryer to the writer. His brother Albert, another old boy of Bates' school, became County Surveyor.
7. See n. 4.
8. See n. 5.
9. *Beds. Standard*, 24 Dec. 1887.
10. *Bedford Mercury*, 16 Feb. 1878.
11. See n. 5.
12. School logbook.
13. Mr. Pryer.
14. Mr. Bushby kindly gave me this reference.
15. *Bedford Mercury*, 14 Jan. 1882.
16. *Beds. Standard*, 5 Oct. 1900.
17. R. Ensor, *England 1870–1914*, 204 n.

CHAPTER 6

1. Mr. Conisbee points out that, though Kipling's *Stalky & Co* (1899) gives a non-Hughes and non-Farrar picture quite early, "the public school aura was most pronounced about the time of H. A. Vachell's *The Hill* (1904)". He adds "There were distinct signs of implied censure in G. F. Bradby's *The Lanchester Tradition* and Arnold Lunn's *The Harrovians*, both of 1913", though "reaction in literature is usually dated from Alec Waugh's *The loom of youth* (1917)".
2. Mr. Conisbee draws my attention to the fact that for a period in the late 1890s, the Modern School is included in a select list "of public schools", probably because Poole was a leading figure in the Headmasters' Association, indeed a founder.
3. A. C. Percival, *The origins of the headmasters' conference*.
4. See Bamford's *Life*.
5. Conisbee, *Modern School*, 33.
6. See B.M.S. MSS., WF 12/2.
7. *Eagle*, vii, 249.
8. Sargeaunt and Hockliffe, *Bedford School*, 249.
9. *Eagle*, xxvii, 43.
10. Sargeaunt and Hockliffe, 163–7.
11. *Op. cit.*, 134–5.
12. The Phillpotts prizes entailed holiday reading, with the object of fostering a love of literature. Where non-literary boys were concerned, they were to make the name of Phillpotts odious to generations yet unborn. However, at the girls' schools, where prizes were almost unknown, book-hungry girls, in a town without a public library, regarded them enviously. In those days Hockliffe's secondhand bookshop was a gold mine, where volumes could be bought for 6d. An old girl who at the time had never heard of Plato remembers discovering *The Republic* there.
13. Sargeaunt and Hockliffe, *op. cit.*, 107–8, 136–41.
14. *Op. cit.*, 143.
15. *Op. cit.*, 144.
16. *Ousel*, 14 Feb.
17. Sargeaunt and Hockliffe, *op. cit.*, 170.
18. County Record Office, MO, 718–20.
19. K. Westaway (ed.), *Bedford High School*. 63.
20. *Op. cit.*, 81, 91.
21. *Uisage*, x, July 1932.
22. Hilda Howe (Mrs. Long) who returned to teach from the 1940s to 1960.
23. Hilda Howe.
24. C. D. Linnell in *The Eagle*, xxvii, 39.

CHAPTER 7

1. There has been remarkable longevity among architects employed by the Trust: Edward Blore, 1787–1879; Basil Champneys, 1842–1935; Oswald Milne, 1881–1968.
2. Bamford, *Public Schools*, p. 66.
3. See article in *Times Ed. Supp.*, 23 June 1972.

CHAPTER 8

1. CRO, W 1/827.
2. *B.H.R.S.* xvi.
3. Godber, *Hist. Beds.*, 368.
4. *V.C.H.* iii, 20. The 1690 ruling arose out of a petition by Sir William Francklin against Christie and Hillersden; Francklin was unsuccessful, but the mayor had to attend the bar of the house and acknowledge shortcomings. At the 1774 election it is said that a sermon was preached on the text "Are not ten sparrows sold for a farthing?" The 1774 case is discussed in S. Douglas, *Controverted elections tried and determined 15–16 Geo. III*, 1775–7, 4 vols., the Bedford case occurring ii, 67–128.
5. Byng, *Torrington Diaries*, iv, 110.
6. *Personal Tour*.
7. Godber, *op. cit.*, 488.

APPENDIX I

Officers of the Trust

Chairmen

(As Mayors of Bedford)

James Chamberlain (1764), Thomas Knight (1765), John Howard (1766), Gidney Phillips (1767, 1773, 1775, 1777), John Heaven (1768), John Cawne (1769, 1774), Richard Cave (1770), William Parker sr. (1771), Edward Chapman (1772), John Parker (1775), Anthony Barton (1776, 1780), John Palmer (1778), William Parker jr. (1779, 1788, 1792), Thomas Howard (1781), William Pateman (1782), John Pheasant (1783), John Cave (1784), William Palmer (1785), Thomas Partridge (1786), William Smith (1787, 1789, 1801), Thomas Clayton (1790), Thomas Small (1791), John Wing (1793, 1808, 1817), Thomas Cockman (1794), Peregrine Nash (1795, 1807), John Day (1796, 1800, 1812, 1820), John Cooke (1797, 1809, 1818), Charles Webb (1798, 1816), Edward Chapman jr. (1799), Isaac Elger (1802), William Long (1803, 1813, 1822, 1829), Francis Green (1804, 1814, 1823), William Campion (1805), Thomas Kidman (1806, 1815, 1824), G. D. Yeats (1810), Charles Short (1811, 1821, 1826, 1836, 1837), Charles Webb (1816), John Green (1819), James Webb (1825), Charles Bailey (1827, 1831), George Livius (1828), T. G. Elger (1830, 1835, 1838), G. P. Nash (1832), Thomas Wooldridge (1833), George Witt (1834), T. A. Green (1839), Robert Newland (1840, 1845), W. R. Mesham (1841), Joseph Browne (1842), T. J. Green (1843–4), Alexander Sharman (1846), Henry Leech (1847), Charles Higgins (1848), C. F. Palgrave (1849–50), William Williams (1851–2), William Blower (1853), Thomas Barnard (1854), George Hurst (1855), W. W. Kilpin (1856), G. H. Miller (1857), John Howard (1858–61), Robert Couchman (1862), James Howard (1863–4), W. J. Nash (1865–6), T. T. Gray (1867–8), A. E. Burch (1869), J. R. Bull (1870), James Coombs (1871), F. T. Young (1872).

(Elected by the Trust)

Samuel Whitbread (1873–95), Guy Pym (1895–1905), Geoffrey Howard (1906–21), Lord Ampthill (1921–4), W. R. Bousfield (1924–8), Sir Maurice Craig (1929–34), Sir Reginald Ward Poole (1934–8), Sir Richard Wells (1938–56), W. A. L. Osborn (1956–8), Sir Douglas Gordon (1958–66), Sir John Howard (1966–).

Clerks

Thomas Cave (1764–8), Richard Wakefield (1768–91), Edward Chapman (1791–1807), William Smith (1807–9), John Whitehouse (1809–34), Samuel Bailey (1834–42), H. F. Leech (1842–9), William Jones (1849–58), D. H. Francis (1858–76).

Clerks and Receivers (from 1883)

A. H. Allen (1876–1922), E. D. Hay Currie (1922–8), R. L. Elgie (1929–64), N. A. Smith (1965–6), R. N. Hutchins (1966–).

Receivers (till 1883)

William Waller (1761–86), John Heaven (1786–94), John Gotobed (1795–1804), Thomas Gotobed (1804–42), G. P. Nash jr. (1842–4), John Elger (1844–50), Captain William Jones (1850–60), T. J. Green (1860–8), G. P. Nash (1868–83).

Surveyors (earlier ones not continuously ascertainable)

J. Lavender (1846–82), Lander & Bedells, later Lander, Bedells & Crompton, later Lander, Bedells and Stuart Edwards, later Lander Bedells (1882–).

Surveyors (Bedford)

Samuel Bailey (1835–42), James Horsford (1842–79), Henry Young (1879–1920), George P. Allen (1921–35), Geoffrey M. Inskip (1935–59), Henry T. Inskip (1959–).

Masters of the Hospital (children's home)

John Field (1773), Richard Freeborn (1774–82), Robert Clements (1782–96), Edward Jeffrey (1796–1805), Thomas Sheppard (1805–15), John Furze (1815–46), Maria Furze (1846–7), George Winwood (1847–65), Peter Passmore (1866–71).

APPENDIX 2

Heads of Schools

Free/Grammar/Bedford School

Edmund Green (1548–73), William Smyth (1573–7), Francis White (1577–?), – Chambers (?), Richard Butcher (1597–?), Henry Whitaker (–1601), Robert Barker (1601–10), Daniel Gardner (1610–36), William Varney (1636–56, 1660–3), Thomas Butler (1656–60), John Allanson (1664–5), John Butler (1665–72), John Longworth (1672–7), William Willis (1681–3), Nicholas Aspinall (1683–1718), Matthew Priaulx (1781–39), George Bridle (1739–73), John Hook (1773–1810), John Brereton (1811–55), J. F. Fanshawe (1855–74), J. S. Phillpotts (1874–1903), J. E. King (1903–10), R. Carter (1910–28), H. Grose-Hodge (1928–51), C. M. E. Seaman (1951–5), W. M. Brown (1955–).

Writing/English/Commercial/Modern School

John Whitehouse (1764–5), George Jackson (1765–1803), John Whitehouse (1803–9), Robert Ruffhead (1809–14), William Massey (1814–20), W. H. White (1821–31), John Moore (1831–60), W. Finlinson (1860–77), R. B. Poole (1877–1900), C. W. Kaye (1901–16), A. Powell (1917–22), H. W. Liddle (1922–46), J. E. Taylor (1946–65), B. H. Kemball-Cook (1965–).

High School

Ada Benson (Mrs. McDowall) (1882), Marian Belcher (1883–98), Susan Collie (1898–1920), Emmeline Tanner (1920–4), Kate Westaway (1924–49), Gwendolen Watkins (1949–65), E. K. Wallen (1965–).

Girls' Modern/Dame Alice

Mary Porter (1882–94), Edith E. Dolby (1894–1925), Beatrice Tonkin (1925–46), Irene Forster (1946–55), Hilda Lawson-Brown (1955–70), S. M. Morse (1970–).

General preparatory/"National"/Elementary (boys)

John Furze (1815–31), T. Riley (1831–69), F. Bannister (1869–75), G. M. T. Bates (1875–1911).

Girls' elementary (on central site)

Miss Smith (part-time 1815–31), Miss Poole (1836), Maria Furze (1837–60), Miss Mitchell (1860–99), Miss C. A. Etchells (1899).

Infants' elementary (on central site)

T. Jagg (1839–68), Miss Cooper (1874).

Ampthill Road

A. Corney and Miss Robinson (1876), John Baldwin (1882).

Clapham Road

Miss M. Poynter (1894–1902).

APPENDIX 3

Memorials to Harpur

A Tudor merchant who enriched his town may be presumed to have hoped that at least whatever memorial marked his resting place would be left undisturbed. Harpur has had various memorials, but has been unlucky in this.

His burial in St. Paul's church, Bedford, was not recorded at the time – the register entry is an insertion in a later hand. This is so surprising as to give rise to doubts as to whether he was buried here; yet the desire expressed in his will, coupled with the entry in the corporation accounts for February 1573/4 for wine for his funeral, make a pre-supposition, strengthened by the known fact that his widow, Dame Margaret, was buried here 3 November 1596, and by the contemporary brass inscribed "Hereunder lieth buried the body of Sir William Harper, knight, lord mayor of the city of London, with Dame Margaret his last wife". This brass, which has been described as unique, and therefore engraved expressly, is the only portrait of Harpur which may be authentic; yet its present siting on the south wall (1920) makes "hereunder" not quite correct. (The shield with Dame Margaret's arms has long been missing.)

There have been three further memorials, of which two survive. One was an apparently contemporary altar tomb, seen in 1765 by the antiquary W. Cole "against the east wall of the south chancel"; on it was a "coarse" painting of arms. It has been pointed out by Mr. F. W. Kuhlicke that a sketch by Rudge (who came to Bedford in 1840) shows a tomb against the south wall. Apparently the trustees, about the time of their large-scale building by Blore, commissioned a new tomb in a slightly different place, and the brass was then placed on this tomb. In the 1890s the then vicar, L. Woodward, wanted to restore the brass to its original position and to "lower" the tomb; search was made in the minutes, but committee minutes had not been preserved, and he was informed that nothing could be found to justify the trustees sanctioning such action. None the less, this was done in 1899 (*Ousel*). Not till 1911 was it reported to the Trust estate committee that the "cenotaph in memory of Sir William Harpur in St. Paul's church had been lowered to the floor level and that the brass had been removed and placed on the floor and covered by a mat". One of the workmen concerned, when seriously ill, said that the tomb was removed at night, and parts of it buried in the churchyard outside the south wall of the chapel. Here in fact they were subsequently found by other workmen digging a drain, and they are now (1973) under the tower of the Harpur complex. It seems that at the time this was done, the brass was relaid in its original matrix and covered with a mat. Here, no doubt, Harpur would have wished it to remain; but if covered it would not easily be found, and if uncovered might suffer damage. In 1920 it was moved to the south wall.

The other two monuments were commissioned by the newly established Trust from a minor sculptor, Benjamin Palmer, who had a mason's yard in Holborn. One (in Tudor costume and unconvincing) was put up on the north wall of St. Paul's church, with an erroneous inscription to the effect that Sir William Harpur and his wife Dame Alice are buried below (Dame Alice was buried in St. Mary Woolnoth in 1569). The other (in 18th century costume, but pleasing, and reasonably like the brass) is over the door of the former school building, now the mayoral suite. It bears the inscription: *"Ecce viator corporea effigies Gulielmi Harpur, equitis aurati, scholae istius, quam cernis amplam et ornatam, munificentissimi fundatoris. Si animae picturam spectare velis, in charta beneficiorum invenias deliniatam."* (Traveller! here is a bodily representation of Sir William Harpur, knight, the munificent founder of this school, which you see so spacious and adorned. If you wish to behold a picture of his mind, you will find it delineated in the record of his benefactions.)

For full details of the whole, see F. W. Kuhlicke, "The Harper Brass in St. Paul's, Bedford", in *Trans. Mon. Brass Soc.*, x, 68–73.

The Trust tried in vain to find a portrait of Harpur for the boardroom (ch. 3). In 1836 an annual dinner in his memory was proposed, but the idea seems to have been dropped. Founder's Day began to be celebrated at the schools towards the end of the last century, and for at least the last fifty years the mayor and corporation have attended in their robes the Founder's Day service in Bedford School chapel, while at Bedford Modern School they attend the annual prize-giving.

Despite the fact that Harpur's name is borne in London by a street and by the estate office, and in Bedford by a street, a local government ward, a hospital ward, the modern almshouses, and is to be bestowed on the so-called Harpur Suite (former assembly rooms and library facing the complex) and on the new shopping centre – it was at one time also borne by a public house; yet the closure of Harpur Secondary School in 1965 left the position that no school of Sir William's foundation at present bears his name.

APPENDIX 4

Exchange of part of the Holborn Estate in 1654

PRO/C. 78/1269 No. 2: Chancery decree: Corporation of Bedford against Fisher, bart., and others.

Whereas in Holy Trinity term 1649 the mayor, bailiffs, burgesses and commonalty of Bedford, complaints, complained to Chancery against Sir Thomas Fisher bart., Leonard Street, Sir John Brownlow bart., Sir William Brownlow bart., Grace Fetherston, Anthony Wright gent., John Hooker esq. and John Shalmer (two feoffees for St. Clement Danes), and the mayor, commonalty and citizens of London (governors of the hospital of Christ, Bridewell and St. Thomas the Apostle), Thomas Rant esq., and Ralph Wild, gent., defendants, touching 13 acres and 3 roods in Lyon Field and Little Conduit Shott in the parish of St. Andrew Holborn, and a way thereto; of which lands the complainants were seised to charitable uses by conveyance from Sir William Harpur and Dame Alice; and they and their predecessors had made several long leases thereof at rents paid to them by their farmers during their terms, one of which, near expiration, of the greatest part of the said lands, was made to William Langhorne gent. and others, the interest whereof was by assignments come to Grace Fetherston; and the complainants' lands lying intermingled with the lands of the defendants, the complainants' farmers did not only deface the ancient land marks but lease out the complainants' lands to the defendants and their tenants, whereby through long unity of possession the said boundaries and way were become so obscured that, when the complainants' lands were to revert, they could not know where to make their entry or to find out the way; for relief wherein, and to have a commission to enter into and set forth unto the plaintiffs their lands and way, the said complainants prayed this court. Which being granted, the defendants put in their answers, whereunto the complainants replied, divers witnesses were examined, and 27 June 1650 was appointed for hearing; on which day the defendants' counsel insisted that the setting out of the lands would cut off the houses by the middle and the backsides, but the complainants' counsel offering to accept lands answerable in value, whereupon (Brownlow, Hooker, Shalmer, Rant, Wright and Wild did not appear), this court was satisfied that the complainants made a sufficient title but that through long possession and by reason of the many houses thereupon it would be difficult to distinguish the lands; and therefore it was ordered that a commission should issue to Edward Roberts, George Manley, Edmond Wingate, Richard Powell esqs., Robert Titchborne alderman, Josias Barner esq. and George Almery gent., authorising them to survey the lands, examine witnesses, and end the differences, and to set out for the complainants such a parcel of land as might be answerable to the lands conveyed. In pursuance whereof, and of a commission 14 September 1650, five of the commissioners (Manley, Powell, Roberts, Wyngate and Barners) (reported):

the difference with the inhabitants of St. Clement Danes:

witnesses differ and we are not able to determine anything;

the governors of Bridewell: they pretend no title of inheritance on the north side of a vault (former ditch), neither does Bedford claim on the south side;

the difference between Sir John and Sir William Brownlow is in a fair way to be settled;

the difference with Sir Thomas Fisher: we find Sir William Harpur's grant mentioned 13 acres 3 roods, but in the fine levied about the same time it is mentioned only to contain 13 acres 1 rood. All the rest of the lands lying in the two fields, Lyon Field and Conduit Shott are claimed by Sir Thomas Fisher by deed 15 July (1568) and ought to contain 16 acres 3 roods; both which parcels claimed by Fisher and Bedford contain by deeds 30 acres. But we caused the lands to be twice measured by two surveyors, who do return that the lands contain only 27 acres; howbeit we are not able to discover the bounds, and we did find them willing to make an abatement proportionable. The corporation sent up two aldermen to treat, and having had several meetings, Bedford was persuaded to offer a lease for 21 years at £50 p.a., and Fisher should set out the bounds and maintain them, with promise that Fisher should have first offer of another lease at expiration: upon this difference (Fisher would not accept less than 40 years) the parties broke off. 1 July 1652.

On 19 January 1652/3 the court declared that the complainants should have their proportion only according to the rate of 13 acres 1 rood. It was ordered that a commission should set out to the complainants and to Fisher, to each his just proportion, and the metes and bounds, together with a way to the same. For what concerned the parish of St. Clement Danes, who have had a long possession, it was ordered that the complainants' bill as to them should stand dismissed with 40s. costs.

In pursuance of which order, a commission was issued to the said referees, who made and returned their certificate:

We have viewed the two fields, Lyon Field and Little Conduit Shott, divided by a ditch east-west, Conduit Shott lying north; and finding the plaintiffs have four pieces lying intermingled with as many pieces of Fisher, each of the said two parties' pieces siding with each other east and west and crossing the field through from north to south, we have distributed the 27 acres according to their respective quantities (detailed bounds follow). And so the quantity of the four pieces set out to the plaintiffs is 11 acres 3 roods 27 poles, and to Fisher 15 acres 13 poles; and a way through Theobalds Way. 1 March 1652/3.

And afterwards Fisher put in exceptions, coming to be heard 15 July 1653; and Fisher offered that he would let the complainants have their whole proportion in the field called Conduit Shott, except the bowling grounds; and if not enough there, the rest in Lyon Field; which seeming very reasonable, it was ordered the complainants should have till after Michaelmas to answer. But 20 October 1653, for that the plaintiffs could not consent, it was ordered that the matter be referred to four of the former commissioners to consider of a fitting exchange; and on 28 Nov. last the time was extended, when they reported:

3 December 1653. We have allotted to the complainants pasture containing 8 acres 2 roods 17 poles in Little Conduit Shott, the easternmost part of the shott, comprehending in it the soil of Theobalds Way in its south part next Lyon Field, one entire close, and abutteth south on the north ditch of Lyon Field, east and north on the out ditches of the shott, west on a ditch with quick hedge severing the piece from bowling grounds (assigned to Fisher).

We have also allotted to the plaintiffs in Lyon Field 3 acres 1 rood 10 poles, being the easternmost part, which consisteth partly of alleys, gardens, backsides, yards and buildings in its south part, and partly of pasture, and abutteth eastward partly on the ditch of Sir William Brownlow's pasture and partly on the west wall of his garden, and north on the north ditch of Lyon Field, on which ditch the line extendeth west 170 foot; and the south bound of the piece is the north side of an underground vault or sewer, formerly an open ditch, tending east and west, 264 feet or very little differing, severing it from the freeholds of Brownlow, governors of Bridewell, Wright, Fetherston, and beginneth eastward by Brownlow's wall at the north distance of 184½ feet from Holborn Street, and terminateth westward 141½ feet from the said street, and 12 feet from the east wall of the Red Lyon Inn; from which west point the west bound of the piece is a line drawn northward parallel with the wall of the Lyon Inn 52 feet unto a point 193½ feet from Holborn Street and 264 feet west from Brownlow's wall; then turning eastward it extendeth the space of 27 feet to a point 193½ feet north from Holborn Street and 237 feet from Brownlow's wall; then turning again northward it extendeth 90 feet in a straight course to a point in the brick wall of Fisher's garden next the field or pasture 283½ feet north from Holborn Street and 247½ feet west measured along by the wall next Brownlow's wall, and 39 feet east (measured by the garden wall) from the wall of the Lyon Inn; from which point the line, crossing the plain field northward, extendeth in a straight course to the before described west terminating point of the north line.

All the rest of the 27 acres in Lyon Field westward to Bloomsbury ditch we have allotted to Fisher, 11 acres 3 roods 30 poles.

And for the convenience of each party, outlet and passage to, in and from Lyon Field unto their lands, on the south side of a piece of 6 acres 1 rood 23 poles, formerly the plaintiffs', now Fisher's; and liberty of passage by and through Theobalds Way as the same lieth betwixt the gate called the King's Gate and Gray's Inn Lane Gate.

We are informed that Leonard Street, one of the defendants, took the profits of the greatest part of the plaintiffs' land since Michaelmas 1652.

Afterwards 19 Jan. 1653/4, forasmuch as the exchange was settled and the bounds set out, it was ordered that if Fisher should not by that seven-night show cause to the contrary, the certificate of 1st March should stand ratified by decree, and Street should pay the complainants £50.

It is this 16 February 1653/4 decreed that the exchange be hereby ratified and the bounds be ratified (liberty of passage shall not give the complainants any title to Fisher's lands), and Street shall pay the complainants for 1½ years at the rate of £40 p.a.

APPENDIX 5

Some indication of the contribution made by Trust schools in various fields of endeavour

It is not possible to make a precise estimate of the contribution made to the community by any school. The most important part of it is intangible, the spirit which old boys and old girls derive from teachers who drew out in them unsuspected potential and from those who shared this experience with them. The result in their lives and in their contribution to the community cannot be assessed.

Those old boys and old girls whose names are known beyond Bedford are in a sense the tip of the iceberg. Of these at least some indication can be given, though not with precision. Some names may be inadvertently omitted from this list where a boy or girl has gone far afield and has not maintained home links; old boys in industry are harder to trace than those in professions and services. Difficulty applies more particularly to girls, who in any case go back only to 1882, of whom at first few took up careers, and for whom less full records are available. In the case of girls, sometimes a career which promised to be notable was given up on marriage. (Some eminent husbands and sons are known, but to cover these would extend the enquiry too far.) For boys and girls, decorations are given where known, but are believed incomplete.

The lists were compiled as follows: Bedford School: Mr. M. Barlen with the help of the Upper History VI and OBs; Modern School: Mr. A. Underwood with the help of the Local History Group and OBMs; High School: Miss D. Kitchener with the help of Miss Burnip; Dame Alice: Mrs. Long. For the Harpur Elementary School, a few names are taken from a presentation volume to G. M. T. Bates, preserved at the Town Hall, and later annotated by an old boy.

The schools will welcome notification of omissions and correction of errors, in order to correct and complete their own records.

The two pairs of schools do not show a clear-cut dividing line. Some families and indeed some individuals appear on both lists.

Families are sometimes represented by more than one individual, and sometimes the same family recurs over a long period. These families may have sent day-pupils, either native-born, like the Howards, or "squatters" like the Smyths, or boarders from overseas.

Over the years part of the pattern of careers has remained stable, especially that of education and medicine. Part however has changed: the high proportion once taken by the army has dwindled, and there are no recent bishops; but art, television, and (for girls) fashion designing have come forward. The interest in history at two of the schools may reflect good teaching at the time. In the arts section are some architects, artists and musicians, and a few writers such as Mark Rutherford and Christopher Fry. Industry has few representatives, perhaps a disadvantage to the country and the schools. Under politics will be found a prime minister (South Australia). On the debit side, Bedford must acknowledge Baillie-Stewart, but not the notorious William Joyce (Lord Haw-Haw) with whom he has been confused.

Quality varies over the period. Notable heads probably helped to promote florescence *c.* 1900. Later the impact of World War I is starkly apparent.

With regard to numbers, Bedford School, with its longer history and prestige, accounts for more than half the total; and again preponderates with those in higher échelons; but the Modern School, though as an important school it is of more recent date, makes a good showing in most of the same fields. Though the two girls' schools began in the same year, the much earlier concentration on academic work at the High School is reflected. Dame Alice has only recently entered on its period of fruition. The pattern of products of the four schools, as distinct from numbers, is remarkably similar.

The Harpur contribution appears to be not in spectacular brilliance, but in sound and faithful service, especially in education and medicine; much of it (about 1:5) overseas.

Except on one occasion, the chairman of the Harpur Trust has since 1906 always been an Old Bedfordian or Old Modernian, and many old boys and girls have served on the governing body.

The date in the right-hand column indicates the decade of leaving school.

ACADEMIC, EDUCATIONAL, SCIENTIFIC

Bedford School

Sir Warington Smyth, Professor of Mineralogy, Royal School of Mines. Rowed in the Cambridge boat, 1839. 1830–1830

Rev. C. G. Wilkinson, Headmaster, Pocklington Grammar School.

T. G. E. Elger, astronomer, secretary of the Natural History Society. .. .. .. ?

Dr. A. C. Burnell, C.I.E., oriental scholar and author. .. .. .. ?

C. P. Smyth, F.R.S., Astronomer Royal for Scotland 1845. 1830–1840

E. T. Hartley, Headmaster, Skipton Grammar School.

Rev. R. Alliott, Headmaster, Bishop's Stortford School. 1850–1860

Sir W. Hillier, Professor of Chinese, King's College, London 1904. 1860–1870

W. C. Green, Headmaster, Pynsent's Grammar School, Chudleigh 1874.

Rev. T. C. Fry, D.D., Headmaster of Oundle and Berkhamstead Schools.

Sir Wyndham R. Dunstan, F.R.S., Director, Imperial Institute 1903. 1870–1880

Rev. C. F. Farrar, Headmaster, Elstow School.

John Sargeaunt, VIth Form Master at Westminster School, 1890–1918.

F. Jacob, inventor. Work on submarine cables and telegraphy.

Professor Langdon Brown, Regius Professor of Physic at Cambridge. 1880–1890

Rev. T. C. Fitzpatrick, President of Queen's College, Cambridge. Vice-Chancellor, Cambridge 1915–16, 1928. .. .. ..

Rev. H. M. Burge, Headmaster of Repton and Winchester, 1902. Bishop of Southwark and Oxford.

C. H. Greene, Headmaster of Berkhamstead School, 1910.

Professor E. Hockliffe, Queen's College, London 1921.

Sir A. Symonds, K.C.B., Permanent Secretary to Board of Education. 1890–1900

E. G. Morris, Director of Education in Kenya and Nigeria. 1900–1910

Sir W. Cleary, K.B.E., C.B., Deputy-Secretary at Ministry of Education.

Professor W. Rowan, Professor of Zoology, Alberta.

W. J. Walker, Headmaster, Woodhouse Grove School, 1914.

Professor J. D. Bernal, F.R.S., Member Soviet Academy, Lenin Peace Prize 1910–1920

A. J. P. Martin, F.R.S., C.B.E., Nobel Prize for Chemistry 1952.

J. S. Carter, Headmaster, St. John's Leatherhead and Blundell's 1948.

Rev. G. K. Tibbatts, Headmaster, Boys' Central School, Chidya.

Professor H. R. X. D'Aeth. 1920–1930

Professor J. H. Bromley, Professor of History, Southampton. 1930–1940

Professor C. E. M. Hansel, Professor of Psychology, Swansea.

Professor H. C. Allen, University College, London.

Professor J. P. C. Roach, Professor of Education, Sheffield.

J. R. Grover, Headmaster, King Edward VI School, Retford.

W. M. Brown, Headmaster, King's School, Ely, and Bedford School.

Brigadier R. V. M. Benn, O.B.E., Head of Army School of Education.

Professor J. F. Adams, F.R.S., Professor of Astronomy, Cambridge. 1940–1950

Professor V. G. Emsley, Prof. of Biology, George Mason Univ., Virginia.

Professor M. D. Warren, University of Kent.

Dr. V. C. Runeckles, Director of Plant Science, Univ. of British Columbia.

Bedford Modern School

Sir William Tilden (1856–) Professor of Chemistry at Imperial College. Dean of the Royal College of Science and Principal of the Royal School of Mines. The first chemist to prepare a specimen of synthetic rubber.

E. M. Langley (1863–8) mathematician and schoolmaster. Author of text books and founder of the *Mathematical Gazette*. Also a noted botanist with a cultivated blackberry named after him.
W. Hillhouse (1860s) Professor of Botany and Vegetable Physiology, Birmingham.
W. R. Bousfield, K.C., M.P., F.R.S. (1866–70) Lecturer in Maths and Engineering, Bristol University. Authority on Patent Law.
W. Greenwell, Lax LL.D. (1869–76) Mathematician and Legal authority. Presiding Examiner, Cambridge Locals 1887–1927.
A. J. Pressland (1875–83) Educational theorist. Author of Royal Commission Report on *Physical Training in Switzerland*, 1902.
Prof Henry Payne (1879–84) Established Chair of Engineering, South Africa. Then at University of Melbourne, Australia.
G. J. Gibbs (1881–85) Inventor of the Heliochronometer [a sundial for recording *mean* solar time as opposed to the traditional *apparent* solar time].
C. A. Worth (1884–7). Ophthalmologist. Author of standard work on the squint. Inventor of "Worth's Amblyoscope" and "Four Light Test".
Dr. E. T. Bell (1898–1900) mathematical theorist in U.S.A., and discoverer of proofs and generalisations. Science fiction writer [John Taine].
Revd. F. L. McCarthy (1915–21) Dean of Balliol College, Oxford.
C. W. Oatley, F.R.S., O.B.E. (1916–22) Professor of Electrical Engineering, Cambridge.
N. B. Larby, O.B.E. (1917–24) Deputy Director of African Education, Kenya.
Dr. D. C. Riddy, C.B.E. (1919–26) H.M.I. of schools. Chief Modern Languages Inspector of Board of Education.
Dr. W. C. A. Hutchinson (1929–36) Lecturer in Natural Philosophy, University College, Dundee.
Dr. R. Maude (1934–46) Lecturer in mathematics, University College of Wales, Aberystwyth.
N. M. Savage (1946–53) Associate Professor of Geology, University of Oregon, U.S.A.
Dr. J. Holland Rose (1867–73) Vere Harmsworth Professor of Naval History, Cambridge. Fellow of the British Academy. Author of standard (short) life of Napoleon I, etc., etc.
J. Steele Elliott (1878–87) archaeologist and ornithologist.
L. R. Conisbee (1904–15) B.M.S. Historian. Compiler of Bedfordshire Bibliography, editor Hastings and East Sussex Naturalist, etc.
Dr. F. G. Emmison, F.S.A., F.R.Hist.S. (1918–23) Beds. County Archivist 1924–38, Essex County Archivist 1938–69.
Prof. W. F. Grimes, C.B.E. (1920–21) Keeper and Secretary of the London Museum, Director of the Institute of Archaeology and Professor of Archaeology, London University, etc., etc.
G. C. Dunning (1920–4) Archaeologist. Inspector of Ancient Monuments.
H. G. Tibbutt, F.S.A., F.R.Hist.S. (1925–9) authority on non-conformity in Bedfordshire and the Civil War period. Record Officer, Air Force Dept., Ministry of Defence.
I. P. Collis, F.S.A. (1928–34) County Archivist, Somerset.

Harpur Elementary School

O. A. Le Bean, chief examiner in mathematics, Board of Education.

Bedford High School

P. Spafford, O.B.E., Secretary, The Ling Institute, and Principal, Bedford Physical Training College, 1949.
M. Spence, Principal, Bedford Froebel Training College, 1927.
Constance Stewart, Principal, Lincoln Training College, 1924.
Beatrix Havergal, M.B.E., founder of Waterperry Horticultural Training College; R. H. S. Veitch Memorial Medal, 1961.
Laura Jackson, Principal, College of the Ascension, Selly Oak.
Florence Sutton, Principal, N. England and Manchester Kindergarten Training College, 1914.
May McKisack, Professor of History, Westfield College, London, 1955 (published works).
Agnes Leys (*née* Sandys), Vice-Principal, St. Hilda's College, Oxford.
Mary Coate, Fellow, Lady Margaret Hall, Oxford, 1922 (published works).
Dr. Janet Matthews (*née* Brown), Lecturer in Science.
Teresa Hankey, History tutor, Bedford College, London, 1955.
I. M. Sampson, Headmistress, Muree, 1900, Madras, 1906.
A. T. Scott, Headmistress, Bingley Grammar School, 1904.
A. M. Stephenson, Headmistress, Preston High School, 1906, F. Holland School, London, 1912.
K. Wragge, Headmistress, Peterborough Girls' County School, 1907.

H. M. Footman, Headmistress, Chester School for Girls, 1911.
M. A. Grant, O.B.E., Headmistress, Withington Girls' School, Manchester, 1908.
Sybil Turing, Headmistress, Simla, 1908, Lahore, 1919.
M. Spurling, Headmistress, Alice Ottley School, Worcester, 1912.
E. M. Russell (*née* Columbine), Headmistress, Pietermaritzburg, 1913.
E. M. Belcher, Headmistress, Crediton High School, 1914, James Allen's Girls' School, Dulwich, 1920.
E. I. Sutton, Headmistress, Carmarthen High School, 1914.
E. M. Edghill, Headmistress, King's High School, Warwick, 1914, Redland High School, Bristol, 1921, St. Felix, Southwold, 1926.
E. Lowde, Headmistress, County Secondary School, Petersfield, 1919.
M. D. Hall, Headmistress, Tranmere High School, Birkenhead, 1921.
D. Coate, Headmistress, Truro High School, 1922.
K. M. Westaway, Headmistress, Bedford High School, 1924.
M. Norris, Headmistress, County High School, Walthamstow, 1924.
W. Coate, Headmistress, Cairo, 1924, and Jerusalem, 1928; reclaimer of desert, Zerka.
D. Carruthers, Headmistress, Green Secondary School, Isleworth, 1925.
E. Wainwright, Headmistress, Jersey Ladies' College, 1926; Penrhos College, 1928.
M. Salmond, Headmistress, Timaru, New Zealand, 1927.
M. Malim, Headmistress, School for the Deaf, Stockton-on-Tees, 1929.
A. Langley, Headmistress, Old Polar School, Croydon, 1930.
May Prickett, Headmistress, Framlingham High School, 1933; *Officier d'Academie*, 1937.
M. Oakley-Hill, Headmistress, Royal Naval School, Twickenham, 1933.
W. Appleton, Headmistress, Norwich Secondary School, 1934.
F. Skerman, Headmistress, Queen's Park Girls' School.
D. Stokes, Headmistress, Kempston Junior School, 1942.
C. Smith, Headmistress, Penrhos College, 1938.
E. Goodman, Headmistress, Halifax, 1954.
D. Smith, Headmistress, Bulawayo Junior School.
Phyllis Robinson, Headmistress, St. Elphin's School, Darley Dale.
Muriel Hardy, Headmistress, Speech Therapy Centre, Moorhouse.
Dr. Mary Pocock, Crisp medal (Linnean Society).
Dr. Dina Dobson Hinton (*née* Portaway), archaeologist.
Mona Hensman (*née* Mitter), O.B.E., work in Madras.
Joyce Godber, County Archivist and Beds. historian.

Girls' Modern/Dame Alice School

Violet Driver (left 1906) taught in Johannesburg High School.
Gwyneth Davey, headmistress in London 1929–61; her school took part in film "Women in our time".
Brenda Bollard, PH.D., did scientific research at McGill university, Montreal, and Columbia university, New York.
Anne Kirkby (*née* Whyte), research in Mexico and at Johns Hopkins university, U.S.A.
Jose Harris (*née* Chambers), research at Cambridge and London; now lecturer at London School of Economics.
Pauline Hedgecock, PH.D., lecturer at Wye College.
Sara Barrett, PH.D., lecturer in mathematics, Durham university.
Doris Lee, professor of education, London university, 1965–71; various publications.
Jancis Dolby (*née* Ford), PH.D., researching at Perth university, Western Australia.
Doreen Playne, lecturer at St. Chad's College, Ladysmith.

THE CHURCH

Bedford School

Rev. F. Barham Zincke, Chaplain to H.M.	1830–1840
Rev. R. Carson, tractarian.	?
Rev. Canon Maclear, Warden of St. Augustine's College, Canterbury.	1850–1860
Rev. T. C. Fry, Dean of Lincoln, 1910.	1860–1870
Rev. A. F. Kirkpatrick, Dean of Ely, 1907.	?

Rt. Rev. W. R. Pym, D.D., Bishop of Bombay, 1903–8. 1870–1880
Archdeacon W. P. Johnson, D.D., Universities Mission to Africa.
Rev. T. Hill, Principal of Gloucester Theological College.
Rt. Rev. H. M. Burge, D.D., Bishop of Southwark and Bishop of Oxford. Headmaster of Repton and Winchester. 1880–1890
Rt. Rev. E. A. Anderson, Bishop of Rivernia, N.S.W.
Rev. Canon R. A. Aitken, Canon of Norwich.
Archdeacon Byrde, Archdeacon of Kwangsi, 1914.
J. Perkins, Sacrist of Westminster Abbey.
The Most Rev. J. A. Fitzgerald-Gregg, Archbishop of Dublin and Primate of All Ireland. 1890–1900
Rt. Rev. W. T. Carey, Bishop of Blomfontein and Bishop of Ely.
Rt. Rev. W. F. Surtees, Bishop of Crediton.
Rt. Rev. J. R. Weller, Bishop of Falkland Islands.
Rt. Rev. C. F. Urquhart, Bishop of Liverpool.
Rt. Rev. R. D. Acland, Bishop of Bombay, 1954.
Rt. Rev. W. M. Askwith, K.C.M.G., D.D., Bishop of Gloucester 1900–1910
Rt. Rev. B. Lasbrey, Bishop of West Equatorial Africa.
Rev. T. W. Pym, Chaplain to Trinity College, Cambridge, Chaplain to H.M.
Rt. Rev. G. N. Lankester-Hall, Bishop of Chota, Nagpur. 1910–1920

Bedford Modern School

W. E. Toll, D.D. (1873–8) Archdeacon and Suffragan Bishop of Chicago, U.S.A. .. ..
Arthur Sheppard, M.V.O. (1875–) Private secretary to the Archbishops of Canterbury (Randall Davidson and Cosmo Lang).
Rev. F. Noel Palmer (1907–15) Principal of the Church Army Training College.
Ven. T. H. M. Dix (1920–6) Archdeacon of Zanzibar.

THE CIVIL SERVICE: HOME

Bedford School

Sir Whitmore Smith, Assistant Sec. India Office. 1850–1860
Sir H. Trustram Eve, K.B.E. 1880–1890
Sir A. Symonds, K.C.B., Permanent Sec. to Board of Education. 1890–1900
Sir C. E. Fitzroy, Solicitor to H.M. Customs and Excise.
Sir E. T. F. Crowe, Head of the Foreign Office.
Lt. Col. Lemon, Chief Constable of Nottingham and Leeds.
Sir P. D. Butler, Secretary for the Foreign Service. 1900–1910
Sir W. Cleary, Deputy Sec. at Ministry of Education. 1910–1920
Sir Bruce Fraser, Controller General. 1920–1930
Sir George Godber, Chief Medical Officer, Dept. of Health.
H. H. Hobbs, C.B., C.V.O.
A. C. Miller, M.B.E., Governor of Pentonville.
Major N. H. Golding, Governor of Dartmoor. 1930–1940
J. Gilbert Cook, C.V.O., C.B.E.

Bedford Modern School

C. Pedley, C.B. (1868–75).
Sir Ralph Harwood, K.C.V.O., K.C.B., C.B.E. (1896–8), Financial Secretary to King George V.
Sir Clement T. Hallam (1904–8), Solicitor to the G.P.O.
P. L. Burton, C.B.E., Civil Service Pay Research Unit.
Sir Henry Johnson, C.B.E. (1917–23), Chairman of British Rail.
Sir George Godber, K.C.B. (1917–20), Chief Medical Officer, Dept. of Health.

Bedford High School

Violet Carruthers, Librarian, Treasury and Cabinet Office.

THE CIVIL SERVICE: OVERSEAS

Bedford School

T. A. Le Mesurier, India Survey. 1860–1870
M. Turner, South Australia Survey. .. .. ?
Col. J. A. C. Somervelle, Military Attache in Tokyo. .. .. ?
A. Beaman, Vice-Consul in Syria. 1870–1880
Lt.-Col. G. S. Elliott, Nigeria Boundary Commission 1904.
Sir B. S. Carey, C.I.E., K.C.S.I., Commissioner in Burma 1890. 1780–1890
Hon. H. T. Creasy, M.B.E., Director Public Works, Hong Kong.
G. F. Adams, C.B.E., Chief of Mines in India.
Lt.-Col. F. G. Beville, Sec. to Gov.-Gen. Central Provinces, India.
Sir W. Hillier, K.C.M.G., Consul-General in Korea. 1890–1900
F. A. Hamilton, C.I.E., Inspector-General, Indian Police.
J. C. Boyce, Deputy Director of Supplies, India.
F. G. Brooks, Chairman, Public Services Board, S. Rhodesia.
F. B. Brooks, Head of Agr. and Lands, Rhodesia.
L. A. N. Brooks, Commissioner of Mines, Rhodesia.
Sir H. MacMichael, Governor of Tanganyka, High Commissioner for Palestine and Transjordan. 1900–1910
Sir C. Bristow, Governor of Bombay.
Sir C. C. Chitham, Inspector-General Police, Central Provinces.
Sir A. D. Gordon, Inspector-General Police, Bengal.
Sir Paul Butler, K.C.M.G., UNRRA Far East representative.
A. V. Askwith, C.I.E., C.S.I., Chief Commissioner, Delhi.
J. R. M. Fell, Minister and Consul-General in Paraguay.
Sir P. Liesching, K.C.M.G., High Commissioner in South Africa. 1910–1920
Sir C. D. Belgrave, K.B.E., Financial Adviser in Bahrein.
M. D. Carter, Director of Land Records and Surveys, Bengal.
Sir George Clutton, K.C.M.G., British Ambassador to Poland.
Lt.-Col. N. G. Maclean, Commissioner of Police, Aden.
Sir Pierson J. Dixon, G.C.M.G., British Ambassador to France. Permanent Rep. at U.N.O. 1920–1930
Sir S. Gillett, C.M.G., Chairman Overseas Food Corporation.
T. E. Rogers, C.M.G., H.M. Ambassador to Colombia. 1930–1940
K. B. Keith, President Kenya Law Society.
Sir Philip Bridges, C.M.G., Chief Justice of Gambia. 1940–1950

Bedford Modern School

Sir Ernest Wilton, K.C.M.G. (1876–87), Consul-General Canton, Chengtu, Hankow. British Minister for Estonia and Latvia. President Saar Governing Commission.
Sir William Pell Barton, K.C.I.E., C.S.I. (1885–88) Author. Resident in Hyderabad.
J. T. Wawn (1888–94), British Consul, Nagasaki.
C. A. Pickwood (1890–4), Administrator of St. Lucia, West Indies.
H. Pickwood (1890–5), Receiver General British East Africa, British Honduras and Mauritius.
Sir Daniel Richmond, K.C.I.E. (1890–6) Chief Conservator, Indian Woods and Forests.
Sir Francis Kerr-Jarrett (1893–1903), Custos [Lord Lieutenant] of St. James's, Jamaica.
D. S. Ingram (1894–7) Ranger Examiner U.S. Forestry Service. The Oregon plant *Silene Ingrami* named after him.
S. W. Smith (1897–1905), British Consul at Foochow, Swatow. Consul-General, Manila, Honolulu.
F. Williamson (1904–9), Consul-General in Kashgar, Chinese Turkestan.
W. I. J. Wallace, C.M.G., I.C.S. (1916–23), Judge of Township Court, Magme, Burma. Chief Secretary to the Government of Burma. Assistant Under Secretary of State, the Colonial Office.
Sir George Mooring, K.C.M.G. (1918–27), Last British Governor of Zanzibar.
T. K. Ramakrishna (1924–9) Under Secretary, Ministry of Home Affairs, India.

THE ARMED FORCES: ROYAL NAVY

Bedford School

Vice-Admiral Fawcett Wray. 1880–1890
Rear-Admiral A. C. Ransom.

Vice-Admirals	Sir R. H. O. Lane-Poole, K.B.E., C.B., O.B.E.	1890–1900
	Sir C. P. Talbot, K.C.B., D.S.O.	
Rear-Admirals	Sir R. Burnett, K.B.E., C.B., D.S.O., Order of Suvorov, Murmansk Convoys.	
	F. L. D. Acland.	
	H. R. M. Woodhouse, C.B., O.B.E.	1900–1910
Vice-Admirals	Sir Charles Hughes-Hallett, K.B.E.	1910–1920
	J. Hughes-Hallett, D.S.O., M.P., Cmdr. Dieppe raid.	
Rear-Admirals	L. A. Boutwood.	
	Campbell-Walter.	
Admiral of Fleet	Sir Michael le Fanu, First Sea Lord.	1920–1930
Vice-Admiral	Sir R. S. Hawkins, K.C.B., Chief of Naval Supplies.	1930–1940

Bedford Modern School

Rear-Admiral J. K. Highton, C.B., C.B.E., R.N. (1914–21), Aide-de-Camp to the Queen.
Capt. A. L. Tapper, R.N., (1915–18), Aide-de-Camp to the Queen.

THE ARMED FORCES: THE ARMY

Bedford School

Major-Generals	W. C. Russell, role in Indian Mutiny.	1830–1840
	G. E. Erskine, role in Indian Mutiny.	?
	F. R. Glanville, R.A.	
General	Sir Henry A. Smyth, Cmdr. South Africa 1887–9. Governor of Malta.	1840–1850
Major-Generals	W. C. S. Clarke, in China War 1860.	1850–1860
	G. H. More-Molyneux, I.S.C., in Afghan Wars 1878–80. Cmdr. in Aden 1901.	1860–1870
Brig.-Generals	E. A. W. S. Grove, C.B., C.B.E.	
	H. S. Sloman, C.M.G.	1870–1880
	A. Slade Baker, C.M.G.	
Major-General	W. C. Barratt, C.B., C.S.I., D.S.O.	
Generals	Sir Walter Braithwaite, G.C.B., Legion of Honour, Croix de Guerre.	1880–1890
	J. Hill, D.S.O., A.D.C.	
Major-General	F. M. G. Hutchinson, C.I.E., I.M.S., Surg.-Gen. Madras.	
Brig.-Generals	W. St.C. Bland, C.M.G., C.B., R.A.	
	L. M. Phillpotts, D.S.O., R.F.A.	
	A. C. Roberts, C.M.G., D.S.O.	
	W. K. Legge, C.M.G., D.S.O.	
	F. W. H. Walshe, C.M.G., D.S.O.	
	G. M. Morris, C.M.G.	
	H. F. Brooke, C.B., C.M.G., C.B.E.	
Lt.-Col. the Hon.	Sir H. B. St. John, C.I.E., C.B.E., K.C.I.E.	
Field Marshal	Sir Cyril Deverell.	1890–1900
Lieut.-General	Sir W. M. Thompson, K.C.M.G., M.C.	
Major-Generals	Sir W. O. Twiss, C.B.E., M.C.	
	Sir W. S. Branker, Comdt. Equipment, Air Council.	
	L. J. Lipsett, C.M.G., D.S.O.	
	Sir H. J. Huddlestone, K.C.B., C.M.G., D.S.O., M.C., Gov.-General, Sudan.	
	H. F. E. MacMahon, C.B., C.B.E., D.S.O.	
	Digby I. Shuttleworth, C.B., C.B.E., D.S.O.	
Brig.-Generals	Sir H. O. Mance, C.B., C.M.G., R.E.	
	A. S. Holme.	
	R. B. Worgan, Mil. Secretary to Viceroy of India.	
	W. M. Fordham.	
	A. W. S. Grove.	
	R. E. T. Hogg, C.I.E.	
	C. R. Harbord.	
	C. E. Heathcote.	
	S. G. Francis.	
	J. K. Cochrane.	
General	Sir Colville Wemyss, K.B.E., D.S.O., Military Secretary	1900–1910
Lieut.-General	Sir W. H. G. Baker, C.B., D.S.O., O.B.E.	

Major-Generals Sir Noel G. Holmes, C.B., C.B.E., Deputy Q.M.G.
L. D. Hickes, C.B., O.B.E., M.C.
R. Briggs, D.S.O., M.C.
H. C. Martelli, A.D.C. to Governor, Jersey.
M. S. Brander, Comdt. R.A.S.C.
Sir L. G. Phillips, C.B., C.B.E., M.C., Director Signals.
Sir H. G. Riley, K.B.E., C.B., Chief Paymaster 1938.
A. T. Miller, M.C., C.B.
A. C. Fuller, Director of Engineers and Signals 1940. Invented Fullerphone and Dynaphone.
J. M. Kirkman, C.B.E.

Brig.-General C. S. Clarke, C.M.G., C.B., D.S.O., R.A.

Generals Sir Sidney Kirkman, C.B., C.B.E., M.C., Dir.-Gen. Civil Defence. 1910–1920
Sir F. E. W. Simpson, K.C.B., D.S.O.

Major-Generals Sir E. F. Tickell, C.B., C.B.E., M.C., Chief Engineer.
Sir H. R. Kerr, K.B.E., C.B., O.B.E., M.C., Comdt. R.A.S.C.
B. E. C. Dixon, C.B.E., M.C.
F. St. D. B. Lejeune, C.B.E., N.A.T.O., Staff.
H. R. Briggs, C.B., D.S.O., M.C.
N. P. H. Tapp, D.S.O.
A. C. Curtis, D.S.O., M.C., A.D.C., Cmdr. Lucknow 1946.

Major-Generals Sir C. F. Liardet, K.B.E., C.B., D.S.O. 1920–1930
R. C. Cotrell-Hill, O.B.E., M.C., D.S.O.
R. W. Urquhart, D.S.O., Comdt. Sandhurst.
H. M. Liardet, C.B., C.B.E., D.S.O., D.L., Comdt. Royal Tank Regiment 1961.
H. R. B. Foote, V.C., D.S.O., Comdt. Royal Tank Regiment.
G. Kellett, Director General Artillery, 1957.

Bedford Modern School

Major G. G. M. Wheeler (1886–91) Victoria Cross, 1915.
Lieut.-Col. A. C. R. Nutt, D.S.O. (1886–90) Inventor of the Artillery Miniature Range.
Brig.-Gen. H. C. Potter, C.B., C.M.G., D.S.O. (1887–93) Bey in the Egyptian Army.
Maj.-Gen. H. P. W. Barrow, C.B., C.M.G., D.S.O., O.B.E. (1889–93) Colonel Commandant Royal Army Medical Corps. Hon. Surgeon to King George V.
Maj.-Gen. C. H. Foulkes, C.B., C.M.G., D.S.O. (1889–93) Colonel Commandant Royal Engineers.
Brig.-Gen. A. J. Turner, C.B., C.M.G., D.S.O. (1891–5), Soldier and prominent Essex cricketer (batsman).
Capt. A. W. Byrne, T.D. (1895–8) Artists' Rifles. Hon. Secretary, the Royal Tournament.
Brig. H. E. W. Bell Kingsley, C.I.E., D.S.O. (1895–03) Commandant of the Indian Military Academy. Aide-de-Camp to King Edward VII and George VI.
Brig. C. G. Hawes, C.I.E., M.C. (1898–1905) Hydrologist in India.
Lt.-Col. C. H. G. H. Harvey-Kelly, D.S.O. (1899–1903) Military Attache, Kabul. Military Governor of Jerusalem after Allenby's entry, 1917.
Maj. G. F. Turner, M.C., (1906–9) Commander, Nayar Brigade, Indian Army.
Brig. T. H. S. Galletly, M.C., D.S.O. (1914–23) Commander 1st Brigade, Arab Legion (under Glubb Pasha).
Capt. A. L. Tapper, R.N. (1915–8) Aide-de-Camp to the Queen.
Brig. E. D. Dynes, O.B.E. (1915–21) Aide-de-Camp to the Queen.
Maj. Gen. R. B. Stockdale, C.B., O.B.E. (1920–5) Colonel Commandant Royal Electrical and Mechanical Engineers.

THE ARMED FORCES: ROYAL MARINES

Bedford School

Sir Walter G. Windham, Royal Indian Marines 1880–1890
Maj.-Gen. R. C. A. Glunicke. 1890–

Bedford Modern School

Lieut.-Gen. R. D. H. Lough, D.S.O., O.B.E. (1896–1902), Colonel Commandant of Marines. Aide-de-Camp to King George VI.

Sir Ernest Huddleston, C.I.E., C.B.E., R.I.N. (1881–8), Shipping Surveyor and Adviser to the High Commissioner for India. Deputy Director, Royal Indian Marines.

THE ARMED FORCES: ROYAL AIR FORCE

Bedford School

Air Chief Marshal	Sir C. S. Burnett, K.B.E., C.B.E., D.S.O.	1890–1900
Air Vice-Marshal	Sir W. S. Branker.	
Air Commodores	Sir Frank Nelson, K.C.M.G.	
	H. V. S. Wells, C.B.E.	

Sir Graham White, aviation pioneer, landed on school field in 1913, appointed keeper of the Royal Motor-Cars in 1902.

Marshal of R.A.F.	the Lord Newall, O.M., Gov. Gen. of New Zealand.	1900–1910
Air Vice-Marshal	Sir P. C. Maltby, C.B., M.C.	1910–1920
Air Commodore	H. I. Messiter.	
Air Commodore	J. E. R. Sowman	

Marshal of R.A.F. Sir Thomas Pike, G.C.B., D.F.C., Chief of the Air Staff, Deputy Allied Cmdr. in Europe. .. 1920–1930

Air Marshal	Sir D. J. P. Lee, K.B.E., Comdt. R.A.F. Staff Col.	1930–1940
Air Vice-Marshals	H. H. Brookes, D.F.C.	
	M. H. Chapman.	
	D. W. R. Ryley, C.B.E.	
	B. C. Yarde, in charge of Berlin Air Lift.	
Air Commodores	W. H. Ewing, O.B.E.	
	C. D. C. Boyce, C.B.E.	
	R. Kellett, A.F.C., D.F.C.	
	A. D. Panton, D.F.C.	
	R. H. Crompton.	

Lt.-Col. L. V. Stewart Blacker – first flight over Mt. Everest (1933).

Air Vice-Marshal Sir W. S. Branker was a Major-General before transferring to the Air Council in 1918. He died in the R101.

Notes

Some 150 O.Bs served in the South African War. There are 22 on the Roll of Honour.
In 1900 some 30 O.B. Officers were listed in the China Exped. Force.
In 1904 11 were listed on the 'Mission to Thibet'.
Some 451 are listed in the Roll of Honour for the First World War, over 1,500 are listed as serving.
Some 269 are listed in the Roll of Honour for the Second World War.
In 1945 Old Bedfordians on the Imperial General Staff included: the Deputy C.I.G.S.; Deputy Q.M.G.; Director of Supply; Director of Forts and Works; Director of Signals; Director of Royal Engineers; and the Military Secretary.

Bedford Modern School

Air Vice-Marshal R. D. Oxland, C.B., C.B.E. (1896–1907), played a leading part in originating the first R.A.F. four-engined bomber in 1936.

Brig.-Gen. P. R. C. Groves, C.B., C.M.G., D.S.O. (1891–6), air strategist.

Notes

South African War – 9 killed.

World War 1

Over 1,028 served, 166 killed.

Honours: 1 V.C., 4 C.B., 7 C.M.G., 1 C.I.E., 23 D.S.O., 34 M.C., 2 D.S.C., 5 Croix de Chevalier. Legion of Honour, 1 Croix de Guerre, 1 D.C.M., 1 D.S.M., 6 M.M., 1 Certificate of Distinguished Service, 2 Serbian Order of the White Eagle, 1 Serbian Order of Karageorge, 2 Russian St. George's Cross, 1 Belgian Order de la Couronne, 1 O.B.E., 70 Mentioned in Despatches.

World War 2

Over 1,230 served, 126 killed.

Honours: 2 C.B., 1 C.I.E., 2 C.B.E., 11 O.B.E., 2 D.S.O. (1 bar), 9 M.B.E., 2 D.S.C., 23 M.C., 14 D.F.C. (1 bar), 2 A.F.C., 1 D.S.M., 1 M.M., 3 D.F.M., 1 B.E.M., 2 King's Commendation, 2 Croix de Guerre, 1 Croix de Guerre with Silver Star, 1 Order Polonia Restituta, 1 Legion of Merit (French), 1 Greek War Cross, 1 King Feisal's (Iraq) Medal, 65 Mentioned in Despatches.

TRINITY HOUSE

Bedford School

Sir A. R. Morrell, Deputy Master, Trinity House. 1890–1900

POLICE

Bedford Modern School

H. C. Prescott (1892–9), Inspector-General, the Iraq Police.
H. R. Alexander (1901–7), Principal, Burmese Training School.
Maj.-Gen. R. O. Alexander, C.B., D.S.O. (1901–6), Canadian Mounted Police.

LITERATURE AND THE ARTS

Bedford School

F. C. Penrose, F.R.S., P.R.I.B.A. Surveyor to St. Paul's Cathedral; in Cambridge University crew, 1840–2. .. .. –1830
Sir T. Erskine-May; 'Standard Parliamentary Procedure'. 'Constitutional History of England'.
J. P. Seddon, F.R.I.B.A. 1830–1840
H. C. Blackden, R.A. .. .. ?
A. Fraser ? 1840–1850
1850–1860
F. Bullen. 'The Cruise of the Cachalot' and other novels. 1860–1870
Percy Godfrey, composer. 1870–1880
J. Sargeaunt, 'Pronunciation of English words from Latin'. .. ..
H. H. Munro. 'Saki'. Short stories. Killed in action 1916. 1880–1890
W. S. Bates, R.A.
O. P. Milne, F.R.I.B.A. 1890–1900
R. Hutton, actor.
H. B. Warner, actor.
N. Tharp, actor – member of Tree's company.
C. W. Parkins – Cyril Harcourt – actor. .. .. ?
Hesketh Pearson, historical biographer. 1900–1910
Leonard Handley, 'Hunters Moon' and other novels.
Sir H. A. MacMichael, 'History of the Arabs in the Sudan'.
Capt. L. V. S. Blacker, 'On Secret Patrol in China'.
D. F. L. Leverson – Daryl Fancourt – D'Oyly Carte Opera Co.
Dr. H. K. Andrews, organist of New College, Oxford. 1910–1920
Patrick Turnbull, 'A Bullet for the General' and other novels. 1920–1930
B. M. Feilden, O.B.E., Surveyor to St. Paul's Cathedral. 1930–1940
J. R. Fowles, 'The French Lieutenant's Woman' and other novels. Smith's Literary Prize 1971. .. 1940–1950
John Wood, actor Stratford Co.
R. Elphick, TV reporter.
S. J. Ross-Macdonald, author. 1950–
Robin Clarke, author.
R. Spence, architect British Museum extension.
R. France, architect.
B. Bagot, architect.
M. Freyhan, pianist, accompanist Festival Hall recital.

Bedford Modern School

W. H. White (Mark Rutherford), (1841–), writer.
J. K. Peel (John Capel), (1901–6), author.

T. C. Morgan (John Muir), (1926–31), author and agricultural journalist.
H. B. Kampf (H. B. Kaye), (1927–33), author.
Rowland Hill (1850s), Editor, *Bedford Mercury*.
W. E. Palmer (1907–13) and R. A. Parrott (1904–8), editors, *Bedfordshire Times*.
J. C. Hamson (1913–6), General Manager, *Bedfordshire Times*.
Richard Capell, O.B.E., M.M. (1898–1900), music critic and war correspondent, *Daily Telegraph*.
V. J. Head (1944–8), Assistant Editor, *The Field*; Rugby correspondent, *Daily Telegraph*.
F. Graves, Editor, *Northampton Mercury*.
G. L. Matthews (1928–32), Editor, *Morning Star*.
H. R. Bocquet (1890–5), composer. Professor at Dresden Conservatory, 1936.
E. D. Potter (1892–8), assistant organist, Westminster Abbey.
Cyril Gell (1916–25), musician; conductor B.B.C. Singers and Men's Chorus.
H. Marshal Palmer (1917–23), musician.
R. T. Stanbridge (1940–5), violinist.
P. J. Simms (1946–54), Director, the Thomas Tallis Society.
T. A. J. Souster (1952–61), composer of electronic music.
H. Sylvester Stannard, R.B.A. (1883–6), artist.
B. C. Elger (1870s), A. M. Stannard (1887–95), C. Lindley (1915–21), Royal Academicians.
G. L. Stampa (1889–91) illustrator for *Punch*.
Frank Mole (1906–9), artist.
G. K. Branson (W. H. Murray) (1916–19), portrait painter, illustrator for *Punch*.
J. Woodward Hill (1850s), civil engineer; designed Bedford suspension bridge, 1888; mayor of Bedford.
H. P. G. Maule (1887–91), architect, Royal Veterinary College, London, etc.
Bernard West (1935–44), artist and architect.
Sir Archibald Flower (1881–3), Chairman of the Governors of the Memorial Theatre, Stratford-on-Avon.
Capt. R. Berkeley, M.P. (1906–8), dramatist: *The Lady with a Lamp*; screen version of Sir Nöel Coward's *Cavalcade*.
C. Whitbread (Marcus Custance) (1916–22), author and playwright.
A. S. Daniell (David Scott Daniell) (1917–24), author, broadcaster and journalist.
A. H. Harris (Christopher Fry) (1918–26), poet (Queen's Gold Medal), dramatist, translator, producer, etc.
H. W. Peel (Gillie Potter) (1898–1903), broadcaster, satirist.
N. M. Bligh (1910–7), theatrical historian.
W. A. Tate (1926–9), head of B.B.C. Overseas Dept., Portuguese and Latin American services.
R. C. W. Luff (1925–30), theatrical agent, co-presenter of the Black and White Ministrel Show.
D. F. Coleman (David Firth) (1954–64), actor, National Theatre and Old Vic.

Bedford High School

Joyce Redman, actress.
Lady Playfair (*née* Mabel Platts), actress.
Pat Pleasance, actress.
Dorothy Tetley, actress.
Eve Turner, actress.
Gertrude Buchanan, actress, South Africa.
Helen Haye, actress.
Nancy Roberts, actress.
Lady Harty (*née* Agnes Nicholls), C.B.E., singer.
Sheila McShee, singer.
Grace Hawkins (Mrs. St. George Kirke), accompanist to Dame Clara Butt.
Jewel Evans (Mary Madden), pianist.
Thea King, clarinettist.
Sylvia Cleaver, member of Boyd Neal orchestra.
Nancy Neild, member of Covent Garden orchestra.
Katherine Eggar, composer.
Carla Attree, member of Royal Ballet Company.
Nancy Harding, teacher of dancing.
Kate Parbury, sculptress.
Mary Penny, artist (Academy 1912).
Margaret Lanaway, artist.
Dora Carrington, artist.
Phyllis fforde, contributor to *Punch*.
Rosemary Churchill, authoress.

E. Capstick (*née* Hargreaves), authoress.
G. Maw (*née* Rideal), authoress.
Ena Hooper (*née* Osborne), authoress.
Gertrude Dimmock, authoress.

THE LAW

Bedford School

Sir Henry Hawkins, first Lord Brampton, Q.C.	1830–1840
W. D. Foulkes, Editor of the Law Journal.	
E. C. T. Petgrave, solicitor and author.	1840–1850
Sir William Verey.	1850–1860
J. Scott Fox, K.C., Judge of County Courts 1915.	1870–1880
A. Parsons, K.C., Judge of County Courts 1916.	
Sir F. Beaman, Judge of Bombay High Court.	
Sir H. J. Gompertz, Chief Justice of Malay States 1926.	1880–1890
Sir B. Newbould, Puisne Judge, High Court, Calcutta.	
Sir George A. H. Branson, Judge of the King's Bench 1920.	
Sir Reginald Ward Poole, President of the Law Society.	
Sir Cecil Fforde, Judicial Commissioner, Bechuanaland.	1890–1900
S. Solomon, Judge of Transvaal Supreme Court.	
Sir G. O. Slade, Judge of the High Court 1948.	1900–1910
Sir J. T. Gilbert, Chief Justice of Bermuda.	
	1910–1920
W. A. Sime, Q.C., M.B.E., Recorder of Grimsby.	1920–1930
Sir P. R. Bridges, Chief Justice of the Gambia, 1972.	1930–1940

Bedford Modern School

Sir William Tudball (1877–84), Puisne Judge of the High Court of Allahabad, 1909–22.
Sir Sidney Abrahams (1893–1902), Chief Justice of Uganda. Attorney-General of the Gold Coast. Chief Justice of Tanganyika. Chief Justice of Ceylon. Privy Councillor.
Dr. J. Mould (1907–10), Q.C.
His Honour Judge J. B. Willis (1915–23).

Bedford High School

Lady Chatterjee (*née* G. Broughton), O.B.E., barrister, 1933.

Girls' Modern/Dame Alice School

Elizabeth Smith (*née* Roberts), first old girl to qualify as solicitor.

MEDICINE

Bedford School

H. O. Lucas, Senior Surgeon, Newark.	1860–1870
Dr. T. Chavasse, President B.M.A. 1905.	
Dr. O. F. Wyer, President B.M.A. 1906.	
Mr. A. Bruce Roxburgh, Surgeon, London Hospital 1898.	1870–1880
Dr. E. W. Goodall, O.B.E., M.D., B.S.	
Dr. A. Clarkson, demonstrator in psychology, Yorkshire College, Leeds.	
Sir Walter Langdon-Brown, Vice-Pres. Royal Society of Medicine.	1880–1890
Sir Maurice Craig, Gold Medalist.	
Capt. R. H. Elliott, D.SC., Ophthalmic Hospital, Madras 1903.	

H. V. S. Wells, O.B.E., hon. physician to H.M. 1890–1900
Sir Adolphe Abrahams, O.B.E., F.R.C.P., author and consultant (see below). 1900–1910
James Startin, M.R.C.S., inventor of hypodermic syringe etc.
Dr. N. R. Rawson, Public Health Officer, Manitoba, Canada. 1910–1920
Dr. F. W. Brown, F.R.C.P., leading psychiatrist. 1920–1930
Dr. P. J. Talalay, Cancer Research U.S.A. 1930–1940
Dr. J. P. Woodall, Research Unit, Yale School of Medicine. 1940–
Professor M. D. Warren, University of Kent.

Bedford Modern School

Maj.-Gen. G. F. A. Harris (1870–2), Professor and Physician, Calcutta Medical School. Inspector General of Hospitals in Punjab and United Provinces. Hon. Surgeon to the King and Viceroy.
John Linnell (1888–96), consultant physician.
H. R. Nutt (1889–94), Surgeon General to the Government of Bombay. Hon. Surgeon to King George V.
Sir Henry H. Bashford (1889–94), Senior Medical Officer to the G.P.O. Hon. Physician to King George VI. Novelist and short story writer.
Sir Adolphe Abrahams, O.B.E. (1891–9). Athlete and Physician. Olympic Medical Officer from 1912. Dean of Westminster Hospital Medical School from 1934.
F. Cook (1903–5). Obstetric and Gynaecological Surgeon, Guy's Hospital.
T. G. Bosworth (1904–11), Professor of Pathology, Royal Veterinary College.
A. T. Andreasen (1919–25), Professor Surgery, University of Calcutta.
W. E. Lancaster, C.B.E. (1921–7), Director of Veterinary Services, Federation of Malaya.
R. Churchill Frost (1933–41), Lecturer in Surgery, Royal Veterinary College.
Dr. R. N. Smith (1937–44), Lecturer in Veterinary Anatomy, Bristol.
E. Cotchin (1939–48), Professor of Pathology, Royal Veterinary College.

Bedford High School

Maud Forrester Brown, M.D., M.S., orthopaedic surgeon, first woman consultant of British Orthopaedic Association, member of International Orthopaedic Association.
Sylvia Costin (*née* Gadsden), orthopaedic surgeon, Gloucester City Hospital, E.M.S. Plastic Unit. Luton and Dunstable Hospital.
Sister Leonore Cooke, medical work in India and Bangladesh.
Catherine Lucas, lecturer, Royal Free Hospital, London.
Joyce Wenham (*née* Partridge), R.F.C.S., surgeon and psychiatrist.
Agnes Kelynack, M.D., Assistant Secretary to British Medical Association (first woman).
Paddy Downie, rehabilitation officer for Marie Curie Foundation.
Noel Goddard, first woman President of British Chiropractors' Association.
Dr. Ethel Landon, M.B., C.M.B., Government Hospital in Lahore.
Dr. Lucy Molony, C.M.S., Yezd, Persia.
Dr. Katherine Sampson, M.D., China.
Dr. Lilias Blackett, C.M.S., Zenana Hospital, Punjab.
Dr. Lily Iliff, China.
Mabel Chappell (*née* Beatty), C.B.E., founder with Mrs. Kenyon of Green Cross Society (Women's Reserve Ambulance).
Daisy Kenyon (*née* Kilroy) (as above for Mabel Chappell).
Evelyn Faulder, First Aid Nursing Yeomanry, Military Medal for gallantry.
Dr. Marjorie Morton, St. Catherine's Hospital, Amritsar.
C. Byrde, chemist, C.M.S. Hospital, Cairo.
Margaret Stewart Brown, matron, Selly Oak Hospital.
Kathleen Bell, matron, Lister Hospital, Hitchin.
May Purdie, R.R.C., O.B.E., nursed King George V.
Eva Lancaster, M.B.E., matron in Egypt; Red Cross work in Malaysia.
Elizabeth Bolton, British Red Cross, Distinguished war service medal.
Phyllis Kilby (*née* Ennals), British Red Cross, Distinguished war service medal.
Queenie Thompson (*née* Curtois), Sister, Order of St. John, Kaisar-i-Hind medal.
Margaret Owens (*née* Bayes), Sister, Order of St. John, Kaisar-i-Hind medal.
M. Hewlett Johnson (*née* Taylor), Commandant of Military Hospital near Manchester, 1918.
Mollie Church, Q.A.A.N.C., M.B.E.
Joyce Pickford (*née* Harris), matron, Brooke Bond Hospital, Kericho, Kenya.

Girls' Modern/Dame Alice School

Ethel Davey. Served as Queen Alexandra nurse in World War I; awarded Mons star; also decorated by Belgian government for nursing soldiers with plague; 1923–44 matron of St. Pancras hospital (hit 8 times in blitz in World War II). Invented for demonstrations life-size doll with internal organs, still in general use.

Annie Madin, senior demonstrator of anatomy, Edinburgh Medical School; R.M.O. at Royal Hants. County Hospital in World War I.

Diane Elliott (*née* Weston), psychiatrist at Shenley hospital.

Angela Robinson (*née* Jeffs), L.R.C.P., Senior Registrar, Seacroft Hospital, Leeds, 1971.

Elizabeth Cowburn, researching for Ph.D. with Medical Research Council.

POLITICS

Bedford School

Sir T. Erskine May, Lord Farnborough, Clerk of House of Commons. .. .. –1830

Thomas Barnard, M.P. for Bedford 1857–9. 1840–1850

N. C. Craig, K.C., M.P., Thanet Division of Kent 1910. 1880–1890

W. Crooks, M.P. 1914. .. .. ?

Sir Nelson Shaw, M.P. .. .. ?

Col. the Hon. G. R. Richards, M.P., Natal 1903, Union S.A. 1924. .. ..

Sir W. Preston, M.P., Cheltenham.

Sir Richard Wells, M.P., Bedford. 1890–1900

Lord Lucas, Private Sec. to Mr. Haldane (Sec. for War) 1905. Secretary for T.A. dept. of War Office 1909. President of Board of Agriculture in Cabinet 1914. .. ..

R. C. Cooper, M.P., Vancouver 1918.

L. R. Pym, M.P. 1900–1910

Lord Campion, Clerk to House of Commons. 'Introduction to Precedent'.

C. te Water, High Commissioner for Union S.A. in London. President of the Assembly of the League of Nations, 1933.

A. W. Smith, M.P., British Columbia. .. ..

Vice-Admiral J. Hughes-Hallett, M.P., Croydon 1954–64. British Rep. at Council of Europe. .. 1910–1920

1920–1930

Rt. Hon. J. B. Godber, P.C., M.P., Grantham. Minister of Agriculture. 1930–1940

Anthony Fell, M.P., Yarmouth 1951–66, 1970–.

A. G. Brown, M.P.

Bedford Modern School

James Howard (1830), M.P.

Sir William Morgan (1840s). Prime Minister of South Australia.

W. R. Bousefield (1866–70), K.C., M.P.

H. G. Graves (1874–81), Member of the Indian Legislative Council.

E. D. Morel, M.P. (1888–9), defeated Winston Churchill at Dundee, 1922. Exposed cruelty in collecting rubber in equatorial Africa in *Red Rubber* (1906), a highly sensational paperback. A founder of the Union of Democratic Control (of foreign policy).

Capt. R. Berkeley (1906–8), M.P.

A. A. Jones, M.P. (1926–32).

V. R. H. Yarnell (1928–37), Member, Legislative Assembly, Pennsylvania.

H. Keith Speed (1942–7), M.P., Under Secretary of State, Department of the Environment.

LOCAL GOVERNMENT AND CIVIC WORK

Bedford School

T. W. Pearse, Town Clerk for Bedford, 1836 .. .. –1830

T. G. Archer, Town Clerk for Lynn, 1864–8. 1840–1850

Thomas Barnard, Mayor of Bedford, 1854. 1840–1850

C. Verey, Chief Constable of Bedford, 1871–83. 1850–1860

J. Scott Fox, Recorder for Sheffield, 1904.	1860–1870
E. C. Byrne, Town Clerk for Sandwich, 1907.	1880–1890
Lt.-Col. G. Hayward Wells, Mayor of Bedford, 1932.	1880–1890
G. J. M. Whyley, coroner.	1880–1890
B. E. Sargeaunt, Govt. Sec. to Isle of Man, 1910.	1880–1890
Dr. R. E. McLaren, Mayor of Tenterden.	?
H. J. C. Shuttleworth King, Town Clerk for Worcester.	1900–1910
Sir B. McFarland, Mayor of Londonderry.	1910–1920
A. H. Randall, Mayor of Bedford, 1960–1.	
G. C. Godber, C.B.E., Clerk to West Sussex County Council.	1920–

Bedford Modern School

H. Thody (1850–9), Founder of the Bedford Volunteer Fire Brigade.
H. Laver (1903–6), ten times Mayor of Middelburg, Transvaal.
John Howard, Mayor of Bedford 1858–61.
James Howard, Mayor of Bedford, 1863–4.
Hedley Baxter, Mayor of Bedford, 1899, 1902.
Henry Burridge, Mayor of Bedford, 1900, 1904.
George Haynes, Mayor of Bedford, 1905–6.
S. L. Kilpin, Mayor of Bedford, 1907.
Commander H. R. Newton, R.N.R., O.B.E., J.P., D.L. (1910–18), Alderman Beds. C.C.
W. Roff, Mayor of Bedford, 1911.
F. R. Hockliffe, Mayor of Bedford, 1915–6, 1918.
W. Nicholls, Mayor of Bedford, 1921, 1927.
A. Braggins, Mayor of Bedford, 1938–9.
A. M. Dudeney, Mayor of Bedford, 1940–1.
J. A. Canvin, Mayor of Bedford, 1944–6.
C. A. E. C. Howard, Mayor of Bedford, 1953–4.
R. G. Gale, Mayor of Bedford, 1955–6.
A. A. Jones, Mayor of Bedford, 1957–8.
G. M. Bates, Mayor of Bedford, 1973.

Notes

High Sheriffs include for Bedfordshire: Lt.-Col. C. Villiers Downes, 1896, Geoffrey Howard, J.P., 1907 (also mayor of Bedford), Mayor Charles Wells, 1928, R. Skinner, 1937, W. W. S. Robertson, C.B.E. 1963; for Cambridgeshire, J. G. P. Crowden; for Huntingdonshire, D. R. S. Moore; for Middlesex, Sir G. Craig; all from Bedford School; for Buckinghamshire, Sir Noel Mobbs, K.C.V.O., O.B.E. (1892–6); for Leicestershire, E. C. Atkins (1882–6), both from the Modern School.

Deputy Lieutenants include Sir Richard Wells and E. J. Skinner, Bedfordshire, from Bedford School, and Commander H. R. Newton, R.N.R., O.B.E., J.P. (1910–8), from the Modern School.

Harpur Elementary School

Henry Burridge, Mayor of Bedford 1900, 1904.
A. L. Nicholls, Mayor of Bedford, 1947–9.
W. Nicholls, Mayor of Bedford, 1921, 1927.
Richard Turner, Mayor of Bedford, 1950–1.
F. W. Smart, County Surveyor.
A. V. Pryer, County Surveyor.
A. H. Perkins, County Treasurer.

Bedford High School

Dame Ethel Shakespear (*née* Wood), D.B.E., civic work in Birmingham.
Dr. D. Dobson Hinton (*née* Portaway), J.P., civic work in Bristol.
M. Russell (*née* Columbine), 4 times mayor of Pietermaritzburg.
C. Woodley (*née* Laurence), mayor of Higham Ferrers.
The Lady Jaqueta Williams (*née* Northcote), chairman of magistrates, chairman, County Library Committee, Red Cross commandant.
H. Taynton Evans (*née* Hiley), chairman, Welfare Committee, Newport, Mon., City Council.

M. Symonds (*née* Askwith), M.B.E., work with W.V.S.
Eva Atherton, O.B.E., public work in Gloucestershire.
Mona Hensman (*née* Millar), O.B.E., work in India.
Florence Harrison, M.B.E.
Mary Hogben, Health inspector, City of London.
Anne Bryant, First Secretary, British Embassy, Lagos, Nigeria.
Elspeth Corry Smith, manager, Erith Employment Exchange.
Cara Watson, Youth Employment.
Ann Shortland Jones (*née* Young), Ministry of Defence, Lagos.
Jacqueline Clark, M.V.O., one of the Queen's secretaries.
Pat Cameron, secretary to late Queen Elizabeth of the Belgians.
Dyne Steele, work for U.N.R.A. and I.R.O.
E. Barker (*née* Blake), O.B.E., work for War Graves' Commission.
Margaret Greenshields, curator, Cecil Higgins Museum.
Irene Lamb, secretary to Clerk of Beds. C.C.

Girls Modern/Dame Alice School

Mary Wilkinson, served 8 years as policewoman; then 25 years as probation officer; chairman, Chiltern counties branch of National Association of Probation Officers.
Winifred Fowler, Mayor of Bedford, 1972–3.

AGRICULTURE, INDUSTRY, COMMERCE & BANKING

Bedford School

Thomas Barnard, Head of Barnard & Co. Bankers. 1840–1850
C. N. Goodall, Man. Dir. of R. Stephenson & Co. 1870–1880
Irwin Adams, Gen. Manager Naval Colliers, S. Wales. 1880–1890
1890–1900
O. J. Barnes, Sr. Manager, Hong Kong & Shanghai Bank.
Sir Harold Yarrow, Chairman of Yarrow & Co. 1900–1910
E. F. V. Wells, Gen. Manager, Witbank Collieries.
Sir John Howard, Chairman of John Howard & Co. 1910–1920
H. G. G. MacKay, Vice-Chairman, Indian Tea Association.
J. B. Simpson, President of Institute of Mining.
W. W. S. Robertson, C.B.E., O.B.E., Director, Davy Ashmore. 1920–1930
W. T. Gill, Rolls-Royce, Derby.
J. W. S. Brancker, Traffic Director, B.O.A.C.
G. T. Davies, Chairman, County Agricultural Committee.
G. B. R. Feilden, F.R.S., C.B.E., work on jet engines. 1930–1940
P. Parker, M.V.O., Chairman, National Ports Authority.
Sir Richard Wells, Lt.-Col. G. Hayward Wells, Charles Wells, Messrs. C. Wells.

Bedford Modern School

John Howard (*c.* 1810), industrialist.
James Howard (1830s), industrialist; M.P.
Frederick Howard (1830s), industrialist.
Sir George Farrar, D.S.O., Bart. (1875–), Leader in Transvaal at time of Jameson Raid. Founder and planner of the town of Benoni, Transvaal.
C. G. Huddleston (1877–83), mining engineer. Discoverer of the Dharwar gold reefs.
E. A. L. Laxton (1878–83), expert on fruit production and evolution of new strains, e.g. Laxton Superb apples.
F. W. Potter (1887–91), engineer-in-chief, Shanghai Gas Co.
J. L. Rose (1888–94), cabinet maker (examples of his work in V. and A.).
E. E. Blake (1888–95), pioneer in motion pictures; managing director for Kodak.
J. M. D. Wrench (1893–9), chief mechanical engineer, Gt. Indian Peninsula Railway, Bombay.
W. A. Pickwoad (1896–1900), manager, Central Argentine Railway.

W. T. Reid (1896–1903), chief designer to the British Aeroplane Co.
L. T. Neck, M.C. (1905–11), managing director, Columbia Graphophone Co.
W. T. Godber, C.B.E. (1915–22), chairman, County Agricultural Committee, chairman of governors of Shuttleworth College.
D. de Villiers (1936–40), chief test pilot, De Havilland and then English Electric Aviation.
R. Stock (1945–50), senior test pilot, British Aircraft Corporation.

Harpur Elementary School

J. H. Pryer, Gold Coast Railway.
R. Turner, Gas Manager.

Bedford High School

Margaret Partridge, President of Society of Women Engineers.
Beatrice Havergal, founder of Waterperry Horticultural Training College.

Girls' Modern/Dame Alice School

Avril Dinsdale, distinction in National Diploma in business studies, 1967.
Jean Muir, fashion designer; 1964 British Fashion World's designer of the year; received presentation from Princess Margaret, 1965.
Bridget Truscott, studying fashion design at Royal College of Arts Fashion School, has had designs accepted by national press.
Diane Bell (*née* Drought), M.DES.R.C.A., designer of textiles.

SPORT

Bedford School

W. B. Weightall, cricket, Camb. university and Sussex. 1860–
W. B. Jessop, first captain, Bedford Rowing Club, 1886. 1870–
P. Christopherson, Rugby, England 1819. 1880–1890
F. H. Palmer, Rugby, England. 1890–1900
P. G. Jacob, Rugby, England.
C. E. L. Hammond, Rugby, England.
B. Maclear, Rugby, Ireland.
J. R. Anthony, Hockey, Wales 1905.
F. Burnett Stuart, Hockey, Scotland 1905.
H. J. Henman, Capt. Ipswich Town.
E. H. D. Sewell, cricket author, cricket, Essex.
Col. R. N. B. Campbell, Sabre Champion of Gt. Britain; Navy and Army (Middleweight) Boxing Champion, 1905, 1907.
Lt. H. O. Mance, Pioneer balloonist.
A. E. Field, new climbs in the Alps.
J. G. Milton, Rugby, England. 1900–1910
C. H. Milton, Rugby, England.
F. G. Brooks, Rugby, England.
S. W. Harris, C.B.E., Rugby, England, vice-captain S.A. and Canada tours.
E. L. Chambers, Rugby, England.
H. H. Vassall, Rugby, England.
P. H. Lawless, Rugby author.
H. V. Baumgartner, cricket, South Africa 1908–13.
F. M. Joyce, cricket, Leicester.
B. L. Peel, cricket, Scotland, 1907.
F. R. Radici, King's Medal, Bisley.
S. W. Harris, Davis Cup for South Africa.
J. de Hazard, 3rd Everest expedition.
R. Robertson-Sheresby-Harvie, motor racing.
H. Grierson, founder of XL Club.
Sir B. MacFarland, Rugby, Ireland. 1910–1920

R. Jones, Rugby, Wales.
B. F. Holland, Rugby, Canada. .. .. ?
J. Beresford, C.B.E., Diamond Sculls, Olympic Gold Medalist.
H. L. Morphy, 1924 Olympics – rowing.
J. D. P. Wheatley, Davis Cup, 1924 Olympics.
Brig. L. Bolton, 1948 Equestrian Olympics.
J. G. Cook, C.V.O., C.B.E., Rugby, England. 1920–1930
E. V. Bevan, Olympic Gold Medalist 1928.
W. A. Sime, Capt. Notts cricket.
F. R. Webster, athlete, 1936 Olympics. 1930–1940
L. F. L. Oakley, Rugby, England. 1940–1950
J. P. G. Crowden, rowing 1952 Olympics.
W. A. D. Windham, rowing 1952 Olympics.
M. H. S. Allen, cricket, Northants.
B. E. Disbury, cricket, Kent.
A. P. R. Dawes, Open Fives Singles and Doubles Champion.
D. P. Rogers, O.B.E., England Rugby Captain and most number of caps. 1950–1960

Note: *Totals include – 16 Rugby Internationals for British Isles*
5 Olympic Oarsmen – 2 Gold Medalists.
2 Davis Cup players.
2 Hockey Internationals.

Bedford Modern School

R. C. Stafford (1900–10), W. B. Thomson (1879–87), H. W. Finlinson (1887–9), E. R. Mobbs (1892–8), H. L. V. Day (1910–5), A. G. Bull ( ), R. E. G. Jeeps, J.P. (1943–9) [Captain of England], L. Weston (1958–66) Rugby Internationals.

A. O. Jones (1881–90) [Captain of England], G. Millman (1943–52), R. A. Gale (1943–53), Cricket Internationals.

Bedford High School

Valerie Scott, tennis player, Wightman Cup; professional in U.S.A.
Audrey Disbany, played cricket for England.
June Wheating (*née* Goodall), badminton champion of South Africa.
Daphne Young, British badminton champion.
Brenda Newell, played hockey for England.
Muriel Madden, on Council and Selection Committee of All England Hockey Association.

MISCELLANEOUS

Bedford Modern School

A. L. A. Mackintosh (1891–4), explorer, lost life on Shackleton's expedition.

Girls' Modern/Dame Alice School

Ethel Gillions, founder of Old Girls' Association, 1911.
Tessa Gillett, explorer (member of Cambridge university expedition to measure glacier movement in Norway).
Madge Nightall (*née* Grimmer) first woman in Bedfordshire to have a pilot's licence.

INDEX

Note: This index does not cover App. 5.

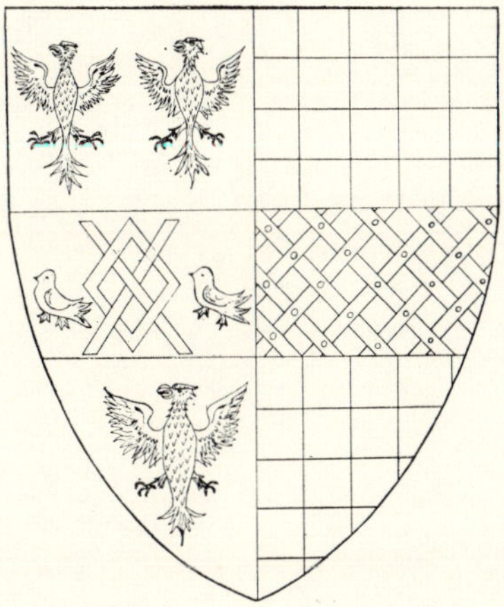

Arms used by the Harpur Trust

The arms displayed upon the seal of the Harpur Trust are those of Harpur, impaling those ascribed to his wife, Alice. The arms granted to Sir William Harpur, knight, by Barker, Garter King at Arms in 1561, are:

azure, on a fess between three eagles displayed or,
a fret between two martlets of the first,

i.e., on a blue shield a broad gold band passes between three golden eagles with spread wings, and on the band is a blue fret with a small blue bird (martlet) on each side. With these arms are impaled the following:

chequy or and azure, a fess argent fretty gules bezanty,

i.e., the shield is chequered gold and blue, and has across the centre a broad silver band covered with a red trellis with gold nail heads. This second coat is ascribed to Sir William Harpur's wife, Alice, but no record of its grant is to be found. According to the Heralds' visitation of London in 1568, the maiden name of Dame Alice was Tomlinson, and her first husband was Richard Harrison. However, a more correct pedigree occurs in the 1623 Heralds' visitation of Gloucestershire. This gives Dame Alice's maiden name as Thorne, and her first husband's name as Thomas Jackman. The question arises, whose arms did she bear? Those described were not granted to either Tomlinson or Harrison. The arms of Thorne are quite different, and those of Jackman bear no resemblance either. In the funeral roll of the College of Arms there is an illuminated record of Dame Alice Harpur's funeral, and the arms as recorded above, impaled with Sir William's, are there shown on her hearse and standard. It must be assumed, therefore, that whatever the origin of the arms, they were recognised as hers by the supreme heraldic authority of the day. The arms ascribed to Dame Alice are not to be found in Papworth's *Ordinary of Arms.*

F. W. Kuhlicke

Arms used by the Harpur Trust

[illegible]

[illegible]

[illegible]

THE BEDFORD CHARITY

(THE HARPUR TRUST)

MAP OF HOLBORN ESTATE

Based on O.S. Plans TQ 3081 NE, NW.

LANDER BEDELLS on the advice of F. KELSALL, Historic Buildings Division, Greater London Council.

COUNTY OF GREATER LONDON
LONDON BOROUGH OF CAMDEN
HOLBORN WARD

Formerly the Parishes of St. Andrew Holborn and St. George the Martyr.

× × × × × Boundary of the ground in Holborn given to Bedford Corporation by Sir William Harpur in 1566.

[box] Estate as reorganised by the Court of Chancery in 1654.

'//////////// Present extent of the Harpur Trust Property.

This plan reproduces on the current Ordnance Survey map the boundaries of the ground in Holborn given to Bedford Corporation by Sir William Harpur in 1566, and the estate as reorganised by the Court of Chancery in 1654. It also shows the present extent of the Harpur Trust property.

The arrangement of the four plots of ground given by Sir William Harpur is shown in the sketch plan in the Corporation archives, but the measurements of the plots have been taken from the bounds set out in the Chancery decree of 16 February 1653/4. (PRO/C. 78/1269 No. 2.) This decree was based upon two surveys of the two fields, Red Lyon Field and Conduit Shott, made by Chancery Commissioners on 1 July 1652 and 1 March 1652/3, and the redistribution made by the same Commissioners on 3 December 1653. The object was to reorganise the eight separate plots of ground, four belonging to Bedford Corporation and four to Sir Thomas Fisher, into two blocks, each owner retaining the same area of ground.

The measurements, especially of area, in the early documents were far from accurate; Bedford Corporation claimed 13 acres 3 roods in the two fields and Sir Thomas Fisher 16 acres 3 roods; but the total area, on survey, was found to be only 27 acres. The total holding of Bedford Corporation was therefore reduced to 11 acres 3 roods 27 poles. The surveys and redistribution of 1652 and 1653 were done with some precision: for example, the northwest corner of the eastern section of Red Lyon Field was moved in the redistribution some 13 feet 3 inches westwards, in order to increase the area of that plot by 10 poles.

The Chancery decree refers to Theobalds Road as lying along the south side of Conduit Shott, and forming the boundary with Red Lyon Field. The road was moved about 50 feet northwards in later years, apparently by Nicholas Barbon in the 1680s when he began the development of both the Harpur Trust estate and the Fisher property. Subsequent rebuildings, especially at the western ends of both Red Lyon Field and Conduit Shott, have been extensive. This plan was first drawn on the 1/1056 first edition Ordnance Survey map of 1875, when redevelopment had not been so considerable, and then transferred to the current Ordnance Survey map at 1/1250.

The redistribution of the holdings of Bedford Corporation and Sir Thomas Fisher in Red Lyon Field and Conduit Shott may be tabulated as follows:

Before 1654,		*Fisher*		*Bedford*		*Total*
	Red Lyon	2.3.00		3.1.00		
	Field	2.3.17		6.1.23		
			5.2.17		9.2.23	15.1.00
	Conduit	7.1.33		0.3.36		
	Shott	2.0.03		1.1.08		
			9.1.36		2.1.04	11.3.00
			15.0.13		11.3.27	27.0.00

After 1654,		*Fisher*		*Bedford*		*Total*
	Red Lyon Field	11.3.30		3.1.10		15.1.00
	Conduit Shott	3.0.23		8.2.17		11.3.00
			15.0.13		11.3.27	27.0.00

F.K.

Queen Square Garden
QUEEN SQUARE
THE ROYAL LONDON HOMŒOPATHIC HOSPITAL
GREAT ORMOND STREET
ORMOND CLOSE
Chancellors' Court
ORDE HALL STREET
Nurses Home
Babington Court
York House
Pump
Posts
COSMO PLACE
St George the Martyr Church (C of E)
Grand Hotel
St George the Martyr Junior School
The Stanhope Institute
ITALIAN HOSPITAL
St George's Infants School
GAGE STREET
Devonshire Court
BOSWELL COURT
Blemundsbury
DOMBEY ST
DOMBEY STREET
Windmill
HARPUR STREET
Boswell House
Springwater
NEW NORTH STREET
Adastral House
BOSWELL STREET
Hostel
Bevan House
Playground
Richbell
Ormonde Mansions
OLD GLOUCESTER STREET
Bonnington Hotel
Falcon
Mercury House
SOUTHAMPTON ROW
BLOOMSBURY PLACE
Bristol House
Faraday House
Rochdale House
OLD NORTH STREET
Hanway House (Ministry of Labour)
RED LION SQUARE
Victoria House
Bank
Sentinel House
THEOBALD'S ROAD
Subway
DRAKE STREET
Theatre
Holborn College of Law Language & Commerce
Central School of Arts & Crafts
Bloomsbury Square Gardens
BLOOMSBURY SQUARE
VERNON PLACE
SICILIAN AVENUE
FISHER STREET
PROCTER STREET
Procter House (West)
Procter House (North and East)
YORKSHIRE GREY YARD
EAGLE STREET
Kingsgate House